YESHIVA UNIVERSITY
is pleased to provide this complimentary edition of

SEVENTY FACES: ARTICLES OF FAITH
a two-volume compendium of many of
Dr. Norman Lamm's most important writings
over the years on issues of critical
importance to education, world Jewry,
and Modern Orthodoxy

•

Thank you for your participation in our

SEVENTY-SEVENTH ANNUAL
HANUKKAH DINNER & CONVOCATION.

The Waldorf=Astoria
Sunday, December 2, 2001

SEVENTY FACES

Articles of Faith

BOOKS BY NORMAN LAMM

A HEDGE OF ROSES:
Jewish Insights into Marriage and Married Life (1966)

A TREASURY OF TRADITION
Co-edited with Walter S. Wurzburger (1967)

THE ROYAL REACH:
*Discourses on the Jewish Tradition
and the World Today (1970)*

FAITH AND DOUBT:
Studies in Traditional Jewish Thought (1971)

"TORAH LISHMAH"
*—Torah for Torah's Sake—
in the Works of Rabbi Hayyim of Volozhin and his Contemporaries
(Hebrew 1972; English 1989)*

THE GOOD SOCIETY:
Jewish Ethics in Action (1974)

TORAH UMADDA:
*The Encounter of Religious Learning and Worldly
Knowledge in the Jewish Tradition (1990)*

HALAKHOT VE'HALIKHOT
*(Hebrew)—Jewish Law and the Legacy of Judaism:
Essays and Inquiries in Jewish Law (1990)*

THE SHEMA:
Spirituality and Law in Judaism (1998)

THE RELIGIOUS THOUGHT OF HASIDISM:
Text and Commentary (1999)

SEVENTY FACES
Articles of Faith (2001)

SEVENTY FACES

Articles of Faith

VOLUME I

BY

NORMAN LAMM

KTAV PUBLISHING HOUSE, INC.
HOBOKEN, NEW JERSEY

Lamm, Norman
Seventy Faces: Articles of Faith Volume 1.
p. cm.
ISBN 0-88125-768-0

Distributed by
Ktav Publishing House, Inc.
900 Jefferson Street
Hoboken, NJ 07030
201-963-9524 FAX 201-963-0102
Email orders@ktav.com
Web www.ktav.com

This book is dedicated to my grandchildren

Tova, Tamar, Ariela, Ahuva, Penina
Yonatan, Daniel, Yehuda
Ari, Peninah, Shmuel, Bracha, Devorah
Tova, Bracha, Yael, Shmuel

and my students, too many to mention individually,
for they too are as my children and grandchildren

May the Almighty grant them long and full years in health
and happiness, to live creative lives of Torah and wisdom

I am pleased to acknowledge with gratitude

Debbie and Elliot Gibber

*who have graciously sponsored publication of these volumes
in memory of their revered father and father-in-law*

CHARLES K. GOLDNER ז"ל
(1900–2001)

*High principle and commitment to Torah and Israel have
characterized his full life on earth and he has been a role model
for his beloved children and grandchildren*

OF MAKING
BOOKS

"And furthermore, my son, be admonished: of making books there is no end"

—Ecclesiastes 12:12

A Hasidic interpretation: Why do people write books? Because they seek to achieve "no end," or immortality.

"By speech first, but far more by writing, and more again by printing, man has been able to put something of himself beyond death. In tradition and in books an integral part of the individual persists, and a part which still works and is active, for it can influence the minds and actions of other individuals in different places and at different times: a row of black marks on a page can move a man to tears, though the bones of him that wrote it are long ago crumbled to dust. In truth, the whole of the progress of civilization is based on this power."

—Julian Huxley, *The Individual in the Animal Kingdom*, 1912

Contents

Volume I

Volume II

CHAPTER 9. ISRAEL AND ZIONISM 171

CHAPTER 10. THE HOLOCAUST 251

Epilogue 293

INTRODUCTION

The present two volume set consists of a selection of articles intended for the general public (to call them "popular" may be assuming too much on my part) and published in a variety of journals and magazines over the course of several decades. Not all the articles that fit this description are reprinted here, and I hope that at least some of those that do appear will prove of interest to the reader. I have not included the more scholarly or "heavy" pieces, and I reserve them for, possibly, a later volume.

The ten chapters (consisting of sixty individual articles) represent most of my major interests in the course of my career over the past fifty years. Because they were written over a relatively long time span, they will inevitably bear traces of differing emphases and occasionally different conclusions. Were it not so, it would be an admission that time, experience, and facts have had no effect on my thinking; I cannot summon up enough humility to make such a public confession . . .

The title of this work requires some explanation. "Seventy Faces," which refers to vol. 1, chapter III, article 12, in many ways is the gist of my position on many of the controversial issues that have engaged the attention of the Jewish community and that have agitated the minds and hearts of those of us who are both fully committed to the classical Jewish heritage and eager to keep the Jewish community from exploding in a burst of centrifugal ideological individualism. That there are "seventy faces" or facets to Torah, as the Sages taught, implies that there is a variety of ways to express one's Jewishness—but not an infinite number of ways. This idea underlies much of the rest of the book.

A word about the very first article in the book, "A Fallen Giant." I have known many eminent and distinguished personalities who qualify as "giants," and losing them to the inexorable victories of the Grim Reaper have left us, the survivors, impoverished. While, somehow, new leaders emerge to take their place and stake their claim to giant-hood, we keenly miss those who most directly affected our lives.

One such person who has been, for me, the "giant" of both my youth and adult life, was the late Rabbi Joseph B. Soloveitchik (1903–1993), of blessed memory, known widely as "The Rav" (the Rabbi), an honorific which attests to the almost universal veneration felt for him. The influence he has exerted upon the thousands of students who were privileged to hear his Talmud *sheurim* (lectures), the thousands more whom he has ordained, and the many who thronged to his special public lectures, often lasting four to five hours of spellbinding oratory and intellectual stimulation, is incalculable. Thus, the opening article is the eulogy—or perhaps combined eulogy and threnody—I spoke at the Yeshiva University assembly memorializing our great teacher and master. It begins with a quotation from Scripture, "A prince and giant has fallen this day." The Rav was preeminently *the* "Giant" for me, and hence the opening piece is reserved for him.

———

A NUMBER OF PEOPLE deserve to be included in a "psalm of thanksgiving" for urging me and helping me in the publication of this volume. My publisher, Bernard Scharfstein, has long pressured me to collect the more accessible of my articles in one work, and I had successfully resisted his insistence, persistence, and importuning. However, when my dear friend Elliot Gibber joined forces with him and suggested that I produce this collection, one that he wishes to present as a gift to his father-in-law in honor of the latter's 100th birthday, I felt outvoted, outmaneuvered—and encouraged.

Dr. Joel B. Wolowelsky volunteered to wade through my publications and both select and categorize them most wisely. Although the final form is my responsibility—for which he should not be blamed—I am indebted to him for his constructive efforts to turn rather disparate articles into a book.

My Academic Assistant, Prof. Jeffrey S. Gurock—a distinguished scholar in his own right—gave freely of his time and critical advice in the editorial phase of this book. I owe much to him.

Those with whom I am in almost daily contact were most helpful in the constant, mundane efforts without which no book is published and no effort succeeds. My long-time and always indispensable Administrative Assistant, Mrs. Gladys Cherny, facilitated my labors without ever a complaint and always with encouragement. Mrs. Ida M. Schwartz, who expended much effort on this volume, has been for me not only a competent and devoted secretary, but in many ways a surrogate mother for whose concern I shall always be grateful. Mrs. Hilda Tejada was ever gracious in her role as receptionist and typist. Mrs. Els Bendheim, a lady of intelligence and learning made many excellent suggestions in the course of proof reading parts of this work. All the above share in whatever virtues may be attributed to this enterprise, without bearing any of the responsibility for its inevitable errors.

No expression of gratitude can ever be complete without recording my most sincere gratitude to my wife Mindella who, for the past 47 years, has put up with my erratic schedule and workaholic afflictions without objection, save to ensure both my physical and mental health.

I mentioned above my reluctance to having this work published. My hesitation is based upon a charming piece of Hasidic lore concerning Rabbi Menachem Mendel of Kotzk, known as "The Kotzker Rebbe." The Kotzker was asked why he never published a volume of his truly profound teachings. His explanation: "If I had such a book printed, who would read it other than my devoted Hasidim? Now, they are all hard-working people who would not have time to peruse it during their overburdened week. Only on Shabbat would they have the opportunity to do so—after the synagogue services, after Kiddush, after a hearty and heavy Shabbat meal. Then a Hasid would repair to his easy chair (if he had one!), open my *sefer*, and begin to read. But the weariness of the whole week, reinforced by the wine and heavy Shabbat meal, would quickly make him drowsy and, unwittingly, the book would drop to the floor. For that I have to write a book?"

Such negative thoughts occurred to me as well. I feared that my work would be neglected, even by those closest to me in this age of information overload. Why, then, did I finally succumb to the importuning of my good friends, Bernard Scharfstein and Elliott Gibber?

In one of the front pages I offer an apology for writing this book—a Hasidic interpretation of a verse from *Kohelet*, and a parallel citation from Julian Huxley. Both speak of authorship as a human effort at attaining immortality. I do not believe either of them intended the mere appearance of yet another volume gathering dust unread on some neglected shelf as a serious challenge to the nefarious workings of the Angel of Death. They did intend the ideas and values that continue with those who follow us.

It is in this sense that I dedicate this volume to my students, too many to mention individually, and to my grandchildren who I hope will, in time, become my students, whether formally or informally.

"Abraham was saved from the fiery furnace because of the merit of [his grandson] Jacob"—Gen. R. 63

The presidency of Yeshiva University is a veritable "hot seat," and the temperature of controversy in the Jewish community is often elevated. If I have survived this "fiery furnace" with at least a modicum of approval from those whose judgment I respect, and with just enough humor not to take myself too seriously—it is in the merit of my grandchildren.

Norman Lamm
New York City
July 2, 2001
וְאֶתְחַנַּן תשס״א

11 Tammuz, 5761

Chapter 1

MODERN
ORTHODOXY

This first chapter of the book begins with the "Fallen Giant" who has had such a powerful influence on Modern Orthodoxy—although I do not recall if he ever used the term as such. Rabbi Joseph B. Soloveitchik, reverently called "The Rav" (The Rabbi), was a seminal thinker, a master teacher, and an eloquent lecturer. It is his spirit and his teachings—both direct and indirect—that have inspired much if not all of this volume.

The five articles following represent my thinking on Modern Orthodoxy over the course of three decades, from 1966 to 1997.

If the reader is perplexed by my use of the terms "Modern Orthodoxy" and "Centrist Orthodoxy," the confusion is justified. The former term has been is use for some time, to distinguish it from the Haredi or more reclusive branch of Orthodoxy (often referred to as "Ultra-Orthodox" or "Fervently Orthodox"; I prefer the Hebrew term Haredi because it is not pejorative and is the one used by the Haredim to identify themselves). For a while, I rejected the title because I considered the adjective "modern" as objectionable; it appeared as if we were boasting of our modernity when, indeed, we were hardly uncritical of it even though we stand for engaging it openly and forthrightly. I therefore introduced the term "Centrist" Orthodoxy, intending not a mathematical mean between two extremes, but those who follow Maimonides' principle of moderation (see "Some Comments on Centrist Orthodoxy" in this chapter.) However, this did not prove to be an inspired decision; most people assumed it meant we were situating ourselves mid-way between Reform and the Satmarer group. Nothing, of course, could be more wrong-headed. I have therefore reverted to the term Modern Orthodoxy. I assure the reader that there was and is no difference in my mind between the two, and I apologize to the sociologists and other pundits for having wasted their time and intellectual effort as they labored to define the differences between the two.

~ 1 ~

A FALLEN GIANT
The Rav

"A prince and giant has fallen this day in Israel"
—Samuel II, 3:38

Surely, such a prince and such a giant, who became a legend in his own lifetime, deserves an appropriate eulogy.

I therefore begin with a confession: I feel uncomfortable and totally inadequate in the role of one delivering a eulogy for my *rebbe,* the Rav. Only one person could possibly have done justice to this task, and that is—the Rav himself; everyone and anyone else remains a *maspid she'lo ke'halakhah*—"one who eulogizes without authorization." Nevertheless, we owe it to him to try our best. And so I ask your—and his—forgiveness at the very outset.

———

THE RAV DEPARTED from us on the exact same day that, 17 years ago, we lost Dr. Samuel Belkin *z.l.,* the late President of Yeshiva University, and the Rav eulogized him from this very podium on the day that he himself would be interred, *erev* the last days of Pesach. He referred to him then in the words of the Haggadah, as *arami oved,* a "wandering Aramean," and paraphrased that as a "wandering Litvak," who as a youngster was forced from his native town and took the wanderer's staff to these shores all by himself.

———

UNLIKE DR. BELKIN, the Rav was not a wandering Aramean. He was not orphaned at an early age. On the contrary, he had the

A eulogy for my teacher, Rabbi Joseph B. Soloveitchik, zt"l on April 25, 1993. It has been reprinted several times.

advantage of a stable, aristocratic home, of encouraging and even doting parents. He was heir, at birth, to a distinguished lineage—the *bet ha-Rav*, that of R. Moshe, R. Hayyim Brisker, the *Bet Halevi*, the Netziv, back to R. Hayyim Volozhiner.

His genius was recognized while he was still in the crib. At age 6, his father had hired a *melamed* to come to the house to teach him. The tutor was a Lubavitcher Hasid who taught him *Tanya* without asking leave of his parents. He learned it so well, that his Mitnagdic father was shocked and fired the *melamed* . . . (His affection for Habad, however, would remain with him to the end.) He then became a disciple of his own father—demanding, challenging, and critical, yet approving and proud.

At the age of 10 he presented his father with his written Torah *chiddushim*. His father was so impressed that he showed it to *his* father, R. Hayyim Brisker, who was so impressed that he sent it to his *dayyan*, R. Simcha Zelig. And, of course, he prophesied greatness for his precocious grandson.

The Rav's development continued unimpeded, and fulfilled and exceeded the hopes of father and grandfather.

———

THE FORMER CHIEF Rabbi of Israel, Rabbi Avraham Shapira, told me the following story to which he was a personal witness.

When the Rav came to visit Israel, the one and only time during his life, in 1935, it was the last year of the life of the elder Rav Kook. The Rav spoke at several places—at Mercaz Harav, at the Harry Fischel Institute, and at several other yeshivot. At every *sheur* that he gave, Rav Kook's son, R. Zvi Yehuda, attended and listened attentively.

When Rabbi Shapira asked R. Zvi Yehuda why he was doing so, he answered as follows: His father received Rabbi Soloveitchik and they "talked in learning." When Rabbi Soloveitchik left, the elder Rav Kook told his son that the experience of speaking with the young Rabbi Soloveitchik reminded him of his earliest years when he was a student at the Yeshiva of Volozhin, during the time that Rabbi Soloveitchik's grandfather, Reb Hayyim Soloveitchik, first started to give *sheurim*. I believe, Rav Kook said, that the power of genius of the grandfather now resides with the grandson—and therefore, he said to his son, you should not miss a single *sheur* by Reb Yoshe Ber Soloveitchik.

———

BUT IF, UNLIKE Dr. Belkin, the Rav was not a wandering Aramean, then we may say of him that he embodied another passage in the Hagadah: "Know full well that your seed shall be a stranger in a land not their own" (Gen. 15:13), that Avraham's children will be strangers in another land. He was not a "wandering Aramean" but a "lonely Abrahamite," a lonely Litvak, and this loneliness was one of the most painful and enduring characteristics of his inner life. This giant who was at home in every discipline, a master of an astounding variety of branches of wisdom, familiar with almost every significant area of human intellectual creativity, felt, ultimately, like a stranger dwelling in another's land. He somehow did not fit into any of the conventional categories. His genius was such that the loneliness attendant upon it could not be avoided— a fact which caused him no end of emotional anguish, yet gave us the gift of his phenomenal, creative originality. He was both destined and condemned to greatness and its consequences.

———

THIS SENSE OF loneliness, isolation, and differentness had a number of different sources, all of which reinforced each other. One of them was emotional and began quite early in his life. The Rav poignantly describes (in his *Uvikashtem Misham*) his early experiences of fear of the world and of social detachment, his feelings of being mocked and rejected and friendless. The only friend he had was—the (12th century) Rambam and, as he grew older, all the other giants of the Talmudic tradition whom he encountered in his learning. The Rav identifies this as more than imagination and fantasy but as a profound experience—the experience of the tradition of the Oral Law. Yet, the sense of social loneliness and emotional solitude was not dissipated.

Indeed, that was the way he was brought up: he was taught to hide his emotions. He was never kissed by his father. He had no real friends in his childhood or youth and no truly intimate comrades in his adulthood.

THIS SENSE OF alienation was not only a psychological and social factor in the various roles the Rav played in life; it was also
central to his whole conception of life. His most characteristic
form of analysis in his philosophic essays and oral discourses
was the setting up of typological conflicts, of theoretical antitheses: Adam I and Adam II; *Ish ha-Halakhah* and *Ish ha-Elohim*; the
covenant of fate and the covenant of destiny; majesty and humility . . . And, ultimately, conflict and dissonance make not only for
dynamism but also for alienation and loneliness.

This philosophical approach stems from two sources. One was
his attempt, probably developed in his days in Berlin, to defend
Judaism from the encroachments of a self-confident and aggres-
sive natural science and equally arrogant then-modern philosophy. To counter them, he adopted the Neo-Kantian view in
which there is a distinct chasm that separates the natural order of
objectivity, quantification, and determinism (at least on a macro
scale), from the internal human realm of the subjective, qualita-
tive, and passionate where freedom reigns.

The second source is, I believe, the *hashkafah* of his Mitnagdic
forbear, R. Hayyim Volozhiner, who saw the world and all existence as multi-layered and plural, as reflected in the Halakhah with
its multiple judgments as in the Mishna of Ten Degrees of Sanctity,
as against the Hasidic view of a monistic and unified world, one
which blurred distinctions and sought to overcome contraries.

Thus, for instance, Rav Kook, strongly influenced by the Hasidic side of his lineage, saw underlying unity beyond all phenomena of fragmentation and opposition, while the Rav's view
was anything but harmonistic. He saw not wholeness but conflict, chaos, and confrontation in the very warp and woof of life.
Man was constantly beset by a torn soul and a shattered spirit, by
painful paradoxes, bedeviled by dualities, and each day was
forced to make choices, often fateful ones, in the confrontation of
savage contraries, of the jarring clash of claims and counter-
claims in both conception and conduct.

Both these sources—the neo-Kantian and the thought of R.
Hayyim Volozhin—see fundamental disunity and a fractiona-
tion of experience in the world.

SUCH A VISION of contradiction and incongruity leads inexorably to anxiety and tension and restlessness, to a denial of existential comfort and spiritual security. It results in *loneliness*—the Rav truly was "The Lonely Man of Faith"—and this philosophically articulated loneliness with its depth crises becomes enduring and especially poignant when superimposed on a natural tendency to solitude and feelings of being a stranger in a foreign land.

Yet, paradoxically, in practice he made strenuous efforts to overcome these dichotomies, to heal the wounds of the sundering of experience and even of existence itself, to achieve the unity of man with himself, with nature, with society, and with the divine Master of the Universe—even though he knew that such attempts were ultimately doomed to frustration. Hence, his efforts to bridge the worlds of emotion and reason, of Halakhah and Agadah, of Hasidism and Mitnagedism. Perhaps the very attempt to achieve unity and wholeness reflected his penchant for peace—a goal he valued and cherished—although he knew that in reality disharmony and the pain of inexorable conflict and contradiction controlled.

THUS, FOR INSTANCE, in the area of Jewish thought, where his fertile mind reigned supreme, he was a stranger amongst those who worked in Jewish philosophy. For he came to it from another world—one of greatness in Torah and mastery of Halakhah as well as the classics of both general and Jewish philosophy; and his assumptions and aspirations and insights were derived from the Halakhah, rather than seeing Halakhah as irrelevant to Jewish philosophy. Hence, for example, the Rav's reconciliation of the differing viewpoints of Maimonides and Nahmanides as regards the obligation to pray, whether its source was rabbinic or in Torah law, became the source of his teaching on the "depth crisis" of everyday life. Amongst such Jewish thinkers, he remained a *ger*, a stranger and alien in a foreign land. The Rav was a lonely Litvak.

————

SIMILARLY, HE WAS a master *darshan* endowed with a richness of homiletic ingenuity combined with charismatic rhetorical prowess and stellar oratory—undoubtedly the greatest *darshan* of our, or even several, generations. Yet he had no peer, no companion, no friend even in this area. The kind of *derush* that even the best of them practiced was not his home, not his way. He could be as ingenious—and more so—than the cleverest of them, with a sense of timing and drama that was astounding, but his uniqueness lay in his synthesis of both Halakhah and Jewish thought in homiletic guise rather than the conventional *derush*. Here too he was a *ger*, and the world of the other *baalei derush* was for him "a land not their own." It was not his home.

————

EVEN IN HALAKHAH, where he was our generation's undisputed master, he still was a stranger in a foreign land. Other great scholars were also gifted thinkers capable of incisive insights, but he alone—in addition to his cognitive supremacy, his dazzling halakhic definitions, and his brilliant formulations—had a broader scope by virtue of his wider knowledge and his exposure to other modes of reasoning, which helped him in his halakhic creativity, so that he was singular amongst the giants of Halakhah of our time. Thus, his quality as a "lonely Litvak" expressed itself as well in his defiance of convention in dress and demeanor. He simply refused to conform to standards imposed from without, whether intellectually or in the form of stylistic niceties.

————

HOW DID THE Rav as a "lonely man of faith" overcome these bouts of loneliness, given his conception of dialectic and conflict as inscribed in human nature and existence itself?

First of all, his early emotional and social loneliness became bearable when he found fulfillment in his domestic life. Anyone who was privileged to visit with him and the late Rebbitzen in their home in Roxbury could tell immediately that for the Rav, his home was a haven—and a heaven. Do we not recall the bitter tears he shed at his eulogy for her?

The second way, in response to his existential loneliness, was spiritual. This man whose goal was never mere peace or happiness but truth, was able to assuage his feelings of being a stranger in a foreign land by his deep and unshakable faith. The "lonely Abrahamite" knew not only the anguish of alienation inflicted upon Abraham's children, but he also knew the secret of our ancient forefather—that of "You found his heart faithful to You" (Neh. 9:8): a faithful heart, a heart of faith.

———

HOW DOES FAITH overcome the loneliness of the stranger, the alien, the *ger*? Perhaps by understanding that none is more lonely, so to speak, than the One Who Is Without Peer Himself! Man's loneliness and Israel's loneliness as "a nation which dwells alone" (Nu. 23:9) are both reflections of the divine loneliness. Even as He is One, the unsurpassably and ineffably One, so is He incomparably alone—He has no peer (Dt. 4:35); and does not such absolute and transcendent *aloneness* imply, from a human perspective, unparalleled and unimaginable *loneliness*?

The Almighty reaches out to His human creatures, seeking, as it were, the spiritual companionship of humans: the commandment of loving God can be understood by the talmudic dictum that "the Holy One, blessed be He, desires the prayers of the righteous"; and man eases his own pitiful terrestrial solitude by linking his loneliness to the majestic loneliness of the Divine. So does loneliness join loneliness, and out of this encounter is born the divine-human companionship, nourished by divine grace and human faith. Bonds of friendship are created, as man gratefully acknowledges God as "my Beloved," and God regards the lonely Abrahamite as "Abraham My Friend."

———

SUCH EXULTATION CAME to the Rav during prayer. During these precious moments and hours, suffused with the purest faith, the Rav found both the truth and the peace to which he devoted his life, as his riven soul was healed and unified. Recall his moving description, in his article "Majesty and Humility" (in *Tradition*, v. 17 [1978], p.33), of his experience of prayer when his late wife, o.b.m, lay dying in the hospital. Reread so many other of his famous essays where he bares his soul and reveals the depths and heights of his pure faith as expressed in prayer and the companionship of the Master of the Universe.

Here did the Rav, in his most intimate and private moments, reveal the true dimensions of his spiritual *Gestalt* by dint of his profound faith. He was no longer a stranger, no longer an alien, no longer the lonely Litvak.

FINALLY, HE WAS able to abolish or at least moderate both forms of his loneliness intellectually—and that, in a paradoxical manner: He found peace and tranquility—on the battlefield of Halakhah during his *sheurim* here at Yeshiva! Often, the Sages speak of halakhic debate as the "give and take" of Halakhah, *massa umattan*, which is also the term for—business. It is a negotiation in the coin of ideas. But often they speak of a rougher kind of dialogue, as halakhic contention, *esek ba-Halakhah*, which refers not to a commercial analogy, but to strife, battles, as in Gen. 26:20, "they contended with him," referring to a struggle over the wells. *That* was the Rav's kind of *sheur!* That is what I think of when I recite the daily blessing, *la-asok be'divrei Torah*, "to **engage** in the study of Torah" . . . Engaged in a war of wits with his own students, parrying ideas and interpretations, entering the fray between Rashi and Tosafot, between Rambam and Ramban—and Ramban with the Baal Hamaor—and trying to resolve their differences in a manner typical of the Brisker *derekh* which he inherited and then modified and perfected, he found his peace and his companionship.

PERMIT ME TO relate a story that throws light on other aspects of the Rav's character. It was my second year in his *sheur*, and I was intimidated and in awe of him as was every other *talmid*—that is, *almost* everyone else. There was one student, the youngest and one of the brightest, who was clearly the least frightened or awed. The Rav had been developing one line of thought for two or three weeks, when this *talmid* casually said, "But *Rebbe*, the Hiddushei Ha-Ran says such-and-such which contradicts your whole argument." The Rav was stunned, held his head in his hands for three agonizingly long minutes while all of us were silent, then pulled out a sheaf of papers from his breast pocket, crossed out page after page, said that we should forget everything he had said, and announced that the *sheur* was over and he would see us the next day.

———

I LEARNED TWO things from this remarkable episode. First, we were overwhelmed by his astounding intellectual honesty. With his mind, he could easily have wormed his way out of the dilemma, manipulated a text here and an argument there, maybe insulted an obstreperous student, and rescued his theory and his ego. *But the Rav did nothing of the sort!* He taught, by example, that the overarching goal of all Torah study is the search for Truth. That search for Truth was the essence of his activity in Torah, and we witnessed it in action. He encouraged independent thinking by his pupils as a way to ensure his own search for the truth of Torah. The Rav was authoritative, but not authoritarian. No "musar shmuess"—no lecture in ethics— could have so successfully inculcated in us respect for the truth at all costs.

The second lesson came with the anti-climax to the story. The very next day, it was a Wednesday, the Rav walked into class with a broad, happy grin on his face, held out his copy of the Hiddushei Ha-Ran, and said to the *talmid*, "Here—now read it *correctly!*" The Rav had been right all along . . .

What we learned was a secret of his greatness and success as a teacher, namely, his attention to preparation. I always thought that there was a vast difference between his formal, public *derashot* and his *sheurim* in class. The former were finished, polished, conceptually and oratorically complete products, a joy to behold, each of them a marvel of architectonics. The *sheurim* he gave in class were of an altogether different genre. They were dynamic and stormy, as he formulated ideas, experimenting with a variety of arguments, testing, advocating and discarding, proving and disproving, as he brought us into his circle of creativity and forced us to think as he thinks and thus learn his methodology in practice. A *sheur* by the Rav was always a no-holds-barred contest, a halakhic free-for-all, an open-ended process instead of a predetermined lecture.

Well, this incident proved otherwise. The Rav actually pulled out of his breast pocket his hand-written notes for this *sheur!* We were confounded: It was all prepared in advance! Yet his greatness was that, on the one hand, he prepared assiduously for every *sheur,* leaving as little as possible to chance. On the other hand, despite this thorough preparation, the *sheur* indeed *was* open-ended, because he listened carefully to any serious challenge by even the youngest of his students and was ready to concede an error. And all through this, so successful was he in engaging us in the act of creation, that we never realized that he had thought it all out ahead of time! Attending his class, I always felt, was like being present at the moment of genesis, like witnessing the act of Creation in all its raw and primordial drama, as conceptual galaxies emerged from the chaos of objections and difficulties, as mountains collided and separated, "as he uprooted mountains and crushed them together" (as the Talmudic phrase has it), until, finally, a clear and pellucid light shone upon us, bringing forth new and exciting worlds. He combined preparation and openness, determination and freedom, the fixed and the fluid. What a master pedagogue!

So AWESOME WAS his performance as both a thinker and a teacher, that emerging from an encounter with the Rav, whether publicly or privately, in a class or in an article, in Halakhah or in Jewish thought, it was impossible to avoid feelings of grave inadequacy, a vast inferiority. Each of us would think: How could I ever attain such depths, such heights of content or style, of thought or language? In students, that usually resulted in hero-worship; in colleagues and contemporaries—it often eventuated in envy and even enmity.

It is a measure of the Rav's character that he was not spoiled by our adulation, and he ignored the slurs against him; never, publicly or privately, did he mention them. Giants pay no attention to such slings and arrows.

WHENEVER I THINK back to the Rav as a teacher I recall the fascinating tale recorded in *Pirkei de'R. Eliezer* (chap.2): R. Eliezer comes to Jerusalem where he meets his rebbe, R. Yochanan b. Zakkai. The latter invites his pupil to "say Torah," and he declines, explaining that he has derived all his Torah from R. Yochanan b. Zakkai and therefore has nothing to tell *him*. But, replies R. Yochanan b. Zakkai, you **can** do so; indeed, you can produce new Torah thoughts, such as were beyond what was received at Sinai! Sensitive to the fact that R. Eliezer is shy about displaying originality in the presence of his teacher, R. Yochanan b. Zakkai stands outside the study hall:

> R. Eliezer sat and expounded, his face as bright as the sun, with rays of light shining forth as they had from Moses' face [after God had appeared to him]; no one knew whether it was day or night. [Finally,] R. Yochanan came up behind him and kissed him on his head, saying to him: "Happy are you, Abraham, Isaac, and Jacob, that such a one as this one has issued from your loins." Said Horkenos, R. Eliezer's father: ". . . He ought not have said that, but rather: 'Happy am I that such a one has issued from my loins.'"

Similarly, the Rav's Torah was a revelation of Torah in its own right. There was something radiant about him, his vigor, his dynamism, as the original analyses and pursuit of truth and creative gestures poured forth from him in such triumphant excitement. Moreover, as a *rebbe* or teacher, he was simply unsurpassed. His gift for explanation, for elucidating a difficult concept or controversy or text, was that of sheer genius; who could compare to him? Happy are the Patriarchs of our people, happy are his father and grandfather *zikhronam liverakhah*—and happiest of all are we, we who had the good fortune to study under him. How sad I am for our younger students who did not and will never be so privileged; at best they can get only a reflection of his greatness at second hand.

WHAT KIND OF person was the Rav?

Despite his no-nonsense attitude while teaching, he was a man of sensitivity and graciousness. It would not be a mistake to say that he was, in the best sense of the word, a gentleman. He might have been a terror in the classroom, but he was attentive and polite and accepting and warm outside the *sheur*. Above all, he possessed great kindness and he was a *baal tzedakah*, a charitable person.

He was also very vigorous. In the days of his strength, his *yemei ha'aliyah*, he never walked; he ran. It is almost as if his body was rushing to keep up with the flow of his ideas. Vigor, dynamism, vibrancy dominated his being, from his "lomdus" to his gait.

———

ABOVE ALL, THE Rav was a man of independence. He was a true heir of his great-great-grandfather, R. Hayyim Volozhiner, who held that in Torah study you must go after the truth no matter who stands in your way; respect no person and accept no authority but your own healthy reason. So, the Rav was his own man, and often went against the grain of accepted truths and conventional opinion. Once, after a particularly original *sheur*, a stranger who was not used to such unusual independent creativity, asked him, "But Rabbi Soloveitchik, what is your source?" He answered, "a clear and logical mind" . . .

He was an independent thinker not only in his Halakha and his philosophy but also in his communal leadership. He had great respect for some of his peers—eminent *Rabbanim* and *Rashei Yeshivot* of the generation—but he did not allow that respect to intimidate him. He rejected fanaticism or zealotry as well as small-mindedness, even as he deplored lack of faith. He was not afraid to be in the minority, and refused to be cowed by pressure of the majority. He was horrified by extremism and overzealousness as well as superficiality and phoniness in communal policy-making almost as much as he contemptuously dismissed them in "learning." And if he sometimes seemed to waver in setting policy or rendering a decision in communal matters, it was because he saw all sides of an argument and was loathe to offend or hurt even ideological opponents.

———

THUS, FOR INSTANCE, almost alone amongst contemporary *Gedolei Torah* (talmudic authorities), he viewed the emergence of the State of Israel as evidence of divine grace; he saw its appearance as opening a new chapter in Jewish history, one in which we enter the world stage once again. He was not afraid—despite the opinions of the majority of *Rashei Yeshiva* and his own distinguished family members—to identify with the goals and aspirations of Religious Zionism.

———

PERHAPS THE MOST significant area where he diverged from other *Gedolim* and followed an independent way was with regard to secular studies, to *Torah Umadda*. The Rav was an intellectual Colossus astride the various continents of human intellectual achievement and all forms of Jewish thought. Culturally and psychologically as well as intellectually, this made him a loner amongst the halakhic authorities of this century. How many preeminent Halakhists in the world, after all, have read Greek philosophy in Greek, and German philosophy in German, and the Vatican's document on the Jews in Latin? A Ph.D. from the University of Berlin in mathematics and especially philosophy, he took these disciplines seriously, not as an inconsequential academic flirtation or a superficial cultural ornamentation, or as a way of impressing benighted and naive American Jewish students who did not know better. There is no doubt where his priorities lay—obviously, in Torah—but he did not regard *Madda* as a *de facto* compromise. The Rav believed that the great thinkers of mankind had truths to teach to all of us, truths which were not necessarily invalid or unimportant because they derived from non-sacred sources. Moreover, the language of philosophy was for him the way that the ideas and ideals of Torah can best be communicated to cultured people, it is Torah expressed universally; and he held as well that his philosophic studies helped him enormously in the formulation of halakhic ideas.

The Rav had no use for the currently popular transcendent parochialism that considers whole areas of human knowledge and creativity as outside the pale. We must guard, therefore, against any revisionism, any attempts to misinterpret the Rav's work in both worlds, akin to the distortion that has been perpetrated on the ideas of R. Samson Raphael Hirsch. The Rav was not a *lamdan* who **happened** to have and use a smattering of general culture, and he was certainly not a philosopher who **happened** to be a *talmid chakham,* a Torah scholar. He was who he was, and he was not a simple man. We must accept him on his terms, as a highly complicated, profound, and broad-minded personality, and we must be thankful for him. Certain burgeoning revisionisms may well attempt to disguise and distort the Rav's uniqueness by trivializing one or the other aspect of his rich personality and work, but they must be confronted at once. When the late R. Yehezkel Abramski eulogized R. Hayyim Brisker, he quoted the Talmudic eulogy, "If a fire has blazed up among the cedars, what shall the hyssop do," and interpreted that as: after the giants have been taken from us, who knows what the dwarfs who follow them will do to their teachings . . .

———

THE RAV WAS exceedingly loyal to Yeshiva University. Thus, when some 14–15 years ago we faced the threat of bankruptcy, I asked him to help rescue our Yeshiva, and he immediately accepted. At a critical meeting in the late Herbert Tenzer's office in 1978 he appeared before our leaders and read to them his confession of gratitude to Yeshiva University. He spoke of how much Yeshiva meant to him, how it afforded him a platform, how critical it was to whatever he had attained in his life, how much it meant to his family.

It was he who gave *semikhah* to some 2000 rabbis and thus influenced hundreds of thousands of Jews in America and throughout the world. And he graciously allowed us to name the Semikhah Program the Rabbi Joseph B. Soloveitchik Center for Rabbinic Studies, because he knew it would help the Yeshiva. He was, indeed, the *ruach chayyim* of the Yeshiva.

———

ADDITIONALLY, THE RAV refused to isolate himself in an ivory tower. He sought contact with ordinary Jews—whom he **never** disdained. This practical turn of mind and interest served him well. Thus, the Rav functioned not only as a *Rosh Yeshiva* but also as a *Rav,* as a Rabbi for ordinary Boston *baalebatim.* As such, he was in contact with the realities of American Jewish life, and as a result his halakhic decisions and communal policies were leavened by an intimate awareness of their lives and loves, their needs and limitations and aspirations, their strengths and their weaknesses. His *rabbanut* in Boston was the perfect counterpoint to his life as *Rosh Yeshiva* in Manhattan, and protected him from making decisions that were appropriate, perhaps, for the high ideals of a yeshiva but not for *amkha*, for ordinary laymen. He dominated the ivory tower; it did not dominate him.

———

THE RAV WAS deeply devoted to his family. Just as his father was *his* teacher, so did he teach his three children—and he treated his daughters the same as his son. He was fortunate to have brilliant children, illustrious sons-in-law, and gifted grandchildren; all are involved, in one way or another, in the world of Torah, many of them educated at Yeshiva and some teaching here.

———

BUT MOST IMPORTANT to us—his students and their students and the thousands who came under his or his students' influence—is what he meant to us as our *Rebbe*.

Despite the austere majesty and the irrepressible dynamism of his *sheurim*, and despite the fear of coming to a class of the Rav unprepared, we intuitively knew that we had a friend—a father, an older brother—in him. We invited him to our weddings, and later to our children's weddings; and he came. We consulted him on our personal as well as rabbinic problems; and he listened and advised. We presented our halakhic inquiries; and he taught us "the way in which they shall follow," as God said to Abraham regarding his descendants.

———

HE EXERTED A POWERFUL emotional pull on his students: I know so many, each of whom secretly (and sometimes not so secretly) *knows* that *he* was the Rav's favorite disciple! Who knows?—perhaps all were and, then again, perhaps *none* were. He so profoundly affected the lives of so many of us—in the thousands—and yet he remains somewhat remote, because not one of us *fully* encompasses all of his diverse areas of expertise, let alone the acuity of his intellect. Those who were his *talmidim* in Halakhah generally were not fully informed or sensitive to his philosophic thought, and those who considered themselves his disciples in philosophy hardly appreciated his genius in Halakhah. So, he had many students, and no students . . . But cannot the same be said of the Rambam—some of whose students followed his Halakhah, and some his philosophy, and very few, if any at all, both?

———

THE RAV NEVER blurred the distinctions between the roles of Rosh Yeshiva and Hasidic Rebbe. He aspired to have *talmidim*, not *hasidim*—challenging, questioning, independent-minded disciples, not fawning, accepting, unquestioning acolytes. That is why at the same time that he forced us into systematic thinking and molded our *derekh*, our methodology, he also gave us "space," insisting that we think and decide certain halakhic questions on our own. He lived his interpretation of the injunction in *Pirkei Avot* to proliferate students—literally, "set up many students"—as, "make a great effort to have your students *stand on their own*" and not be permanently tied to your apron-strings. But so great was his personal charisma that many of us ended up as both *talmidim and hasidim* . . .

———

IN II KINGS 1 we read of the last moments in the life of the prophet Elijah as he is accompanied by his disciple Elisha. Elijah has been told that he must prepare to be swept up to Heaven in a whirlwind, and so he wishes to take leave of his *talmid*. But three times Elisha refuses to leave his *rebbe*. Elijah casually splits the waters of the Jordan, and teacher and pupil cross the river. Elijah and Elisha continue their conversation—an important one, but not relevant to my point—and then we read: "And it came to pass as they were walking, *walking and talking*, that there appeared a chariot of fire and horses of fire which separated the two men, whereupon Elijah was swept up by a whirlwind to heaven."

I have often wondered about that last, fateful, conversation as the two walked, each to his own destiny, "walking and talk-ing." What did they talk about, that *Rebbe* and his *talmid*, during that somber but very brief period of time? How I would have wanted to be privy to that incredible conversation! Further, I was always troubled by the peripatetic nature of that conversa-tion, *walking and talking;* why a *walking* discussion, why not seated or standing?

In response, I put myself in Elisha's position vis-a-vis my own *Rebbe*, and wonder: if I were granted but 10 minutes with the Rav, both of us certain that this was the last chance to talk before the winds bore him away, what words would pass between us? I would not presume to suggest what he would say to me; but what would I say to him? What last message, last impression, would I want to leave with him?

———

TWO THINGS: First, I would walk with him rather than sit or stand because when walking you do not look at each other; I would be too embarrassed to do that. For I would say to him: Rebbe, forgive us for taking you for granted. You were so much a part of our lives, so permanent a fixture of our intellectual and spiritual experience, that we too often failed to tell you how much you meant to us, as children often neglect to let their par-ents know how much they love them. We were so engrossed in our own growth that we ignored your feelings. I leave you with a feeling of shame.

Second, we thank you. Our hearts overflow with gratitude to you, our master in Torah and in life itself.

There is not one of us who does not owe you an undying debt of gratitude. You inspired us; we bathed in admiration of your genius, fought to be accepted as *talmidim* in your *sheur,* and were actually proud when you took note of us—even to be singled out for rebuke for a "krumer sevoro," for our intellectual sloth or slovenliness. You were our ideal, our role model, even though we all knew that our natural limitations prevented us from ever reaching your level. We thrilled at the sheer virtuosity of your creativity and the brilliance of your originality in your *sheurim* in which you forced us to join you in bold experiments to dissect a *sugya,* understand a *machloket Rishonim* (a halakhic dispute among early authorities), propose a solution to a puzzling Ramban, and—to be critical of you! You gave shape and direction to our lives. We knew we were in the presence of greatness, that our *Rebbe* was a unique historical phenomenon. And deep down we were secretly frightened at the prospect that some day we would no longer have you with us.

———

WHAT CONSOLATION CAN make up for our enormous loss now that his greatness is gone, hijacked from us by history? No more for us the exquisite intellectual delight of his incomparable *sheurim,* the esthetic pleasure of discerning the artistic architecton-ics of his masterful *Yahrzeit derashot,* the edification of his eulogies, the wise counsel we sought from him on matters private or public.

———

THE YEARS OF his decline have drained us of most of our tears. But with the finality of his passing, we utter a collective sigh to the very heavens, a composite sigh composed of one part of dis-consolate *avelut,* of an endless and bottomless sadness; one part of pity for the world, "rachmones" for a world now denied the privilege of the presence of the master of Torah of this genera-tion; and one part of a promise to him that neither he nor his *derekh* nor his *hashkafah* will leave our midst or ever be forgotten. And that is why I would *walk* with him, walk and talk, because sitting or standing imply an end, no future, stagnation, whereas walking implies something unfinished, a destination still beck-oning, a sense of ongoing continuity. Our loyalty to the Rav and his teachings will live as long as we do, as long as our *talmidim* do, as long as this yeshiva exists; it will go on and on. Here, in this yeshiva where he presided as *Rosh Yeshiva* for half a century, his presence will always be palpable, his teachings will endure, and the memory of our master the Gaon, Rabbi Joseph Ber Halevi Soloveitchik, "will not cease from among us and our chil-dren forever," in the words of the book of Esther.

———

AND FINALLY, THE sigh contains one part of love. Yes—to this scion of Litvaks for generations, those of emotional restraint who abjured any display of affection as unbecoming ostentation, to this commanding and self-disciplined intellect, we express openly and unabashedly our affection and our love. And so I would conclude my "walk and talk" session with him by saying: "We loved you, Rebbe, and if we felt inhibited and embarrassed to say it to your face, we profess it to you now. We feared you, we admired you, but we loved you as well."

———

HOW APPROPRIATE IT would have been for the Rav, that living dynamo, to leave this world as Elijah did, carried off to heaven in a whirlwind . . . But alas, that was not granted to him.

When R. Avraham Shapira came here a few years ago to give a *sheur* and he met the Rav for the first time, he kissed him publicly, and whispered to me, as an aside, "it's a mitzvah to kiss a *sefer Torah.*"

Nothing lasts forever. Even a Torah scroll does not endure forever. Sometimes, we know of a Torah scroll which was burnt, such as the one consumed together with the martyred R. Hanina ben Teradyon. At other times, a Torah scroll does not have the fortune of such a dramatic end when the parchment burns but the letters fly away to their Source; instead, it is a Torah scroll which wears out, it suffers, withering away slowly, as letter by letter is painfully wrenched away from it, until it is no more. That, because of our sins, was the bitter end to the life of our very own Torah scroll. It was the very thing he feared most, and it happened to him. In the words of Job, "that which I feared has come to pass." Alas!

But we know that even if the Torah *scroll* is gone, the Torah *teaching* of the Rav will always live on with us. I recently heard of something that happened some years ago at the Brisker Yeshiva in Jerusalem, led by Rabbi Dovid Soloveitchik, son of R. Velvele Soloveitchik, *z.t.l.* The details may be fuzzy, but the essential story, I am told, is true.

A very, very old, bent-over man wandered into the yeshiva one day, and sat down and began to learn by himself. Reb Dovid came over and greeted him. The old man asked, "is this the Hebron Yeshiva?" No, answered Reb Dovid, this is the Brisker Yeshiva. At which the old man opened his eyes wide and, in disbelief, asked, *Reb Hayyim lebt noch*, "is then Reb Hayyim still alive?"

It transpired that the old man had studied in Brisk when Reb Hayyim was still alive, and left in 1913. Caught up in the Russian Communist Revolution, he was exiled to a remote area in Georgia, completely cut off from any contact with fellow Jews, especially those from Lithuania. He continued his studies for some 75 years all by himself until the great Soviet emigrations to Israel began. He had just arrived, and that is why, upon encountering the Brisker Yeshiva, he thought that Reb Hayyim was still alive . . .

And, indeed, Reb Hayyim still lives . . .

And we are here to testify and promise that *"moreinu verabbenu R. Yoshe Ber lebt noch,"* our *Rebbe* still lives, and always will, in our midst!

I read someplace that the Gaon of Vilna said that in the World of Truth they await the coming of a *talmud hakham,* who is accompanied to the Heavenly study hall in *Gan Eden,* so that he can deliver a *sheur* and expound his best *hiddushim.* He is given 180 days to prepare this public *derashah.*

Farewell, Rebbe. You always prepared for us, well and meticulously, and you no doubt will do the same now. And when you give your *sheur,* your *derashah,* before the Heavenly Court, with all the great *Gedolei Torah* of the ages in attendance, those who were your closest companions and comrades during the years of your lonely sojourn, remember us—your family and your *talmidim*—even as we shall always remember you; and may your merit and the merit of your Torah and your *chiddushim* protect us and grant health of body and mind and soul, peace—peace above all!—in every way, and love of God, love of Torah, love of the people of Israel, love of others and their love of us, to all of us—your family, your disciples and their disciples, and all of this Yeshiva to which you came half a century ago, which you graced with your greatness of mind and heart, and which was your home and our home together—and in which your presence will always be palpable and from which your memory will never fade.

For you were a blessing to us in your life-time. And *zekher tzaddikim liverakhah,* your memory will be a blessing to us forever, until the coming of the Messiah, may he come speedily in our time.

~ 2 ~
A PROGRAM
FOR ORTHODOXY

This is an exciting period for a thinking Orthodox Jew. It is a dangerous time too—when faith threatens to be swept away in the wildly whirling intellectual currents of the times. But the danger enhances the excitement and highlights the opportunities. Rarely before have we been faced with such an array of challenging, stimulating, and provoking ideas. And yet, rarely before have we reacted to such stimuli so passively, so defensively, so apprehensively, so uncreatively.

What does the Torah have to say about the great issues that confront modern man and the modern Jew? Unfortunately, I do not know. My training has left me largely unprepared for them. I have even had to overcome powerful inhibitions in order to reach the stage where I am not suspicious of the very question. Assuming that by the "battle of ideas" we mean something that transcends the petty concerns of institutional rivalry, all I can say is that—to borrow a phrase from the Zohar—the Voice of Torah today is *kol beli dibbur*, it is inchoate: a voice without words, a general cry not yet reduced to clear speech. In an age which stresses the importance of communication, we have not yet developed clear guidelines, not yet formulated convincing approaches, not yet spoken lucidly, to the cardinal issues of our century. I have faith that there *are* clear views and answers within Torah; but we have largely failed to express the *kol Torah* in *dibbur*, to articulate the vision of Torah, to spell out the implications of our tradition. Too often we have even refused to acknowledge the existence or the validity of the questions. I am therefore dispirited and vexed by our apparent unwillingness to engage in the Battle of Ideas, but optimistic as to the ultimate outcome if we finally do begin searching out the judgment of Torah and communicating it effectively.

Published in Jewish Life, *March–April 1967, this was based upon an address entitled* "The Voice of Torah in the Battle of Ideas: A Program for Orthodoxy" *at the convention of the Union of Orthodox Jewish Congregations in November 1966.*

THE RANGE OF intellectual problems that today confronts a thinking Jew—especially a young one—is quite impressive. What is the meaning of chosenness in the modern world? How can I reconcile true *emunah* with my right to question and even doubt? What is unique in the message of Torah that cannot be found elsewhere? What about Biblical criticism? What of the "moral problems" in Torah that bother so many students? What does Torah tell us about the uniqueness of man in an age of genetic engineering and psychological manipulation? How does man encounter God in a world which has yielded more and more of its secrets to scientific inquiry? How are we to advocate Halakha for the community as a whole, when those who accept Halakha are in a minority and when religion in general is becoming more marginal in society?

That Torah does offer guidance on these and all other issues is evident from the fact that *some* efforts have been made to spell out authentic Jewish views—here and there an article, a monograph, a book. In every generation attempts were made to grapple with questions that disturbed people's minds and hearts. But our generation has not yet done so, at least not adequately. Perhaps we were too busy with the exigencies of everyday life and with assuring our material and financial survival. But now survival will be determined by the quality of our ideas, and we must begin to make up for lost time. More students in Yeshivas will not solve the problem, not even bigger institutions of learning. The *size* of our schools will be meaningful only if the *content* of our teaching is germane to the life of our students, only if we succeed in relating our classical literature to life as it is lived today.

Because we barely have begun meeting these challenges, it may be wiser for us to concentrate not on specific responses of Judaism to individual problems, but on a general strategy for its campaigns in the "battle of ideas" and ideals and ideologies.

A battle plan calls, before all else, for defining our attitudes—towards our "enemies," towards other Jews, and towards our fellow Orthodox Jews.

Identifying the Problem

First it is necessary to identify the "enemy" in this battle. I submit that the enemy is not an institution and not a movement—not even Reform or Conservatism. The polemics and counter-polemics against them—and they have almost become a kind of required loyalty oath to Orthodoxy—are, for the most part, vain and fruitless. They would be amusing if they did not involve such a tremendous cost of time and talent and of good will in the community at large.

The "enemy" hovers in the pervasive intellectual climate of the whole Western world. It is the view that religion has been by-passed in our time, a view implicit in the philosophies, both ex-plicit and assumed, of secularism and naturalism, and the values of hedonism and amorality which they bring in their wake. It is not a single, well-defined ideology, but a hodge-podge of ideas of varying subtlety and depth. The adversary of Judaism, and of its endeavor to sanctify all of life through the Mitzvot, is the com-bination of attitudes—so indigenous to modern society that its members are shocked when its validity is questioned—that reli-gion is purely a matter of private conscience; that it is a collection of sacred symbols and ecclesiastical rituals, to be performed at certain times and in special places, wedded to a general and vague system of ethical values; that, as a vital force in daily exis-tence and in public affairs, it is virtually nonexistent; that its con-ception of God is a mythical "grandfather" image, and its cosmogony, taken literally, is based on an outdated world-view and is therefore totally unscientific; that it must be suffered as a historic relic by a Jewish community which is the most Western-ized of all, and indulged as the sentimental whim of some old-timers and die-hards. This potpourri, in its very heterogeneity, is symptomatic of the noxious confusions of the secularist Jew, who cannot see beyond his naturalist nose.

If there is any institutionalization of this unhealthy spiritual mood, it is in the powerful Jewish secular agencies that control the finances and the public relations of the Jewish community. I find more peril for Judaism in the Federations and defense or-ganizations than I do in the various non-Orthodox groups. The spiritual bankruptcy combined with the pecuniary and political power of the former represents a far greater threat than the sanctification of a truncated Torah by the latter. Ten, twenty, or thirty years ago there was a certain cogency to the identification of the various heterodox "Judaisms" as the most pernicious rivals to the authentic Jewish tradition. There was substance, then, to the quest in our ranks for erecting the greatest possible barriers between Orthodoxy and the other "interpretations." Let our positions be firmly marked, we argued, and better a Reformer of the American Council for Judaism type than a right-wing Conservative. Let Jews see the alternatives clearly, and let us do away with the confusions that blur the dividing lines.

I am no longer so sure that this is a valid and effective approach. The conditions of American Jewish life have changed, and yesterday's tactics may be outmoded today. Once, the ranks of Conservatism were replenished by defecting Orthodox Jews, and the Jewish Theological Seminary drew its students, to a large extent, from the dropouts from our Yeshivot. I do not believe that is true any longer, at least not to the same extent. The Conservative movement has accomplished much with its youth organization, especially its Ramah camps, and its theological students now are usually those who are on their way *in* rather than on their way *out*. One does not treat such people as renegades; one welcomes them and regrets only that they have stopped short of the true goal. In a more limited way, one may say the same of the Reform. Their young leadership is not cut of the same cloth as was the old one which considered flirtation with Christianity as far more important than pondering its sorry lack of fidelity to the Jewish tradition.

———

TODAY WE ARE all of us—all who assent to the idea that the Jewish people is more than an ethnic group with certain ethical pretensions and the pioneers of "democracy" and "Americanism," but a people dedicated to a transcendent religious vision—threatened by extinction. Between intermarriage and a depressed birth-rate, both of which are approved or at least condoned by the inner logic of Jewish secularism, the existence of the entire community is threatened. At a time of this sort we are using the wrong weapons against the wrong enemies if we continue to consider Conservatism and Reform as the sole or even the major threats to Torah.

This by no means implies a "Jewish ecumenicism" for our times. We are not now—and should *never* be—ready to give the seal of approval to "kosher-style" Judaisms. It does mean that we must concentrate our energies and talents in those areas which are today most significant and most in need of attention. It means that we must encourage any and every sign of Jewishness and Torah-consciousness, no matter how primitive and truncated, wherever we find it.

Shall we, then, apply the same means we once used against Reform and Conservatism to the various secular agencies and federations? No, decidedly not. The methods we employed in the past have not proven so successful as to be worthy of emulation in new situations. Moreover, I repeat that it is not an *institution* that threatens us, but a climate, a mood, a spirit of the age. This "enemy" is not as clearly identifiable as is an organization or a movement. It infiltrates our own ranks too, and attacks the vitals of Orthodoxy and its institutions from within.

Because this mood, so inimical to our highest interests, is not a single theory, this "enemy" is not necessarily "bad" in the sense of well defined theories antagonistic to Judaism. It is, to some extent, a collection of honest doubts, a mood of individual autonomy rather than submission to authority, a bewilderment in the face of evil of the dimensions of the Age of Auschwitz. It is such that constitutes the spirit of an age that makes it unusually difficult for Torah to prevail, as we should like to see it prevail.

———

WHEN THE ENEMY is a pervasive intellectual mood, bolstered by profound perplexities of people who are not illiterate but cultured and intelligent and honest, you cannot beat it into submission by belligerence and invective. That just does not work, especially in a democratic society. Condemnation, denunciation, and *issurim* will not convince people to return to Torah. Nor can we simply ignore problems. In a society with instantaneous communication and almost universal higher education, everyone is aware of the ideological problems even if we refuse to consider them. There is only one effective attitude to take: analysis, understanding, intelligent persuasion, ethical example, and—yes!—sympathy with and respect for opponents who often would like to believe if only we could convince them.

The right attitude towards other Jews means not to despair of our ultimate victory. It means to recognize the good inherent in the masses of non-observant Jews, a goodness that is waiting to be redeemed, that invites us to save it. The early Hasidic Tzaddik, R. Elimelech of Lizensk, interpreted the words of David: "Surely goodness and mercy shall follow me (yirdefuni) all the days of my life and I shall dwell in the House of the Lord forever" (Psalm 23). Yirdefuni means "will pursue me" more than "follow me." David is not asking merely for his personal "goodness and mercy." He is telling us that the Jew who possesses innate goodness and performs acts of mercy is such that this goodness and mercy will pursue him until they drive him back to the Source of all goodness and mercy: "and I shall dwell in the House of the Lord forever."

———

AMERICAN JEWS HAVE a tremendous reservoir of "goodness" and of "mercy." They have given munificently to Israel, to refugees, even to Yeshivot, to charities of all kinds; they have contributed strength to the cause of the racially and financially oppressed throughout the world. This goodness, if harnessed by us intelligently, can lead them to return to the House of the Lord, to the fold of Torah Judaism. If we fail to exploit this goodness for the sake of Torah, we are foolish. If all we can do is excoriate and villify Jews—we are worse. To reproach an erring Jew is a Biblical commandment. But to do so in a manner which will further alienate him is to compound obvious ineffectiveness with criminal stupidity.

Similarly, our attitude towards our fellow Orthodox Jews must be reexamined. What the times cry out for is—mutual respect. I emphasize respect, not submission. The Left must acknowledge the authenticity of the Right as a fulcrum of Torah learning and living and as a restraint upon those who might otherwise be cast adrift. And the Right must stop looking with suspicion on those who read the facts of American Jewish life differently, on those who are impatient with our patent paralysis in addressing ourselves to the bulk of American Jewry. We must restrain the hot-heads among us from posing as the exclusive Defenders of the Faith. One inane ad in the New York Times can do more to undo the effectiveness and attractiveness of Torah in this country than what the Yeshivot have accomplished in the last five or ten years. Insults lead only to a profanation of the Divine Name. Public re-crimination means the fouling of our own nest. We are not strong enough to afford such dubious luxuries.

The Message and the Medium

Given these attitudes towards the adversary, towards the general Jewish community, and towards those in our own camp, what must we do that has not yet been done in order to triumph in the Battle of Ideas?

I submit that we must reorient ourselves—in our thinking, our scholarship, our teaching, our public posture, our curricula—so that we become *relevant* to man, and Jew. We must search out those themes which address themselves most directly to modern man's yearnings, his fears, his loneliness, his desperate inner void, his magnificent technological achievements, and we must do so in an idiom which he understands, which he respects, and to which he responds.

In every age, the Sages of Israel presented the view of Torah in a manner which their contemporaries understood and which dealt with their most vital concerns. The Sephardic Sages ex-pressed Torah in a rationalist idiom, because it was Greek phi-losophy that bothered their people. R. Yehudah he-Chasid spoke in a different tongue in addressing medieval German Jewry—and struck a responsive chord.

"Both these and those are the words of the Living God." They were making the same Torah relevant to different communities. The Kabbalah, especially after its popularization; Musar in Lithuania; Hasidism in the rest of Eastern Europe—all produced great literatures, each highlighting a different aspect of the "sev-enty faces of Torah." Hirsch in Germany and Kook in Palestine did the same—they talked to the hearts and the minds of *their* contemporaries. The same truth of the same Torah must be pre-sented differently for each age and each cultural climate. Let it be clearly understood—I absolutely do not, Heaven forbid, speak of changing the Halakhah or any of the principles of Judaism. I speak only of making them *relevant*. Relevance does not mean compromise or submission to the presuppositions of Western civilization; it does imply meaningfulness and intelligibility. It means *"reden tzu der zach."* Forms may differ in response to new needs, while contents remain unchanged. The Torah is, to use the Kabbalistic metaphor, *poshet tzurah ve'lovesh tzurah.*

It is for this reason that I believe that if we are to keep our own generation attuned to the Divine Will, we must change the form of our response in a manner germane to our generation. It may not be completely true that, as Marshall McLuhan has put it, "the medium is the message." But certainly the quality of the medium can either enhance or frustrate the message. I do not believe, for instance, that such classics of Musar as the *Shevet Musar* or *Kav Hayashar* will win over Jews to Yiddishkeit in our times as they did in the days they were composed. Neither will speculative metaphysics, nor Hasidic *machshavah*, and certainly not the anti-*hashkafah hashkafah* of many Lithuanian Yeshivot. Nor, for that matter, will any successful method we develop now be very effective 200 years hence.

Insights can be salvaged, but they must be recast and paraphrased, not just translated. No two prophets, said the Rabbis, prophesied in the same style; yet they offered the same message, but applied it to differing circumstances. There are *chiddushim* (novellae) in Halakhah—and it remains the same Halakhah. So there can be—no, *must* be—different styles and even *chiddushim* in Jewish thought without doing violence to its integrity and its continuity.

————

OF COURSE, THIS idea can be taken to an extreme; and I fear that some of my colleagues may be doing just that. We cannot make relevance the *test of validity* of the Jewish tradition and we cannot expect that every item in the catalogue of Jewish belief and practice should be explicated in a manner directly relevant to every individual. That is absurd, and can lead to tragic results. Thus, we may view the Sabbath as a way of addressing man on the creative use of new-found leisure, and "Family Purity" as delineating the views of Judaism on the dignity of woman and the significance of erotic love in life. But we can never make their practice dependent upon such interpretation, nor can we expect every detail to fit into the scheme. We have it on the authority of Maimonides, no mean expositor of relevance, that whoever expects and attempts this is *mishtageia shigaon arokh*—is exceedingly mad. Unfortunately, some of us have occasionally succumbed to this madness, and the result has been an extravagance of expression that borders on the sensational and reflects both immaturity and irresponsibility. We must remember that, paradoxically, a certain amount of irrelevance is always relevant in religion.

———

BUT THIS DOES not excuse us from the task at hand.

Usually, unfortunately, we seem dreadfully irrelevant and appear to confirm the impression that we have simply been bypassed. The finest research of Orthodox Jewish scholars in history and in the editing of texts is usually done is esoteric areas of concern only to their few colleagues. Many of the Kollelim produce experts in *Kodoshim* when there are burning contemporary halakhic questions that require immediate attention—and *pesak* is sometimes disdained as a kind of halakhic technology beneath the dignity of a scholar *lishmah*. Our popular literature is often incredibly childish; it sometimes seems to be directed to backward grade school children of exceptional naiveté. Our Yeshivot shy away from the teaching of *hashkafah*, perhaps fearing the doubts it may arouse, and what they do teach of it has preciously little to do with life outside the Yeshivah. Indeed, our contemporary "Yeshivah circles" have tended to become so centripetal, so ingrown, that they often show no awareness of a Jewish world that might well accept its teachings if only it spoke out. And both the Yeshiva "world" and the "outside world" are the poorer for this abyss that separates them.

Our finest thinkers have not yet come to grips with the great issues of the times. Do we have a valid overview on the population explosion?—not a halakhic decision of Yes, or No, or Maybe, but a genuinely religious approach which sympathizes with the new dimensions of the problem? Here is an instance where we can speak to the rest of mankind without our own vital interests intruding, for Jewry is under-populated, and our judgment, in this case, specifically excludes Jews and other such small communities. Or, take the question of peace. We, the descendants of Isaiah and Micah, have left the spiritual judgments on the issue of World Peace to heterodox Jews, and worse, to Christians—whose concern for *shalom* is written over the continent of Europe in Jewish blood. We ought not merely react to the opinions of others on Viet Nam, either repudiating United States policy because other religious groups do, or supporting it because *our* religion is different. We must, rather, provide an answer that is authentically Jewish; and if we find no answer, or discover that the situation is too complicated for us—let us have the courage of silence. Similarly, despite growing numbers of Orthodox Jewish scientists, our confrontation with issues raised by natural science is about 100 years behind the times—many of us are still fighting Darwin. To the challenge of the various social sciences—which may ultimately prove more consequential than the problems raised by biology and geology—we have not yet begun to respond. That is why the Voice of Torah is a *kol beli dibbur.* We have too often made a virtue, even a dogma, of irrelevance.

Suggestions for a Strategy

What must be done in order to encourage an awareness of the Torah's relevance to life today? I would enumerate briefly, the following considerations in developing a strategy for the attainment of our goals:

1. Nothing in Judaism can have *valid* relevance unless it is based on authentic Jewish sources. Hence—the primacy of Torah and the study of Torah, Talmud and *Poskim.*

2. We must take a positive, non-apologetic attitude to secular education, and not accept it begrudgingly as a vocational necessity. Continuing the debate on Yes-College or No-College is no longer meaningful in an age where the vast majority of Jews we want to speak to are college graduates.

3. Our best and most creative thinkers must undertake the sacred task of the relevant exposition of Orthodox Judaism. That means that they must first acquaint themselves with both the

problematica and the vocabulary of modern man. This exposition must be expressed in an idiom that will be respected in the academic world. This does not imply an exaggerated reverence for "intellectuals"; it implies only that this is the most effective way of reaching most impressionable, thinking Jews.

4. We must rethink the curricula of our Yeshivot so that what our students learn is geared to preparing them for life in the "outside world" of business and the professions and not proceed, as is done now, on the unspoken assumption that they will remain in the Yeshiva forever. The choice of *masekhtot* must be done with this in mind. Most important, we must begin to teach *hashkafah* as an integral part of *talmud torah,* and not treat it as if it were a subtle kind of *bittul torah.* And the *hashkafah* itself must concern youngsters living here and now—not in Lithuania in the nineteenth century.

5. We must attempt to reach out to *all* Jews with the teachings of Torah. We must never allow ourselves the parochial satisfaction of believing that Torah was meant only for the Orthodox, and that "the others" may be scolded but need not be taught. A continuing retrenchment will harm the general Jewish community and prove self-defeating for Orthodoxy.

6. Our popular and semi-popular literature and journalism must do away with or at least minimize polemics and counter polemics, and concentrate instead on relaying the relevant teachings of Torah to all Jews, with respect for their intelligence and integrity.

7. We must willingly concede that we do not have all the answers to every new problem yet. Even in Halakha there are unanswered questions; in *hashkafah* even more so. This openness will spare us the embarrassing dilletantism that often characterizes intellectual improvisation.

8. Above all, we must be receptive to new ideas, to honest questions, and to novel situations. We must examine them objectively and not react with automatic hostility. We must, as Rav Kook taught us, build the *armon ha-torah,* the castle of Torah, around every challenge, whether of modern science or philosophy, see if we can absorb it, reflect on it patiently and then, if we find it inimical to the spirit of Torah, reject it and fight against it. Our battle must be forceful, vigorous, and courageous.

SUCH, TO MY mind, is the grand strategy we ought adopt in order to make the voice of Torah not only audible and articulate but also triumphant in the Battle of Ideas. We most certainly must do it; for if we do not, Heaven forbid, no one else will or can. I may be unhappy with what has been done—or not done—by us so far towards this end. But I know that if our faith in the Almighty and His Torah will outweigh our fear of the modern world we can accomplish our historic task, and succeed splendidly.

I conclude, then, on a more optimistic note. We Jews have remarkable staying power—both physically and spiritually. We can sustain losses and yet rebound miraculously. Our Father Jacob grappled with his mysterious assailant, whom our tradition identified as "the angel of Esau in the guise of a scholar"—the personification of the antagonists of Torah in the Battle of Ideas. In the battle, it is Jacob who is injured, not the angel. Yet we consider Jacob the victor. Why so? Because, answers R. Abraham, the son of the Rambam, Jacob did not give up that fight even *after* he was injured! He held on to the angel until he prevailed; and this special heroic quality of Jacob is an omen, for his descendants, of a powerful persistence and sustaining strength in times of crisis.

Let us proceed, with the courage born of such a tradition, to the great battles ahead of us. We may sustain some losses, and the injuries will hurt; but: *ki alah ha-shachar,* dawn is about to break on a new day for Torah, for Orthodoxy. And, if we act wisely and patiently and heroically, we can yet say to our adversary as Jacob did to his: *Lo ashaleichakha ki im berakhtani,* we shall not let you go until you have blessed us.

For we have come not to conquer you, but to convince you.

~3~

MODERN ORTHODOXY'S
IDENTITY CRISIS

The facts about our community, as represented by the Orthodox Union, are rather encouraging. Numerically and institu-
tionally, in terms of youth and influence, we are a significant
group in this country. But we are beset by many problems. And
our thorniest and most disabling problem is, curiously, an "identity crisis"—perhaps a sign of our youthfulness as an ideological
movement.

Objectively examined, what binds us together as a separate entity is our full commitment to the Torah tradition and our openness, at the same time, to the wider culture of the world about us.
To use the two dreadfully inadequate words which normally describe us as a distinct group, we are both "modern" and "orthodox." I shall be using these terms only with the greatest
hesitation. "Orthodox" is almost pejorative; it implies a stifling
and unthinking narrow-mindedness. And "modern" is amus-
ingly pretentious; it adds nothing to the validity or invalidity of
a proposition. Jacques Maritain recently referred to this as
"chronolatry," the idolatry of what is newest or latest in time.

But while this observation is true enough as far as it goes, it
does not go nearly far enough. Merely to describe what we are is
not a sufficiently convincing reason for being what we are or for
persuading others to acknowledge our rightness and join our
ranks. The great problem of modern American Orthodoxy is that
it has failed to interpret itself to itself. This failure, which reveals
itself in many ways, derives from a remarkable intellectual
timidity which we should have long outgrown.

———

ONE SHOULD NOT be too harsh in judging the past. There were
reasons—good reasons—for our apologetic posture. But it was hu-
miliating. In confronting the outside world and those to the left of

Published in Jewish Life, *May–June 1969*

us, we seemed to be saying that while we hold on to the practices and doctrines of the Jewish tradition, we are really just like everybody else, perhaps even more so. We appeared to be whispering, in unbecoming shyness, that we were not really foreign or dirty.

At the same time, we were and still are apologetic—almost masochistically—towards those to the right of us. We send our children to the universities. And we are going to continue to do so despite the campus' recent notoriety. The far right does not approve of our educational policy, which touches the heart of our distinctiveness, or our educational and congregational institutions. How do we justify ourselves? Neither by scholarship, nor by halakhic reasoning, nor by pointing to historical antecedents, nor by the philosophic validity of our stand. Instead, we present the lamest of all apologies: vocational necessity! Our whole existence is thus based on a practical economic concession—the need of a college degree in order to get a better job.

Our problem, then, is that we have yet to accept ourselves openly and directly on the basis of our major contribution to Jewish life in this century: that it is our *religious* duty, our *sacred* responsibility, to live the whole Torah tradition in the world, instead of retreating from a world in which there is literally no longer any place left to retreat to. As long as this condition of spiritual timidity and intellectual diffidence prevails, we can hardly blame the non-Orthodox world for accusing us of temporizing, the Hasidic world for ignoring us, and the Yeshivah world for disdaining us.

The challenge to our intellectual leadership is clear: to formulate the world-view of "modern Orthodoxy" in a manner that is halakhically legitimate, philosophically persuasive, religiously inspiring, and personally convincing. It is a tall order, admittedly, but one which we must fill if the great centrist mass of American Orthodox Jews is not to be pulled apart in all directions, as they stagnate in impotence and inarticulateness for want of a clear world-view *(shitah)* to which they can feel fully committed in good conscience.

———

IN ITS ENCOUNTER with the "outside world" of non-observant Jewry and the rest of mankind, modern Orthodoxy must offer neither "more of the same" nor the illusory advantages of escape and withdrawal. It must present viable options to the prevalent doctrines of the culture of the West, in terms that men and women born into this culture can understand and appreciate. We must make available attractive Jewish alternatives to the nihilism and permissiveness and meaninglessness and Godlessness of secular life. These alternatives must be neither distorted nor compromised, but they must be expressed and elaborated in the cultural and psychological idioms of the contemporary world.

Judaism was born in protest against the idolatries of a simpler age, and must not fail to reject those of our own, far more complicated day. Our message must always be critical and restless with the complacent dogma of a society content with the correctness of its spiritual paralysis.

I cannot accept the idea that Orthodoxy must defensively retreat and wait for Messiah until it speaks to mankind. We must engage the world right now and, speaking in a cultural idiom it understands, say that we are dissatisfied with it. We must declare forthrightly that its "sexual revolution" is atavistic, a throwback to pagan debauchery; that its conception of man is depressingly shallow; that its prescription for happiness is vulgar and dangerous; that its conception of education is trivial and dehumanizing.

WE MUST, THEN, learn to speak persuasively and intelligibly to the man of today about transcendent purpose, about the meaning of the Covenant, about the significance of halakhic living both for personal meaningfulness and for the fulfillment of our covenantal obligations. Never again must we stoop to the kind of inane religious propaganda, which we once considered so very "modern," which led us to offer as proof of the correctness of our commitment the avoidance of cancer or trichinosis by virtue of the practice of certain observances.

It is equally important that we explain ourselves clearly, forthrightly, and unapologetically to those of our Orthodox Jewish brethren who do not accept our involvement in the wider culture as an integral part of our world outlook. We must make it explicit and clear that we are committed to secular studies, including our willingness to embrace all the risks that this implies, not alone because of vocational or social reasons, but because we consider that it is the will of God that there be a world in which Torah be effective; that all wisdom issues ultimately from the Wisdom of the Creator, and therefore it is the Almighty who legitimates *all* knowledge; that a world cannot exist, and that certainly an independent Jewish state cannot exist in the contemporary world, in which some of the best of its brains and the most sensitive of its religious spirits will condemn as sinful and dangerous those profane disciplines which alone can keep it alive and prosperous. Our *religious* commitment to such principles must be as passionate and as faithful and as *Jewish* as was that of the Hirschian movement, especially in the first two generations of its history, in the context of conditions that prevail in this second third of the twentieth century.

———

FOR OUR OWN times, if we are to make any headway in the "contest for the Jewish mind," we must resolve the central dilemma of the tension between our "two worlds." A transcendental theological schizophrenia is no virtue. We must, in terms of our own tradition, formulate the method whereby we can accord religious significance to the "other"—the so-called profane or modern—world. But which branches of general knowledge are legitimate for the loyal Jew—the one who is not concerned with vocational dispensations but with a religious world-view? May we ever accord the status of *Mitzvah* to a secular discipline? Can we consider it technically as the performance of *talmud torah*—remembering that Maimonides himself felt so inclined? As a minimum, we may grant that scientific, especially medical, studies possess religious significance. As a maximum, they will never attain the rank of Torah and Talmud. But where do they stand in between these two poles?

Rav Kook, of blessed memory, spoke of harmony as the great Jewish ideal, and he included within it the polarities of physicality and spirituality, of the sacred and the profane, even of faith and doubt as part of cosmic unity. It remains for us to elaborate the metaphysical framework and even more, fill in the practical details.

This does not at all mean that we reject or condemn or do not wish to cooperate intensively at all levels with those groupings within Orthodox Jewry which do not accept these premises. On the contrary, with more confidence in the religious rightness of our stand, we will be less subject to intimidation by those who feel sure of their different commitments within the context of the halakhic discipline. Perhaps then we shall come to understand that the rabbinic dictum that "there are seventy faces to Torah" refers to social and cultural patterns and to intellectual formulations and attitudes as well as to exegetical approaches. We shall then realize that the Lithuanian yeshivah world was different from the Spanish world of Maimonides, and the Hasidic world different from that of Rashi, and all of them different from each other and from us and from the world of Rabbi Akiva. All were different—and yet all essentially the same because all are aspects of one Torah, bound by one common halakhic commitment. This firmly and unequivocally excludes the non-Orthodox movements. But it also means that Judaism need not always develop in one mold, whether that of Brisk or Satmar or even Yeshiva University. We have our own contribution to make to these "seventy faces of Torah," and it is no tergiversation or betrayal to state positively those emphases and issues wherein we differ.

I HAVE THE feeling that if Jewry and Judaism are to survive in the Diaspora, it will be indebted largely to our group. I do not mean this as a boast—I think it is frightening. If Israel is not to reduce to another Levantine mini-state, but is to become the political expression of the *am segulah,* then it will be the result of the work and inspiration and self-sacrifice of like-minded groups in Israel, presently inarticulate and inchoate, with whom we must work in tandem. But this requires of us a keen awareness of our own responsibility, a refusal to remain weak-willed and apologetic, and the courage of our convictions that our approach is a legitimate expression of *avodat ha-Shem.*

The intellectual leaders of modern American Orthodoxy have a Herculean but exciting, vital task before them. Unless it is discharged properly and sensitively, we shall continue to bear the progressively heavy burden of a collective inferiority feeling which will earn us disdain from without and engender for us confusion from within.

". . . Ye shall turn aside neither to the right nor to the left—but you shall walk in the way which the Lord your God has commanded you, that you may live and that it might be well with you, and that you may prolong your days in the land which you shall possess" (Deut. 5:29, 30).

~ 4 ~

SOME COMMENTS ON
CENTRIST ORTHODOXY

Carl Becker, the great American historian, once said: "It is important, every so often, to look at the things that go without saying to be sure that they are still going." I would add the need for intellectual vigilance to this reminder for practical caution by paraphrasing his aphorism: "It is important, every so often, to look at what we are saying about the things that go without saying to make sure we know what we are talking about."

In reflecting on some of the foundations of our *Weltanschauung*, I do not presume to be imparting new information. The task I have set for myself is to summarize and clarify, rather than to innovate. Dr. Johnson once said that it is important not only to instruct people but also to remind them. I shall take his sage advice for this discourse.

We seem to be suffering from a terminological identity crisis. We now call ourselves "Centrist Orthodoxy." There was a time, not too long ago, when we referred to ourselves as "Modern Orthodox." Others tell us that we should call ourselves simply "Orthodox," without any qualifiers, and leave it to the other Orthodox groups to conjure up adjectives for themselves. I agree with the last view in principle, but shall defer to the advocates of "Centrist Orthodoxy" for two reasons: First, it is a waste of intellectual effort and precious time to argue about titles when there are so many truly significant issues that clamor for our attention. In no way should the choice of one adjective over the other be invested with any substantive significance or assumed to be a "signal" of ideological position.

We are what we are, and we should neither brag nor be apologetic about it. These days, we do more of the latter than the former, and I find that reprehensible. Let us be open and forthright about our convictions: They are *le'khat'chilah*, to begin with, and not *bi'di'avad*, after the fact. We must not be intimidated by those who question our legitimacy for whatever reason. Nevertheless—or maybe because of our ideological self-confidence—we must be ready to confront, firmly but respectfully, any challenges to our position.

It is in this spirit that I mention an argument that is often offered to refute our Centrist outlook: that, after all, we have introduced "changes," and that such changes bespeak our lack of fealty to Torah and Halakhas. We are taunted by the old aphorism, *chadash assur min ha-torah,* that anything new, any change, constitutes an offense against Torah. (It is interesting how a homiletical *bon mot* by the immortal *Chatam Sofer* has been adopted as an Article of Faith. I wonder how many good Jews really believe that it is an ancient warning against any new ideas and not a halakhic proscription of certain types of grain at certain times of the year . . .)

Have we really introduced "changes?" Yes and No. No, not a single fundamental of Judaism has been disturbed by us. We adhere to the same *ikkarim,* we are loyal to the same Torah, we strive for the same study of Torah and observance of the *mitzvot* that our parents and grandparents before us cherished throughout the generations, from Sinai onward.

But yes, we have introduced innovations, certainly relative to the East European model which is our cherished touchstone, our intellectual and spiritual origin, and the source of our nostalgia. We are Orthodox Jews, most of us of East European descent, who have, however, undergone the modern experience—and survived it; who refuse to accept modernity uncritically, but equally so refuse to reject it unthinkingly; who have lived through the most fateful period of the history of our people and want to derive some invaluable lessons from this experience, truths that may have been latent heretofore. In this sense, we have indeed changed from the idealized, romanticized, and in many ways real picture of the *shtetl,* whether of "lomdisch" Lithuania or the Hasidic courts.

Do these changes delegitimize us as Orthodox Jews, as followers of Halakhah, as *benei Torah?* My answer is a full and unequivocal No.

The "changes" we have introduced into the theory and practice of Orthodox Judaism have resulted not in the diminution of Torah but in its expansion. Some changes are, indeed, for the good. And such positive and welcome changes were introduced at many a critical juncture in Jewish history.

These changes (actually changes in emphasis rather than substance), which we will describe and explain presently, were occasioned by the radically new life experiences of the last several generations. They are genuine Torah responses to unprecedented challenges to our whole way of life and way of thinking. They include: modernity—its openness, its critical stance, its historicism; the democratic experience which, most recently, has raised the serious challenge of the new role of women in family and society; the growth of science and technology, and the scientific method applied to so many fields beyond the natural sciences; almost universal higher worldly education amongst Jews—which destroys the common assumption of bygone generations that an *am ha-aretz* in Torah is an unlettered ignoramus in general; the historically wrenching experience of the Holocaust; the miraculous rise of the State of Israel; and the reduction of observant and believing Jews to a small minority of the Jewish people—a condition unknown since the darkest periods of the Biblical era.

What are some of our contributions to Torah Judaism? Let us adumbrate several of the more characteristic foundations of our *Weltanschauung,* some of which may appear more innovative and some of which are "different" only because of the emphasis we place upon them relative to other ideas and ideals. They deal with the general areas of education, moderation, and the people of Israel.

The first is *Torah Umadda,* the "synthesis" of Torah and worldly knowledge. For the latter term, *Madda,* we can just as well substitute the Hirschian *Derekh Eretz,* though I prefer *Chokhmah* to both; it is the term used both in the Midrash and in the writings of Maimonides.*

For us, the study of worldly wisdom is not a concession to economic necessity. It is *de jure,* not *de facto.* I have never understood how the excuse of permitting "college" for the sake of *parnasah* or earning a living can be advocated by religiously serious people. If all secular learning is regarded as dangerous spiritually and for-

---

*For more on the theme of *Torah Umadda,* see my book of the same name published in 1990.

bidden halakhically, what right does one have to tolerate it at all? Why not restrict careers for Orthodox Jews to the trades and small businesses? Is the difference in wages between a computer programmer and a shoe salesman large enough to dismiss the "halakhic" prohibition of the academic training necessary for the former? The Hasidic communities and part of the Mitnagdic yeshiva world, which indeed proscribe any and all contact with secular academic learning, have at least the virtue of consistency. One cannot say the same for the more moderate or modernist factions of the "yeshiva world" which condone "college" for purposes of a livelihood (while insisting upon rather arbitrary and even bizarre distinctions amongst various courses and disciplines) at the same time that they criticize, usually intemperately, the Centrist Orthodox for their open attitude towards the world of culture.

For us, the study of worldly wisdom *enhances* Torah. It reveals not a lowering of the value of Torah in the hierarchy of values, but a symbiotic or synergistic view.

Critics of the *Torah Umadda* school have argued that our view is premised on a flawed appreciation of Torah, namely, that we do not subscribe to the wholeness and self-sufficiency of Torah. *Torah Umadda* implies, they aver, that Torah is not complete, that it is lacking; else, why the need for secular learning?

This critique is usually based upon the Mishnah in *Avot* (5:26) that *hafakh bah ve'hafakh bah de'kula bah*—delve into Torah intensively, and you will discover that it contains everything. Hence, the Tannaim believed that Torah is the repository of all wisdom, and therefore independent study of other systems of thought and culture is a denial of this authoritative comprehensiveness of Torah.

Truth to tell, this is indeed the interpretation of this particular Mishnah by the Gaon of Vilna in his Commentary: The Torah contains, in hidden as well as revealed form, the totality of knowledge. But does this really imply that there is no independent role for *Madda* or *Chokhmah*?

Not at all. First, the Gaon himself is quoted by one of his students, R. Baruch of Shklov, as saying that ignorance of other forms of wisdom results in a hundredfold ignorance of Torah: "for Torah and wisdom are bound together" (Introduction to *Sefer Euclidos*, 1781). The last clause itself belies the view that all wisdom, including worldly wisdom, is contained within the

Torah. While it is true that the Gaon was extremely adept at demonstrating, through various complex and arcane means, that the many aspects of Torah interpenetrate each other so that, for instance, elements of the Oral Torah are discoverable in the text of Scripture, still we may not be correct in assuming that his interpretation of this Mishnah is anything more than its face value. In all probability it does *not* represent the essence of his encompassing view on the nature of Torah. Moreover, even if one insists upon ascribing to the Gaon such a radical view of Torah based upon this comment, he clearly does maintain that the secular disciplines are necessary to unlock the vault of Torah in order to reveal the profane wisdom that lies latent within it.

Second, we find instances where the Sages clearly delineate Torah from Wisdom, *Chokhmah*. Thus, in Midrash Ekhah, 2, we read: "if you are told that the Gentiles possess wisdom, believe it; that they possess Torah, do not believe it." What we have here is not a confrontation between sacred and secular wisdom, but an expression of their complementarity: Each is valuable, each has its particular sphere. "Torah" is our particularist corpus of sacred wisdom, confined to the people of Israel, while "Wisdom" is the universal heritage of all mankind in which Jews share equally even though it is not their own exclusive preserve.

Finally, the debate on the meaning of the Gaon's words notwithstanding, his is not the only authoritative interpretation of the passage in the Mishnah. Meiri sees this passage as teaching that any problem within Torah itself is solvable without having recourse to sources outside of Torah. Torah, thus, is self-sufficient as sacred teaching; it makes no claims on being the sole repository of all wisdom, divine and human. This much more modest exegesis is certainly more palatable for us, living in an age of the explosion of knowledge and the incredible advances of science and technology. The view some ascribe to the Gaon, that there is no autonomous wisdom other than Torah, because it is all contained in Torah, would leave us profoundly perplexed. No amount of intellectual legerdemain or midrashic pyrotechnics can convince us that the Torah, somehow, possesses within itself the secrets of quantum mechanics and the synthesis of DNA and the mathematics that underlie the prediction of macroeconomic fluctuations and . . . and . . . No such problems arise if we adopt the simpler explanation of Meiri.

For those of us in the Centrist camp, *Torah Umadda* does not imply the coequality of the two poles. Torah remains the unchallenged and pre-eminent center of our lives, our community, our value system. But centrality is not the same as exclusivity. It does not imply the rejection of all other forms or sources of knowledge, such that non-sacred learning constitutes a transgression. It does not yield the astounding conclusion that ignorance of Wisdom becomes a virtue. I cannot reconcile myself, or my reading of the whole Torah tradition, with the idea that ignorance—any ignorance—should be raised to the level of a transcendental good and a source of ideological pride.

Time does not permit a more extensive analysis, based upon appropriate sources, of the relationship between *Torah* and *Madda* within the context of *Torah Umadda.* But this one note should be added: Granting that Wisdom has autonomous rights, it does not remain outside the purview in Torah as a corpus of texts or body of knowledge. Ultimately, as Rav Kook taught, both the sacred and the profane are profoundly interrelated; "the Holy of Holies is the source of both the holy and the profane." The Author of the Book of Exodus, the repository of the beginnings of the halakhic portions of the Torah, is the self-same Author of the Book of Genesis, the teachings about God as the universal Creator, and hence the subject matter of all the non-halakhic disciplines. Truly, "both these and these are the words of the living God!" (This may provide an alternative answer to the famous question of Rashi at the beginning of Genesis, as to why the Torah begins with the story of the genesis of the world rather than with the first *mitzvah* as recorded in Exodus.)

The second important principle that distinguishes Centrist Orthodoxy is that of *moderation.* Of course, this should by no means be considered a "change" or "innovation"; moderation is, if anything, more mainstream than extremism. But in today's environment, true moderation appears as an aberration or, worse, a manifestation of spinelessness, a lack of commitment. And that is precisely what moderation is not. It is the result neither of guile nor of indifference nor of prudence; it is a matter of sacred principle. Moderation must not be understood as the mindless application of an arithmetic average or mean to any and all problems. It is the expression of an earnest, sober, and intelligent assessment of each situation, bearing in mind two things: the need to consider the realities of any particular situation as well as general abstract theories or principles; and the awareness of the complexities of life, the "stubborn and irreducible" facts of existence, as William James called them, which refuse to yield to simplistic or single-minded solutions. Moderation issues from a broad *Weltanschauung* or world view rather than from tunnel vision.

It was, as is well known, Maimonides who established moderation as a principle of Judaism when he elaborated his doctrine of "the middle way," *derekh ha-benonit* or *derekh ha-emetzait*, as the Judaized version of the Aristotelian Golden Mean in his *Hilkhot De'ot* as well as in his earlier "Eight Chapters." The mean is, for Rambam, the right way and the way of the virtuous (*ha-derekh ha-yesharah, derekh ha-tovim*). The mean is not absolute; Maimonides records two standard exceptions and describes certain general situations where the mean does not apply. This alone demonstrates that the principle of moderation is not, as I previously mentioned, a "mindless application of arithmetic averages" to his philosophy of character.

Of course, Maimonides is speaking primarily of moral dispositions and individual personality, not of political or social conduct. Yet, there is good reason to assume that the broad outlines of his doctrine of moderation apply as well to the social and political spheres. First, there is no *prima facie* reason to assume that because Maimonides exemplifies his principle by references to personal or characterological dispositions, that this concept does not apply to collectivities, such as the polis or society or the nation, *mutatis mutandis*. Indeed, there is less justification for mass extremism than for individual imbalance. Second, his own historical record reveals a balanced approach to communal problems which, while often heroic, is not at all extremist. Special mention might be made of his conciliatory attitude towards the Karaites despite his judgment as to their halakhic status. But this is a subject which will take us far afield and must be left for another time.

Third, Maimonides refers to a specific verse which, upon further investigation, reveals significant insights. He identifies the Middle Way with the "way of the Lord," citing Genesis 18:19— "For I have known him to the end that he may command his children and his household after him that they may keep the way of the Lord, to do righteousness and justice." The Middle Way is the Divine Way, the Way of the Lord, and the assurance of a just and moral world ("to do righteousness and justice"). It is the essential legacy that one generation must aspire to bequeath to the next: "that he (Abraham) may command his children and his household after him that they may keep the way of the Lord. . . ."

Now consider the context of this verse, which Maimonides sees as the source of the teaching of moderation. It appears just after the very beginning of the story of the evil of Sodom and Gomorrah. Verses 16, 17, and 18, just preceding the passages we have cited, tell of the angels looking upon Sodom as Abraham accompanies them on their way: "And the Lord said: Shall I hide from Abraham that which I am doing [to Sodom], seeing that Abraham shall surely become a great and mighty nation, and all the nations shall be blessed in him? For I have known him (or, preferably: I love him) to the end that he may command his children and his household after him that they may keep the way of the Lord. . . ." God wants Abraham to exercise his quality of moderation, the Way of the Lord, on the Lord Himself as it were, praying for the Lord to moderate the extreme decree of destruction against Sodom and Gomorrah. And Abraham almost succeeds: What follows is the immortal passage of the Lord informing Abraham of His intention to utterly destroy the two cities of wickedness, and Abraham pleading for their survival if they contain at least ten innocent people.

Surely, the "Way of the Lord" refers to more than personal temperance alone; the doctrine of moderation, which the term implies according to Maimonides, is set in the context of Abraham's office of a blessing to all the peoples of the earth, and of his heroic defense of Sodom and Gomorrah—symbols of the very antithesis of all Abraham stands for. A more political or communal example of moderation and temperance, of tolerance and sensitivity, is hard to come by. Yet for Maimonides, this is the Way of the Lord. The Way of the Lord speaks, therefore, not only of personal attributes but of the widest and broadest scopes of human endeavor as well.

Our times are marked by a painful absence of moderation. Extremism is rampant, especially in our religious life. Of course, there are reasons—unhappily, too often they are very good reasons—for the new expressions of zealotry. There is so very much in contemporary life that is reprehensible and ugly, that it is hard to fault those who reject all of it with unconcealed and indiscriminate contempt. Moreover, extremism is psychologically more satisfying and intellectually easier to handle. It requires fewer fine distinctions, it imposes no burden of selection and evaluation, and substitutes passion for subtlety. Simplicism and extremism go hand in hand. Yet one must always bear in mind what Murray Nicholas Butler once said: The extremes are more logical and more consistent—but they are absurd.

It is this moral recoil from absurdity and the penchant for simplistic solutions and intellectual short-cuts, as well as the positive Jewish teaching of moderation as the "way of the Lord," that must inform our public policy in Jewish matters today. The Way of the Lord that was imparted to Abraham at the eve of the great cataclysm of antiquity must remain the guiding principle for Jews of our era who have emerged from an incomparably greater and more evil catastrophe. Moderation, in our times, requires courage and the willingness to risk not only criticism but abuse.

Test the accuracy of this statement by an exercise of the imagination. Speculate on what the reactions would be to Abraham if he were to be alive today, in the 1980's, pleading for Sodom and Gomorrah. Placards would no doubt rise on every wall of Jerusalem: *"shomu shamayim al zot . . ."*, the scandal of a purportedly Orthodox leader daring to speak out on behalf of the wicked evildoers and defying the opinions of all the "Gedolim" of our times! Emergency meetings of rabbinic organizations in New York would be convened, resulting in a statement to the press that what could one expect of a man who had stooped to a dialogue with the King of Sodom himself. Rumors would fly that the dialogue was occasioned by self-interest—the concern for his nephew Lot. American-born Neturei Karta demonstrators in Israel would parade their signs before the foreign press and TV cameras: "WASTE SODOM . . . NUKE GOMORRAH . . . ABRAHAM DOESN'T SPEAK FOR RELIGIOUS JEWRY." Halakhic periodicals would carry editorials granting that Abraham was indeed a *talmid chakham*, but he has violated the principle of *emunat chakhamim* (assumed to be the warrant for a kind of intellectual authoritarianism) by ignoring the weight of rabbinic opinion that Sodom and Gomorrah, like Amalek, must be exterminated. Indeed, what can one expect other than pernicious results from

one who is well known to have flirted with Zionism . . . ? And beyond words and demonstrations, Abraham would be physically
threatened by the Kach strongmen, shaking their fists and shouting accusations of treason at him. And so on and so on.

I cannot leave the subject of moderation without at least some
reference to a matter which never fails to irritate me, and that is:
bad manners. Some may dismiss this concern as mere etiquette
and unworthy of serious consideration. But I beg to differ. The
chronic nastiness that characterizes so much of our internal
polemics in Jewish life is more than esthetically repugnant; it is
both the cause and effect of extremism, insensitivity, and intolerance in our ranks. We savage each other mercilessly, thinking we
are scoring points with "our side"—whichever side that is—and
are unaware that we are winning naught but scorn from the
"outside world." Our debates are measured in decibels, or numbers of media outlets reached, rather than by the ideas propounded and the cogency of our arguments. True, when one
takes things seriously it is difficult to observe all the canons of
propriety; tolerance comes easier to men of convenience than to
men of conviction. But there is a world of difference between a
crie de coeur that occasionally issues from genuine outrage and
the hoarse cry of coarseness for its own sake that infects our public discourse like a foul plague.

Let others do as they wish. We, of our camp, must know and
do better. If our encounter with our dissenting fellow Jews of any
persuasion is to be conducted out of love and concern rather
than enmity and contempt, then moderation must mark the form
and style as well as substance of our position.

That is our task as part of our affirmation of moderation as a
guiding principle of Centrist Orthodoxy. Our halakhic decisions,
whether favorable or unfavorable to the questioner, whether
strict or liberal, must never be phrased in a manner designed to
repel people and cause Torah to be lowered in their esteem. Unfortunately, that often happens—even in our own circles, especially when we try to outdo others in manifestations of our piety.

The third principle of Centrist Orthodoxy is the centrality of
the people of Israel. *Ahavat Yisrael*, the love of Israel, and the high
significance it attains in our lives is the only value that can in any
way challenge the preeminence of Torah and its corollary, *ahavat
ha-Torah*, the love of Torah.

The tension between these two values, Torah and Israel, has been dormant for centuries. Thus, in the High Middle Ages we find divergent approaches by R. Saadia Gaon and by R. Yehuda Halevi. The former asserts the undisputed primacy of Torah: It is that which fashioned Israel and which remains, therefore, axiologically central. Saadia avers: "our people Israel is a people only by virtue of its Torahs" (i.e., the Written and the Oral Torah; *Emunot ve-De'ot* 3:7). Halevi maintains the reverse position: "If not for the Children of Israel, there would be no Torah in the world" (*Kuzari* 2:56). Israel precedes Torah both chronologically and axiologically. Hints of the one position or the other may be found scattered through the literature, both before and after Saadia and Halevi. Perhaps the most explicit is that of *Tanna de-Vei Eliyahu*, which tells of an encounter between a scholar and an incompletely educated Jew. The scholar records the following conversation:

> He said to me, "Rabbi, two things weigh upon my heart, and I love them both—Torah and Israel—but I do not know which comes first." I said to him, "People usually say that Torah comes first, before all else, as it is said, 'The Lord made me [Torah, wisdom] as the beginning of His way' (Prov. 8:22); but I say that the holy Israel comes first, as it is said, 'Israel is the Lord's hallowed portion, the first fruits of His increase' (Jer. 2:3)"
>
> —*S.E.R.*, Ish Shalom edition, chap. 15, p. 17

Now, these two opposing viewpoints have lived peacefully, side by side, for centuries, their conflict latent—until our own days when, as a result of the trauma of the Holocaust and the reduction of Orthodoxy to a decided minority, the problem assumes large, poignant, and possibly tragic proportions. The confrontation between the two, if allowed to get out of hand, can have the most cataclysmic effects on the future of the House of Israel as well as the State of Israel. History calls upon us to abandon tired formulas and ossified cliches and make a deliberate, conscious effort to develop policies which, even if choices between the two must be made, will lead us to embrace both and retain the maximum of each. We shall have to undertake a difficult analytic calculus: Which of the two leads to the other?—and give primacy to the preference which inexorably moves us on to the next love, so that in the end we lose neither. Ultimately, there can be no Torah without Israel and no Israel without Torah. In the language of the Zohar, *Yisrael ve'oraita echad hu* . . . Israel and Torah are one.

If indeed such a calculus has to be undertaken, then Orthodox Jews will have to rethink their policy. Heretofore, the attitude most prevalent has been that Torah takes precedence—witness the readiness of our fellow Orthodox Jews to turn exclusivist, to the extent that psychologically, though certainly not halakhically, many of our people no longer regard non-Orthodox Jews as part of *Kelal Yisrael.* But this choice of love of Torah over love of Israel is a dead end: Such a decision is a final one, for it cuts off the rest of the Jewish people permanently. Such love of Torah does not lead to love of Israel; most certainly not. The alternative, the precedence given to love of Israel over love of Torah, is more reasonable, for although we may rue the outrageous violations of Torah and Halakhah and their legitimation by non-Orthodox groups, a more open and tolerant attitude to our deviationist brethren *may* somehow lead to their rethinking their positions and returning to identification with Torah and its values; *ahavat Yisrael* may well lead to *ahavat ha-Torah.* A posture of rejection, certainly one of triumphalist arrogance, will most certainly not prove attractive and fruitful.

Moreover, if there ever was a time that a hard choice had to be made to reject Jews, this is not the time to do so. In this post-Holocaust age, when we lost fully one third of our people, and when the combination of negative demography and rampant assimilation and out-marriage threaten our viability as a people, we must seek to hold on to Jews and not repel them. Love of Israel has so often been used as a slogan—and a political one, at that—that it dulls the senses and evokes no reaction. Yet, like cliches, slogans contain nuggets of truth and wisdom, and we ignore them at our own peril.

Included in the rubric of the centrality of the people of Israel as a fundamental distinguishing tenet of Centrist Orthodoxy is the high significance of the State of Israel. If I fail to elaborate on this principle it is not because of its lack of importance but, on the contrary, because it is self-evident. Whether or not we attribute Messianic dimensions to the State of Israel, and I personally do not subscribe to or recite the prayer of *reshit tzemichat ge'ulatenu*, its value to us and all of Jewish history is beyond dispute. Our love of Israel clearly embraces the State of Israel, without which the fate of the people of Israel would have been tragically sealed.

Such, in summary, are some of the major premises of Centrist Orthodoxy. They are not all, of course, but they are important and consequential.

The path we have chosen for ourselves is not an easy one. It requires of us to exercise our Torah responsibility at almost every step, facing new challenges with the courage of constant renewal. It means we must always assess each new situation as it arises and often perform delicate balancing acts as the tension between opposing goods confronts us. But we know that, with confidence in our ultimate convictions, we shall prevail. For our ultimate faith and our greatest love is—the love of God. The great Hasidic thinker, R. Zadok haKohen, taught us in his *Tzidkat ha-Tzaddik* (no. 197) that there are three primary loves—of God and Torah and Israel. The latter two he calls "revealed" loves, and the love of God—the "concealed" love, for even if the religious dimension seems absent, as long as there is genuine love of Torah or love of Israel, we may be sure that it is empowered and energized by the love of God, but that the latter is concealed, and often buried in the unconscious. It is this above all that is the source of our loves, our commitments, our confidences.

Rav Kook used to tell of his school days as a youngster in White Russia. The winters were fierce, the snows massive, the roads impenetrable. He and the others lived on a hill, and the school was at the bottom of that hill. He and his classmates would usually fail to negotiate the difficult downward trek, and appear in school bruised and tattered. At the same time, their teacher would arrive spotless, safe, and clean. When asked by his charges how he managed this feat, he replied: there is a stake fastened into the hill, and another here at school, and a rope connects them. Hold onto this life-line, and you will be safe: "if you are firmly anchored up above, you will not slip here below."

~5~

CENTRIST ORTHODOXY
AND MODERATIONISM
Definitions and Desiderata

Critics of the name "Centrist Orthodoxy" assume that it indi-cates that we locate ourselves mid-point between Ortho-doxy and assimilationism and claim that territory as our religious home. That, of course, is nonsense; such an implication would effectively be tantamount to abandoning Torah Judaism in favor of some compromise of basic principles. Only slightly less absurd is the idea that Centrist Orthodoxy is the "center" be-tween Satmar and the few intellectuals who presumably consti-tute the Orthodox Left. It is no compliment to our intelligence to imagine that in the name of Centrism we advocate walking about the religious terrain with a yard-stick, calipers, and a pocket calculator, measuring the exact distance between Neturei Karta and "Humanistic Judaism" in order to locate the exact middle or "center." We are not, and do no aspire to be, ideologi-cal geographers or spiritual surveyors who search out the exact point between right and wrong, religious and non-religious, *mitzvah* and *averah*, and settle upon that center as our religious goal. Centrism may be wrong-headed, but it is not that spiritu-ally simple-minded or religiously asinine.

Whatever one may think of the term "Centrist Orthodoxy" and its merits relative to "Modern Orthodoxy" or "Dati Ortho-doxy" (a designation that has much to commend it) or no name at all, what it says is something vastly different from the infantile inference I have described.

I begin with these prologomena about our identification not because I attribute any significance to it *per se*, but because the name does indeed indicate a definite point of view, and that is the question of moderation which I take to be so fundamental a

Published in the Year Book of Religious Zionism, 1989–1990

characteristic of our *hashkafah* that we can rightly refer to it as "moderatio*nism*."

Of course, one of the difficulties with this self-definition is that the crown is claimed by many pretenders. Most religious movements in our contemporary Jewish community consider themselves moderate and can point to rival positions on either side of them. But that is not the kind of moderation I have in mind. My concern at this occasion is not the practice of a moderate stance, but the theoretical background out of which such moderation issues; hence, my emphasis on moderatio*nism* and not only moderation as such. It is an ideological policy and not just our collective disposition.

In order to clarify what is meant by moderation and its relation to Centrism, it is worth sketching briefly some of the background of the "theory of the mean" (or center or middle) in Maimonides' thought. (I shall here be elaborating upon [some of] what I began to say in an article in the Fall 1986 issue of *Tradition;* see the previous article.)

It was Maimonides who established moderation as a principle of Judaism when, in his *Mishneh Torah* (*Hil-Deiot*) as well as in his earlier "Eight Chapters," he elaborated his doctrine of the mean or "the middle way" (*ha-derekh ha-emtza'it* or *ha-derekh ha-benonit*) as the Judaized version of the Aristotelian Golden Mean. The mean is, for Maimonides, the "right way" and the "way of the virtuous" (*ha-derekh ha-yesharah, derekh ha-tovim*) and, most significantly, "the way of the Lord" (*derekh Hashem*).

Every disposition or facet of character can be plotted along a line going from one extreme to another. Thus, to take an example from the way we deal with money: one can be greedy or, at the other extreme, extravagant and a squanderer. Some place in the center, in between parsimoniousness and exorbitance, is the intelligent and moderate way of handling money. Another example: concern for one's own well-being. At one end is cowardice, at the other extreme is a foolish boldness that is unnecessarily dangerous, and in the middle is a moderate and sane form of courage.

Now, this doctrine of the mean, the basis of the theory of moderation, is open to attack on several grounds. First, there is objection to our particular use of this doctrine because Maimonides here writes of individual character, not of national or social policy—of personal dispositions, not religious outlooks and ideology. And second, regarding the theory itself, it appears to be highly artificial: a mathematical approach to life and character which should, in truth, be more existential than arithmetic. Does moderationism mean that one must be bloodlessly "parve," never getting angry, excited, revolted, indignant, no matter what the provocation? In truth, in its arithmetic form, the theory appears flat, emotionally inhibiting, passionless, and uninspiring.

Let us respond to these criticisms in order. (Regarding the first criticism, see my *Tradition* article, here reprinted as the previous article.)

We turn now to the second charge against moderationism. It is accused of being too artificial and arithmetic in directing us to the exact middle, mathematically equidistant from both extremes at the ends of the spectrum, and it is thus emotionally inhibiting and spiritually bloodless.

About thirty five years ago, my teacher and mentor, Rabbi Joseph B. Soloveitchik, [for whose recovery I devoutly pray,] addressed a convention of the Rabbinical Council of America in Detroit. Among other things, he said that we err in assuming that Maimonides is prescribing an arithmetic approach to *de'ot*—character traits or dispositions. Rather, Maimonides' approach is far more subtle and dynamic: he favors the ability to go from one end to the other of the spectrum as necessity requires it, so that in sum and on the average we stay in the center, but not that we remain unalterably and unerringly glued to one mid-point.

I recall being enchanted by this interpretation, because I had long been troubled by the flatness of the apparently one-dimensional approach of Maimonides. But I could not at that time agree that this explanation by "the Rav" was indeed consonant with the expressed view of Maimonides. However, one learns never to dismiss an opinion of the Rav without a great deal of thought, and more than three decades of such thought have borne him out.

According to Maimonides, in man's natural state, nature and nurture both combine to place him someplace off-center on each spectrum band of character, We are either too sparing or too spendthrift, too fearsome or too reckless. Nature does not incline us to moderation, because the probability that all the elements that go into our composition will lead us to the exact mid-point of character approaches zero. Rather, moving toward the center is an act of deliberate, conscious choice effected by the exercise of intelligence, "Therefore," writes Maimonides, "our earliest Sages instructed us that a man ought always weigh his dispositions and measure them and direct them to the middle way" (*Hil. De'ot 1:4*).

The key to character for Maimonides is not the mean as such, but this weighing and measuring and directing, the conscious use of reason rather than passively following Nature blindly and supinely. In other words, the process of arriving at a determination of one's own life and character is more important than the results. It is the dynamic quality of rationally weighing and assessing and then, out of freedom, deciding and choosing—the profoundly human act of self-determination of one's own character, one's very self—that qualifies this activity as "the way of the Lord," for we then imitate Him, who created the world out of freedom, in exercising the intellect with which He endowed us and thus directing our very destiny.

The mean itself is not absolute; thus, Maimonides records two standard exceptions and describes certain general situations where the mean does not apply. Moreover, there are different levels of virtue: The *chakham* the merely wise person, aims for the exact mid-point, whereas the *chasid* or pious person, who aspires to supererogatory conduct, will incline to the more ego-denying extreme. This alone is enough to demonstrate that the principle of moderation is not a mindless application of arithmetic averages to the philosophy of character.

In this sense, the Rav's insight is completely correct; the Maimonidean outlook is dynamic, it encourages us to move from point to point as long as we do so with complete awareness of the options (for that is what is meant by the weighing and measuring of the extremes and all points in between) and as long as we are eventually and ultimately expressive of the position of the center, or moderation. Maimonidean centrism is, in this sense, different from the passive Aristotelian theory of the Golden Mean. For Maimonides, one must engage all possibilities—both extreme positions and all that comes between them—and out of this dialectic emerges a choice determined freely by the individual's will and intellect rather than one's congenital personality structure. (By "all options" I obviously do not intend to violate the demands of plausibility; I refer only to those positions which share the fundamental propositions and vision of the stand under discussion.) This interpretation is, at the very least, reasonable, for it demands the exercise of reason and intellect and prevents us from being enchained to emotion and impulse, subservient to external authority, or conforming to social pressure and the narrowness of one's particular upbringing.

Moreover, the "weighing and measuring" in the process of arriving at the—or a—mean necessitates the consideration of *all* available options, including both extremes, thus making sure that no relevant view is ignored and no valid value is overlooked. In this sense, paradoxically, dynamic moderation is more "extreme" than extremism because it must consider both extremes rather than only one.

Thus, if the first chapter of *Hil. De'ot* reveals Maimonides' indebtedness to the Aristotelian Golden Mean (despite the differences mentioned, and yet other significant deviations I have discussed at length in my "The Sage and the Saint in Maimonides' Writings," in the *Samuel Belkin Memorial Volume*), his second chapter shows a bias in favor of the Platonic model of the ideal man as one who like a prince in control of his realm, has all his traits in balance, using each as needed and coordinating all synergistically. Hence Maimonides' recommendation of the physician of character who prescribes one extreme to neutralize a penchant for the other extreme and thus helps reestablish harmony or equipoise in the human soul.

Maimonides, as an eminent physician, naturally chose the Greek metaphor of the medical doctor to illustrate his view of the dynamics of the mean. It is a commonplace that biological systems, like ecosystems on a far larger scale, resist extremes and resort to equal and opposite forces to regain balance. (With equal justice, but resorting to a less picturesque simile, Maimonides could have used the biblical reference to astronomy to illustrate the peril of the extremes. Thus, exposure to the sun in moderation is a source of health: "the sun of righteousness shall arise, healing in its wings" [Mal. 3:20]—but in excess it is harmful: "the sun shall not smite thee by day" [Ps. 121:6]. But these verses would not have allowed for the lesson of utilizing one extreme to combat the excess of the other.) Here is the basis for a dynamic view of moderation.

History is replete with instances of rampant extremism to the everlasting detriment of the Jewish people. One need only mention the well known cruelty and narrowness of the Zealots during the period of the Second Commonwealth who, irate at those who did not share their political perspective, destroyed the food supplies of their fellow Jews at the time that the Romans, their common enemy, were besieging Jerusalem. This does not point to some genetic Jewish predisposition to extremism. It proves only that, for better or for worse (and usually the latter), we are no different from others and we are equally vulnerable to seizures of fanaticism and other forms and varieties of extremist conduct even to the point of self-destruction.

It is ironic that Maimonides himself was the object of extremism on the historic polemic that broke out after his death. Especially deplorable was the extreme to which some anti-Maimunists went in arranging for the burning of the master's *Guide for the Perplexed* on the altar of a Dominican church. At the other end of the spectrum were those who were so enamored of Maimonides' philosophical teachings that they utterly neglected his role as the greatest Halakhist of his time and his immortal contributions to Halakhah, and acted as if all this was just a gesture to the ignorant masses.

Other historical examples of extremism and moderationism abound. The Hasidic-Mitnagdic polemic offers abundant illustrations, especially of extremism. The Hasidic defiance of the communal establishment and especially Rabbinic authority occasionally went beyond the bounds of proper religious discourse, and provoked a far more intense and even violent reaction: excommunication, hatred, violence. It was only the appearance of two distinguished personalities—R. Shneur Zalman of Ladi on the Hasidic side and R. Hayyim Volozhiner on the Mitnagdic—that stilled the controversy and allowed the debate to proceed in a civil fashion. Both were passionate spokesmen for their respective points of view, but both operated as moderates in the best sense of the word.*

I purposely refrain from citing examples from current Jewish history for two reasons. First, there are so very many unfortunate instances of dreadful and unnecessary expressions of extremism

*For more on this, see my *Torah Lishmah: Torah for Torah's Sake in the Works of Rabbi Hayyim of Volozhim and His Contemporaries, 1989.*

that one hardly knows where to begin. And second, I do not want our attention to this theoretical analysis of moderationism to be distracted by what may be considered partisanship in many of the controversies that now divide our people. What this essay loses in the lack of concrete examples from the current scene will, I hope, be more than compensated for in inviting dispassionate reflection on the central theme. And that focus is the Jewish justification of a special kind of moderation that issues from the most reliable sources of the Jewish tradition understood in an appropriately sophisticated manner.

It is this dynamic, radical moderationism which, I believe, leads us to a more certain grasp of the truth of Torah than a narrowly focused insistence upon one view or value alone. In a rather quaint agadic disquisition on the Hebrew alphabet, the Talmud (*Shabbat* 104a) connects the letter *shin* with the word *shekker* falsehood, and the letter *tav* with the word *emet*, truth. The reason, the Talmud explains, is that *shekker mekarvan mileih, emet merachka mileih:* the letters of the word for falsehood, *shekker*, are close together—*sh-k-r* follow upon each other in the alphabet—whereas those for truth, *emet*, are spread apart: *aleph* is the first letter of the alphabet, *mem* the middle one, and *tav* the last letter. What the Talmud seems to be suggesting is that a tunnel view, focusing upon one issue to the exclusion of all others, leads to distortion, whereas a broader view, which is all-encompassing and which takes into account diverse opinions and factors, corrects for such distortion by providing perspective, thus ensuring *emet*, truth.

I submit that this moderationism not only has general relevance to Halakhah, but lies at the heart of the thought processes of every competent *posek* or halakhic decisor. A *posek* is not a computer in human form who accesses his halakhic data-base for the relevant and dominant halakhic opinions and offers them "as is" without considering minority views and without insight into the unique human situation of the one who posed the questions. A true *posek* in the classical sense gathers all his authorities—the extremes and all that come in between them—and relates them to the question or dilemma presented to him in all its general qualities and, as well, its existential singularities. An examination of the literature will generally yield a multiplicity of authoritative approaches, each of a different order of cogency (I have discussed this at length in an article I co-authored with Aaron Kirschenbaum for the very first issue of the *Cardozo Law Review*). He will not opt automatically to be either a *mekil* or a *machmir*, although he may have such tendencies either in general or in specific areas of the Halakha. His ultimate decision will be based upon close analysis of all relevant opinions in conjunction with the individual circumstances of the problem presented to him, and informed by the overarching goals of Torah and the values it seeks to implant in the community of Israel. He will not, except in the most communally harmless of questions, seek to abide by all opinions, by which is meant that the most stringent recorded opinion always prevails.

This "weighing and measuring" and consideration of all viewpoints before deciding, is the halakhic implementation of moderationism. It used to be the accepted hall-mark of a *posek* who was a *gadol*. Our hapless generation can no longer be so certain that its contemporary *poskim* follow that Maimonidean ideal. But the truly great halakhic decisors of past generations were not at all reluctant to broaden their halakhic vistas and include those legal motifs which reckoned with human needs and sensitivities. An example from the Halakhah concerning Passover comes from the writings of R. Naftali Zvi Yehuda Berlin (known as the *Netziv*), Rosh Yeshiva of Volozhin, whose hundredth "yahrzeit" was recently observed. He is writing to his eminent, son, Rabbi Chaim Berlin, who was quite strict about eating the proper amount of *maror*, and for whom these "bitter herbs" was horseradish, with all its harsh spiciness. In a letter dated just 103 years ago, he reprimands his son, suggests that he substitute Romain lettuce for the horseradish which is "like swords for the body," especially after fasting on the eve of Passover, and is thus in violation of the the verse, "its [Torah's] ways are the ways of pleasantness" (*Meromei Ha-sodeh* to *Sanhedrin* 39a).

One of the most brilliant and underestimated rabbinic figures of the pre-World War II East European generation, Rabbi Joseph Engel, once said the following, in commenting on a well known Midrash. On the verse in Genesis that "And God saw that it was very good" (Gen. 1:31), the Midrash comments "*very good* implies death." Rabbi Engel considers this rather astonishing interpretation as a general principle of Torah: all extremes, all "veryism," is deadly! (See his *Otzerot Yosef, derush* 8, p. 45; he mentions two exceptions, both related to the term *me'od*—very: humility and gratitude.)

We have no apologies to offer in adopting the Maimonidean teaching of the Way of the Lord, the "middle way," for our policy of moderation especially in our times, marked as they are by a painful absence of such moderation in all areas. Extremism is rampant, especially in our religious life. Of course, there are reasons—unhappily, they are too often very good reasons—for the new expressions of zealotry. There is so very much in contemporary life that is vulgar, reprehensible, and ugly, that it is hard to fault those who reject all of it with unconcealed and indiscriminate contempt.*

If indeed we adopt this teaching of Maimonides as we have explained it, it means that we do not have an automatic response to each and every problem that we encounter. On the contrary, this approach obligates us to think and reflect and ponder before jumping into the fray. After deliberation, we may even decide to take what is, relative to the circumstances then prevailing, an *extreme* position—but it will not be an *extremist* position! If the process is followed, if the entire spectrum of those options which accord with our ultimate goal is considered and analyzed responsibly, if all factors and options are "weighed and measured," the exact decision is less important than the way it was arrived at; then, any selection will be sane, balanced and, even if wrong, it will at least not be in contempt of the most elementary canons of objectivity and intellectual competence. And it will not necessarily be predetermined by some abstract mathematical formula. Most important, it will avoid the pitfall of fanaticism, by which I mean the espousal of one view to the total exclusion of any circumstances or considerations which may call for modification. Thus one can be a "radical" in any specific position yet a "moderate" overall—a "centrist" even if not in the exact center.

Perhaps this is what is suggested in the saying of our Sages in Avot (1:1), *hevu metunim ba-din*, "be moderate in judgment." The term *din* or judgment may refer not only to a judicial trial but, with some homiletic license, also to *din* as rigor, harshness, or "extremism." Even when one chooses an "extreme" opinion in any subject—he still must remain a moderate . . .

---

*See the previous article, "Some Comments on Centrist Orthodoxy," for further discussion of this point.

Hence, it is a major error to ascribe to moderationism spineless-ness or indifference. True, in today's environment, authentic moderation appears as an aberration or, worse, a manifestation of a lack of commitment. But that is precisely what moderation is not and must not be. It is the result neither of guile nor of indifference nor of prudence; it is a matter of sacred principle. Centrist or Dati Orthodoxy is not a "parve" form of Orthodoxy, although too many moderates do give that impression. It is not a case of ideological wimpishness. The deliberation and reflection and thought processes are all part of coming to a decision. Once the decision is made, however, it must be pursued whole-heartedly, never half-heartedly. As Napoleon told his generals who were contemplating the conquest of Austria: "If you're going to take Vienna, take Vienna!" This whole-heartedness must, it is true, be expressed with civility and sensitivity and understanding, but always with full commitment and the readiness to suffer for the ideal.

The moderation here recommended is neither that of compromise nor that of winning the approval of the masses. It is that of intelligent, deliberate choosing based upon stubborn commitment.

It is this kind of moderationism which is implied in the term "Centrism"—the "middle way" or center which is the "Way of the Lord," the dialectic of the extremes which yields a dynamic moderation based upon the exercise of authentic freedom of choice and self-determination and the assumption of responsibility for the choices so made.

But without genuine self-sacrifice, all our talk and moaning and resolving is just so much excess rhetoric. We must add heat to all the light we strive for: enough heat to inspire as well as light to illumine. We need the gift of passion. Our problem is a pedagogical one: how do we educate our people to be reflective and yet passionate, civil and yet committed, enlightened and yet spirited? Such education requires example but also constant reminder in the form of discussion, persuasion, inculcation, reiteration.

The Zohar (III, 287b) tells the following concerning the death of the great Tanna and mysterious hero of Kabbalah, R. Simeon bar Yochai:

> The day that R. Simeon was dying, as he was putting his affairs in order, the members (of the spiritual group of disciples) came to visit him . . . and the house was filled (with them) . . . R. Simeon raised his eyes and saw that the house was full. Whereupon he

wept and said: once before, when I was very ill, R. Pinchas B. Yair
stood before me . . . and he was surrounded by a flame before me
which never ceased . . . and now I see that the flame has left—and
the house is full . . .

The crowds are not impressive if there is no fire in their bones,
no passion in their souls. Single individuals can prevail if they
are enveloped in the flame of dedication, confidence, and commitment. Cold figures are no match for warm hearts whose flame
endures. Numbers alone, without adequate commitment, are a
cause for much weeping.

That is where we sin today. The chronic failing of any form of
moderation is the lack of passion—a weakness that infects every
area of our activity—from our observance of the mitzvot and our
prayer and our study of Torah, the entire gamut of our personal
religious experience, to our collective posture towards the rest of
the Jewish world where we often tremble and quake when we
should be proclaiming proudly where we stand and why.

The Way of the Lord that was imparted to Abraham on the eve
of the great cataclysm of antiquity must remain the guiding principle for Jews of our era who have emerged from an incomparably greater and more evil catastrophe. Moderation, in our times,
requires courage and the willingness to risk not only criticism
but abuse. If we are willing to take on that challenge and that
burden, we can yet make a major contribution to the unfolding
history of Torah Judaism and to the welfare of our people in
these volcanically unstable times.

I believe *ani maamin*, with perfect faith, in the marriage of
moderation and passion, of fairness and fervor, of deliberation
and dedication, of reasonableness and commitment, of a cool
head and a warm heart.

The time has come for us, Centrist Orthodox or Dati or Modern Orthodox Jews, to cease being apologetic and defensive, shy
and silent and apprehensive, about our "way." It is the *derekh ha-
yesharim*, the "way" of those who march "straight" towards the
goal of all Israel lovingly reaccepting the Torah, and re-establish-
ing *shalom* amongst all Jews and, eventually, all the world.

This, indeed, is "the way of the Lord."

~ 6 ~

SOME THOUGHTS ON
LEADERSHIP

I often ask myself: What does it take to exercise leadership in the Orthodox community in the fading years of this terrible and tormented as well as fantastic and incredible century?

The question is important to us because we Orthodox Jews have a tendency to fight new battles with old weapons and to confront novel predicaments with antiquated strategies . . .

I will mention four items or ingredients of leadership, other than the obvious need to be totally committed to Torah and Halakha with all one's heart and soul.

———

THE FIRST ITEM relates to the heart of this conference, and my thesis is: *leadership of any community requires a number of people, not just one leader, no matter how brilliant or charismatic.* No Lone Rangers need apply for the positions of leadership in any organized community. I admire the contemporary equivalent of the heroic cowboy who defeats the Bad Men single-handedly and goes riding off into the sunset. But I have no confidence that such leadership can endure. True communal leadership requires a *team*, a *community* of leaders, in which one or two or three may be preeminent, but all must pull together.

I heard the following in the name of my teacher, Rabbi Joseph B. Soloveitchik, "the Rav," of blessed memory:

The Torah relates (Nu. 13) that God commanded Moses to send twelve men, each the prince of his tribe, to spy out the land of Canaan which He had promised to give to the Children of Israel. Two of them, Joshua and Caleb, came back with a positive report, affirming the promise of God to Israel and asserting that the campaign would succeed. Ten of the princes, however, were thoroughly discouraging and, in defiance of the divine promise,

Delivered at the Conference of the World Council of Orthodox Leadership in November 1997

maintained that any effort to conquer the Land would fail. This report caused untold grief for generations thereafter.

Remarkable: a whole nation witnessed so many obvious miracles—from the Ten Plagues to the splitting of the Red Sea, from the manna to the well of Miriam—and, despite all this, their faith in God was so thin, so fragile, that ten people out of a total population of probably more than 2,000,000 were able to sway them to doubt the divine promise. What demonic powers the ten must have possessed to cause such a tragic upheaval!

But, the Rav adds, there is one more place in the Torah where we find the possibility of ten people to change the destiny of so many others: the plea of Abraham to save the sin-city of Sodom if at least ten *tzaddikim* (righteous people) would be found therein. So, ten people can overwhelm a vast number and lead them to physical and spiritual perdition, and the same number can save an entire populous city from utter devastation.

To which I humbly add this explanation: Why ten? What properties does that specific number possess such that it can wield such enormous power both for good and for evil? The answer, I suggest, comes from the Halakha, where ten is considered the minimum number to constitute an *edah* (congregation) or *tzibbur* (community). If the ten are cohesive, if they are mutually dedicated to one overarching cause, they can overpower hundreds and thousands and even millions of individuals. A *community* of ten is almost omnipotent compared with far larger numbers of individuals who are unrelated and indifferent.

In the same way, leadership by people who are cemented together with the glue of common ideals and values, constitutes a community of leaders, and such an *edah* of leaders can be truly effective on behalf of our people.

How do we of the Modern Orthodox community fare when measured against this criterion?

Not too bad, but also not too good. We have a fair degree of cooperation (thus, this conference), less coordination, and too often an unhealthy degree of turf rivalry and back-biting and empire-building. We have too many Lone Rangers who may do much good, but far less than if we all worked together as befits a community of leaders. But even more prevalent and more disturbing is another phenomenon that plagues us: an ideological fastidiousness, a spiritual squeamishness, such that the slightest ideological deviation or legitimate difference in halakhic or theological decision is considered anathema and the cause of deliberate alienation. This is an attitude which betrays a curious and paradoxical mixture of arrogant self-righteousness—and a shocking lack of self-confidence. Such leadership does more bad than good.

In order for us to succeed, we have to *deserve* to succeed—and that means to regard each other with respect and affection in a spirit of mutual dedication to the cause of Torah generally and Torah Umadda specifically. I hope that this will be one of the many salutary results of this conference. May we here initiate the beginnings of such an era of enlightened leadership for the entire Modern Orthodox community. And may it be a community of genuine friendship, one which avows that such friendship does not require agreement on every detail.

———

THE SECOND ingredient is this: *Our means must be as honorable as our ends.*

In our opposition to the non-Orthodox movements or actions, we must be trenchant in our criticism—but always fair, *scrupulously* fair, and truthful. When I read some Orthodox publications, I marvel at the total lack of perspective. Not only are the non-Orthodox totally demonized—they are *always* wrong, their intentions *always* evil—but we too, of the Modern Orthodox camp, apparently have no redeeming qualities whatever. Such an attitude is not only dishonest, it is also counter-productive. Overstatement and overkill usually bring one's credibility into disrepute.

Last March or April, for instance, one small group of rabbis, armed with an overzealous PR person and a receptive and ignorant reporter in attendance, proclaimed that it was making a revolutionary announcement: a halakhic decision *(pesak din)* that Orthodox Judaism would henceforth not recognize the legitimacy of Reform or Conservative Judaism. Of course, this was an insensitive and sensationalist announcement. Mainstream Orthodoxy has never and does not now acknowledge Reform and Conservatism as *halakhically* legitimate.*

———

*See my article, "Unity and Integrity," in Moment (June 1986), reproduced below as chapter III, article 13.

The results of this mini-blitz? First, it aggravated an already tense situation in intra-communal relations both here and in Israel and set tempers boiling unnecessarily. Second, it was promptly misinterpreted by the secular press as declaring Reform and Conservative Jews as non-Jewish—a totally false and misleading conclusion based upon an erroneous press report that is still haunting us and will continue to do so with a dogged persistence that defies all our denials and bedevils our attempts to attain *shalom bayit* in the community. All in all, it was a tragic introduction to a long and dreadful chapter of intra-religious strife, the likes of which I have not experienced in the 47 years I am in Jewish public life.

R. Yosef Dov Soloveitchik, the author of *Bet Halevi* is reputed to have said that the difference between "us" and "them" is that they pursue *shekker* (falsehood) with *emet* (truth), while we pursue *emet* with *shekker* . . .

Being honorable in our means as well as ends means to extend the courtesy of ethical and truthful conduct—*emet*—to those with whom we disagree, even to our ideological foes.

For instance: some months ago the Agudath Israel sponsored a *Siyyum Hashas*, a celebration of many thousands of Jews who studied a folio of the Talmud per day for about seven and one half years, thus concluding the study of the entire Talmud. The gala historic event took place at Madison Square Garden. Although, unfortunately, there was no mention of Israel by any of the speakers, the event itself was enormously impressive. Immediately upon my return from the Garden, I wrote a letter to [the late] Rabbi Moshe Sherer, President of Agudath Israel, with whose policies I sometimes disagree, complimenting him and his staff on his remarkable *kiddush Hashem*, whereby some 26,000 people gathered in this one site—with thousands more elsewhere connected by television—and where the recitation of the *Shema* and the *Kaddish* made one feel he was in the *Bet Hamikdash* in Jerusalem on a Yom Tov. The utter silence during the *Shemoneh Esreh* was itself a thunderous approbation of Orthodoxy in general and especially of those who study Torah regularly.

So, we today send warm fraternal greetings to our fellow Orthodox Jews of Agudath Israel who are convening in New Jersey. We say to them *Yeyashar kochakhem* and *Chazak Uvarukh*; may your efforts in this direction continue to be successful!

By the same token, the Reform group—with whom our ideological differences are incomparably more profound than with the Haredim—should be encouraged to keep on intensifying their Jewish education for both young and adult.

I am deeply troubled by the truculence of the Reform and Conservative campaign against Orthodoxy, one which resembles a feeding frenzy against us rather than rational criticism—and it makes little difference whether that campaign is directed against Haredim or the Modern Orthodox. Are Orthodox Jews the only ones expected to be bound by the laws of civility and tolerance, the only ones to be reprimanded if they go to excesses in reproaching the others? Is pluralism a blessing to be bestowed only upon pluralists?

I am even more distressed by the enormous risk that the non-Orthodox groups have undertaken in holding their own communities hostage to Israel's acquiescence to their program. If, for whatever reason, Israel decides not to recognize Reform conversions, will Reform leadership be able to push the genie of Jewish anti-Israelism back into the bottle? And if their people lose contact with Israel, will there be enough in the Jewishness in their lives to keep them Jewish at all?

Moreover, *emet* requires us to say respectfully but bluntly that we cannot and will not acknowledge "patrilineal Jews" or other non-halakhically converted Jews as bona fide Jews, and no amount of political or financial pressure will make us yield on a matter of such principle. Our authority is the Talmud and the *Shulchan Arukh*, not the CJF or the GA or the UJA.

I also admit to being perplexed by the newest Reform suggestion: to observe the *Tikkun Lel Shavuot*, a rather minor tradition—announced at a dinner which was totally non-kosher . . . I am equally puzzled at their adoption of a Jewish version of Orwellian "newspeak," such as appropriating the term "outreach" to mean not teaching Jews to come closer to Torah, but to bring non-Jewish spouses of out-marrying Jews into their temples. Why such instances of terminological hijacking as bestowing the title "Kollel," which implies the highest level of Talmudic learning, on what is essentially an adult-ed institute? Terms such as "Kollel" and "yeshiva" and "Rosh Yeshiva" have clear connotations and to misuse them means to obfuscate, not to clarify.

But all this having been said, we must applaud Reform's genuine efforts to return to Jewish tradition in at least some manner, reversing the trend of recent years. *Emet*, truth, demands that we congratulate them when they work for more Jewish education for their constituents, quantitatively and qualitatively. It is in the interest of all of us to see that most of us are informed Jews who are literate in Torah.

I reject the old policy, which no longer has any validity, that "better nothing than a Reform or Conservative Jew." A *pintelle Yid* is certainly superior to none at all. We should encourage any group that attempts to teach more of our classical texts, and especially to build day schools for that purpose. The same concern for *emet* may well impel us later to criticize them for a lack of depth in their curriculum—but meanwhile, better something than nothing. And day schools, even the watered down Reform or secularist or Yiddishist version, are more of "something" than certain well meant but patently ineffective gimmicks now receiving such enthusiastic endorsement by certain sectors of our community. But that is a subject for another conversation.

Our goal, our aspiration, our Torah is *emet*, and it deserves that we pursue it with *emet*.

———

THE CONCERN for *emet* leads me to the third of the four points I wish to raise. And that is, that *Truth demands that our inner life and outer life correspond with each other*, that we be—in the Talmudic phrase—*tokho ke'varo*, that there be no discrepancy and certainly no contradiction between what we are and what we strive to appear to be. In the words of the *Tanna de'Vei Eliyahu* which we recite every morning as the preface to our *Shacharit* prayer, "A person should always be God-fearing, both inwardly and outwardly, acknowledging the truth [publicly] and speaking the truth in his own heart." True piety must be identical, both within and without. Truth must pervade both our inner thoughts and our public professions.

I mention this because the Orthodox community is more and more getting "hung up" on externals, on *chitzoniyut*, and less and less on *penimiyut* or inwardness, thus enlarging the gap between what we are and what we pretend to be. And it behooves us to be receptive to such criticism, no matter what its source.

I have no problem with people who feel that they have or want to be demonstrative in their "frumkeit." If it makes them feel better to dress in a certain way, why should we deny them the pleasure? But pious clothing *must* be consistent with pious living and believing and behavior. Unethical conduct is twice as reprehensible when done by one who wears a *kippah*, three times as bad as when done by one who insists specifically upon a black velvet *kippah*, four times more for one who wears his *tzitzit* out, five times more for davening with the *tallit* over the head, and so on. The more our externals proclaim our Jewishness, the greater the demands on us for the highest standards of moral excellence.

In looking at photographs of yeshiva men of pre-World War II Europe, I often notice that, except for Hasidic Jews, most of them wore the same clothing as *baalebatim* and not essentially different from any ordinary Jew. The Rav once told me the rationale for this policy: the heads of the Yeshivot wanted their students not to appear too different from the run-of-the-mill Jew so as not to alienate him from Yiddishkeit. Why is it, then, that what was good enough for the illustrious yeshivot of Hevron and Mir and Slobodka is not good enough for our contemporary *yeshiva-leit*? Are we today really that much superior to the students of the great classical yeshivot?

But again I emphasize: I do not in any way want to criticize or discourage anyone from indulging himself in the appurtenances of "frumkeit." But we should insist that that people who do this be aware of the responsibility they bear for avoiding any *chilul Hashem*, any desecration of the divine Name. The price is high indeed and should not be taken lightly.

I refer again to the story of the twelve spies sent by Moses to check out Canaan to see if it was ready to be conquered by the Israelites, as God had promised it would. Two of them—Joshua and Caleb—came back with an optimistic report, confirming the divine promise, and ten came back, negative, discouraging, and disbelieving the promise of the Almighty. The Torah tells us (Nu.14:6) that Joshua and Caleb, who spied out the land, tore their clothing. But why did they react in this particular manner, tearing their clothing? And why mention two of the twelve "of those who spied out the land," something we already know?

The Kotzker Rebbe explains: The spies were princes of the tribes of Israel, distinguished individuals dressed, undoubtedly, in fur *shtreimlech* and handsome *bekishes* and white stockings, etc.—the full regalia of demonstratively *frum* people. Yet they inwardly had no faith in God's word, they spoke ill of *Eretz Yisrael*, they created havoc amongst their people. So Joshua and Caleb said: in that case, who needs the pretentiously religious garb? And so they therefore ripped the ostentatious attire off the backs of the ten traitors, the ten who were of "those who spied out the land." The verse thus reads: Joshua and Caleb, *comma*, tore the clothing off those who spied out the land . . .

The two who were loyal, and the Kotzker in his day, were too devoted to *emet* to tolerate fashionable hypocrisy. If we are in any measure devoted to *emet*, we too should conduct ourselves in a manner not calculated to offend the way we really are inwardly. We need not object to special garments in style or color, but we must insist on consistency, on the equivalence of the inward and the outward.

———

FOURTH OF THE four requirements for Modern Orthodox leadership in our times is: *We must be as open to other Jews as the Halakha permits us.* That means we must abjure and reject an "all or nothing" approach if we want and expect other Jews to react positively to the overtures of Torah and the outreach by us Orthodox.

We in America cannot legislate Jewish observance of Halakha as they do in Israel—and there is legitimate reason to ask whether or not the time has come for Israel itself to desist from any new religious legislation. Therefore we must rely on voluntary action by others. This, in turn, means that we have to be attractive, that we must be "beautiful" Jews, *shayne Yidn*, in order to entice others to a life of Torah.

Recall the Sifre, cited in the Talmud, that the commandment "thou shalt love the Lord thy God," which we recite as part of the *Shema*, implies and is fulfilled when we act in a manner that inspires others to love God. Our conduct must be so exemplary that others will attribute our high moral quality to the God we believe in and the Torah we study. So, if we want to win Jews over to Yiddishkeit, we need not water down Halakha, but we also need not and should not overwhelm them with every last detail, especially *chumrot* or strictures for which they are neither

psychologically nor spiritually ready and which can prove counterproductive to our efforts to bring them "under the wings of
the Shechina." Both formal education and outreach require a
gradual approach. What we ought to do, and what is most successful and honorable, is attract them to Torah by demonstrating
the rectitude and probity of observant Jews. We must become too
ethically attractive to resist.

It is helpful to recall that if the "all or nothing" approach were
turned on *us*, we would all fail and end up with a great deal of
"nothing." Simply, none of us is perfect, no one "has it all." Koheleth (7:20) put it directly: There is no righteous person in the
world who does good and never sins. No human being is perfect.
We should therefore not demand perfection of others . . .

I believe that because of this and a number of other highly co-
gent reasons, we should support vigorously the efforts by Fi-
nance Minister Yaakov Neeman and his commission to solve the
current conversion conundrum that so complicates our lives in
Israel and here. What they will recommend will in all likelihood
not be a perfect solution, for I doubt if one exists; but I trust it will
be the best available—even if it is only a temporary cure. The
Jewish people throughout the world need a breathing space after
all this dreadful confrontation that has confounded us and
caused us so much pain and disruption and fratricidal bickering.

There is a philosophical principle as well as pragmatic justification for the approach I have been advocating. The acknowledgment that we do not and cannot attain the whole truth all at
once, that we have to settle at least temporarily for less than the
ideal we would prefer, is a matter of recognizing the truth about
truth itself.

What I mean by that last phrase, "the truth about truth," is
this: Consider the following well-known Midrash:

> R. Simon said: When the Holy One was about to create the first
> man [Adam], the ministering angels were divided into separate
> groups, some saying man should not be created and some saying
> he should . . . [The angel known as] *Hessed* (Lovingkindness) said:
> Let him be created, for he does acts of kindness. [The angel known
> as] *Emet* (Truth) said he should not be created, for he is full of false-
> hood. [The angel known as] *Tzeddek* (Justice, Charity) said he
> should be created, for he is charitable, whereas [the angel known
> as] *Shalom* [Peace] said he should not be created for he is always

contentious. What did the Holy One do? He took Truth and cast it to the earth, as it is written, "and You cast truth to the earth" (Daniel 8). Whereupon the ministering angels said to the Holy One: Master of All the Worlds! Why do you embarrass Your very own strategy (i.e., Truth is one of the Names of God, and hence very much His own attribute)? Do raise up Truth from the earth! Therefore is it written, "Truth grows from the earth."

—*Bereshit Rabbah, 8*

Question: If the idea was to break the tie, why did God cast away Truth; why did He not choose Peace, which also voted against the creation of man?

I suggest the following answer: Truth, the naked truth, which is (as Saadia Gaon called it) the "bitter truth," is intimidating, even terrifying. It makes absolute demands upon us, usually far more than our human limitations will allow. Looking full face into a psychological and spiritual mirror can be a horrendous experience. Uncompromising and merciless, the *emet* that comes from Heaven in its full and unadulterated state is such that man cannot survive his encounter with it. Yes, we can ultimately attain truth—but only partially, and only over a long period of gradual exposure to it.

Hence: "and You cast truth to the earth" and "Truth grows from the earth." God cast the truth to the earth and had it grow and develop from the soil—because the *emet* that makes life moral and ennobles our journey on earth is one which grows organically, which develops like a plant which begins as a seed, then a sapling, then a small tree, then a stately one . . . and so allows us to accommodate ourselves to it gradually. A truth which originally comes from Heaven but does so via the earth is far more effective and palatable and useable than a truth which comes down ready-made and full-blown straight from Heaven.

In the world of politics (in the best sense of the word!), the whole truth must always be in our minds and hearts as a permanent and beckoning goal, but we cannot seek to impose it on others all at once. In this context, *"compromise" is not a dirty word* as long as we remember the ideal in all its wholeness at all times. Compromise is a practical device that allows us to plant a seed of *emet* and nurture it for later development, without clashing head on with others who have different perceptions. It articulates with *shalom* instead of opposing it. It is respectful of the natural limitations of the human creature. It makes it possible for us to connect somehow with truth without diminishing its ultimate integrity. It is what allows the Almighty Himself to decide, "let man be created," that humans are *worthy* of creation!

This "truth about truth" will instill in us a sense of patience and tolerance that is sorely lacking in our Jewish community.

That is why the efforts of the Neeman Commission to find a workable and honorable compromise appeal to me even though the formula they will devise may be less than perfect and less than we might have wanted. It represents an earthly rather than a heavenly truth.

That same attitude must inform our approach to the non-Orthodox community, especially to those who are still clinging to the margins of Jewish experience, who have strayed, but still long for some connection to Judaism. We must do all in our power to befriend and not distance them, to include rather than exclude them.

Let me illustrate this principle by invoking a *teshuvah* by the immortal Ashkenazi *posek* R. Israel Isserlein of 15th century Germany (*Terumat Ha-deshen* II, 93).

The Talmud (*Men.* 30b) requires a Torah scroll to be written with respect for the margins—what in this computer age would be called "justified" columns. Thus, if the scribe has before him a five-letter word and has place on the line for only two letters, he must not write out the whole word on the same line, thus leaving three letters "off the margin." What if the scribe erred and did indeed write the last letters off the margin? R. Isserlein decides that, on the basis of a close reading of the Talmud text, the prohibition is only *le'khat'chilah, ab initio,* but if the act was already done, *bi-di'avad,* the scroll is kosher and may be used for ritual purposes. And what if there are before us two *sifrei Torah,* one fully kosher and the other a scroll in which the scribe erred but which we accepted *bi-di'avad,* once it was done—may or should we prefer the scroll that is completely valid over the one that contains the "off the margin" writing? Here our author rules that to discriminate against the latter scroll would effectively constitute a disqualification of that scroll, and that would be tantamount to declaring it invalid even *bi-di'avad.* Hence, no discrimination is permitted against an "off the margin" Torah scroll.

Now, what holds true for a *sefer Torah* must hold true for a Jewish *neshamah*, namely, that even if he or she is off the margins, even if a Jew is not totally within the sacred pages of the Torah, the Halakha holds that he is nevertheless one of us *bi-di'avad*, and therefore it behooves us to treat him with love and respect and tenderness and not to be *pogem*—disqualify—him or hurt or insult his dignity in any way.

Not imposing the whole truth of Torah all at once, compromising for the sake of *shalom* of *kelal Yisrael*, embracing Jews who hover on the margins unprepared as yet to come into the whole framework of observance but still wanting to be someplace on the parchment of Torah—is the only way to remain loyal to both the Almighty and to *kelal Yisrael*. It is our sacred task to remember both, to forget neither, to reconcile the one with the other.

———

MOST OF THE dilemmas we face as Modern Orthodox Jews in this critical and confusing period of our history revolve about the conflict between our halakhic commitment and our loyalty to *kelal Yisrael*, our love of Torah and our love of Israel. It is a painful predicament, probably not unprecedented (it was explicitly addressed in the *Tanna de'Vei Eliyahu;* see below, chapter 11) but surely a perplexity most characteristic of our times. It is also an ennobling and elevating one, because ultimately, as the Zohar teaches, *Yisrael ve'oraita chad hu*, Israel and Torah are one, so the love of the one includes the other. But on a practical plane, there is indeed a clash of loyalties.

How shall we deal with it? By a *stubborn denial of elementary logic!* By insisting that inconsistency though there be, we will yield on neither, that—as Koheleth (ch. 6) said—it is best to hold on to the one and the other, for a God-fearing person will remain true to both. There is no perfect solution—life in general is resistant to "perfect solutions"—but it is the best available.

Allow me to illustrate my point via a remarkable scene my wife and I witnessed when we were in Prague only a few weeks ago. We visited the famous synagogues of that ancient city and Jewish community. We wept in the Pinkus Shul where the walls—every inch of them—were covered by the names of the 80,000 Prague Jewish deportees, most of whom perished in various concentration camps. We were enormously inspired in the Alt-Neu shul—at 700 years old, the synagogue in longest continuous use in the world, the shul of the Maharal and R. Ezekiel Landau, author of *Noda Bi'Yehudah*. But nothing could compare to a shul only recently discovered in Terezin, which the Germans called Theresienstadt, a town some 45 minutes north of Prague in an apartment which now stands at the site of the Grand Fortress, which housed the unfortunate Jews of Prague in inhumanly overcrowded barracks from where they were either deported or worked to death and slept in stacks we all recognize from the horrendous photos of Auschwitz and Bergen-Belsen and other death camps. Here was a tiny room, claustrophobia-inspiring, dark and dank, a chamber of about 9 x 9 feet that that had been used for over 50 years to store potatoes—since before the Nazis invaded until a few months ago when it was discovered. Here the interned Jews clandestinely gathered amongst the potatoes for prayer, and those who labored as painters stole paint and brushes to decorate their shul in which they davened, risking their lives and skirting torture. Secretly, they painted words on the bare walls: *Da lifnei mi ata omed*, ("Know before Whom you stand," the standard phrase from the Talmud used in synagogues) on the East wall, towards which they prayed, and on the two others—similar appropriate quotes. But most moving of all was the third, the West wall, on which was inscribed the legend, taken from the *tachanun* prayer. *U-ve'khol zot shimkha lo shakhachnu, na al tishkachenu* "Despite all, O God, we have not forgotten You. Please—do not forget us."

Despite all the blood spilt here, despite the ubiquitous stench, despite the murder of loved ones, despite the gallows and the shooting walls staring us in the face day and night, despite the torture chambers and the incredible cruelty of the Nazi overlords, despite the barking dogs and snarling soldiers, despite the sadism and the indignities visited upon us with abandon—*despite all this, we have not forgotten You. Now, we beg You—do not forget us and do not forsake us in this Hell-hole!*

No wonder the Rabbi of Prague told us he considers this the holiest shul in the Czech Republic—and maybe the world.

This is a heart-rending plea that we and God not forget each other. The mutual bond between God and Israel, formalized in the covenant of the Torah, means an oath never to forget each other.

And that holds doubly true for us. We must forget neither the Almighty and His Torah, nor His Jews—wherever they are and no matter what their condition. We must love each unconditionally, even if the two loves sometimes seem to conflict with each other.

We must remain loyal to the Holy One, never forgetting our obligations and our gratitude to Him; and never never must we forget, not even for a moment, our *ahavat Yisrael,* our love of Israel, our deep love and commitment to *every* Jew and to *all* Jews, all *Kelal Yisrael.*

Only then will we be morally justified in asking of Him, "Please—do not forget us."

Chapter 2

FAITH

The first article reprinted in this chapter was my response to the "God is dead" movement in the 1960's. While new ideas have emerged to take its place on the screen of public attention in matters theological, the original Nietzchean maxim has continued to influence contemporary thinking, often in subterranean ways.

The following two articles were my response to the two famous Commentary symposia on what American Jews believe in. The differences in the responses of most participants to the two issues, separated by thirty years, are quite significant; both they and Commentary had changed much. I do not believe that such changes are evident in my own responses.

The last item is my response to an in interview conducted in 1994, on my religious beliefs.

~ 7 ~

GOD IS ALIVE

A Jewish Reaction to a
Theological Controversy

Orthodox Jews have generally taken a detached and un-alarmed view towards the successive fads and fashions in contemporary *apikorsut*. But when such movements are sponsored by theologians, and are widely discussed in the daily press and in weekly news magazines, it is important to understand them and evaluate them in the light of the sacred sources of the Jewish tradition.

A number of Christian theologians, climaxing a development that has been some years in the making in their circles, have put forth their ideas in a manner as shocking as it is honest, and as scandalous as it is forthright. Instead of clothing their atheism in artificial, long-winded, technical terminology, they have accepted the slogan first coined by a German philosopher of the last century: "God is dead." The very blasphemousness of this expression explains why it makes such good copy for the pseudo-sophisticated weeklies, and tempts young professors of theology to break out of the stifling atmosphere of the ivory towers and into a breathtaking sensationalism. These theologians have made so much noise with their smart slogan that nowadays one expects to look for news of theology not in the Religion section of the press, but in the obituary columns.

Their criticism of the "old-fashioned religion"—especially if we seek to apply it to Judaism—is crude caricature, almost vulgar in its insinuations. They have set up a straw man and now knock it down. No intelligent Jew ever thought of God as a man with a long white beard who lives in a castle beyond the sun. No half-sophisticated human being who believed in God ever imagined Him as orbiting the globe in a space ship, somewhere "out there."

Any imputation of such primitive concepts to religious folk of ages past is merely a species of intellectual dishonesty.

Published in Jewish Life *in the early 1960s*

WHAT DO THESE theologians mean by their intemperate slogan? I believe they are saying three things.

First, they are preaching atheism, pure and simple. Second, they are asserting a form of deism. That is, they reject the idea of divine personality. They believe in a deity, but one who has no relations with man; he is conceived as an immanent principle, an impersonal power. A deity of this kind cannot reveal himself to man, nor can man pray to him. He is infinitely removed from nature and from man.

Of course, contrary to what we are being told about its novelty, this slogan is really old-hat. Atheism and deism have long histories, almost as long as monotheism itself. Both are equally inimical to and obnoxious in the eyes of Judaism, for they deny everything in Torah from "In the beginning God created" to the end of the *Chumash,* that God revealed Himself "in the eyes of all Israel." Neither Creation nor Revelation make sense to an atheist or to a deist.

For whatever such information is worth, and whatever perverse consolation it may offer, let it be known that this intellectual dishonesty of preaching a "religion" which no longer accepts a personal God was already advocated several decades ago by a group of Jews in New York; and that far from signifying the "death of God," it commenced for them their own slow spiritual strangulation. If the new breed of Christian theologians believe that they are original innovators when they speak of a "religionless Christianity," they are in error; they have been anticipated in the Jewish community by the Reconstructionists when the latter proposed "Judaism as a Civilization" and "naturalistic religion" in which it was taught that one can be "Jewish" even though he clearly denies the existence of God as Judaism has taught it throughout the centuries. The consequences of this kind of belief, now exposed for all the world to see, are exemplified by a Reform clergyman who openly preaches agnosticism or atheism, deletes every mention of God from his service, even from the *Shema*—and yet is accepted as a bona fide member of a non-Orthodox rabbinical association!

The Real Question

However, there is a third meaning of interpretation of the "God is dead" slogan that does deserve to be taken seriously by believing Jews. Here there is no denial of theism, the belief in the existence of a personal God. However, it seeks to understand the profound sense of loss, by man, of the experience of God in modern life. Why, this interpretation asks, does man no longer encounter God as personally and as intimately as he once used to?

The question is a real one, and it will not do for us merely to dismiss it lightly. For some reason, modern society and modern life are such that we usually fail to establish dialogue with God, we fail to feel Him as deeply, for instance, as our grandparents did. Our inferior Jewish education is no answer to or explanation of the problem. A familiar phenomenon of former days was the unlettered old lady who could barely read her prayers and certainly could not understand them, but nevertheless was moved by them to have a profound religious experience with her Maker. Prayer was a moving experience, and it was not out of the ordinary to see a tear shed even by one who was intellectually underdeveloped. Today even many of our children are more literate in Judaism than were some of our forebears. Yet seldom does one notice a tear in our synagogues, except on the occasion, heaven forbid, of personal disaster. What has happened to our lives? Why has God, who is alive forever, seemingly abandoned so many of us?

The problem, then, is not God, but man. What does Judaism have to say to this very real challenge? I suggest three answers.

FIRST, WE SHOULD not expect to have a *sustained*, intimate relationship with God, constantly and uninterruptedly. Such expectations are too high if we demand of ourselves that this personal experience, this intimate relationship with God, be constant and continuous. Man, finite and mortal, cannot maintain uninterruptedly such a relationship with God, infinite and eternal. Our great mystics spoke of the phenomenon of *ratzo va-shov*: a principle of alternation; the deep and profound communion with God exists for a short while, and then suddenly man's spirit recoils and he is possessed by a feeling of emptiness and distance and remoteness, only to reestablish contact once again. This is revealed in the very structure of our benedictions. We address God intimately, in the second person: "Blessed are *Thou . . .*" and then, suddenly, we revert to speaking not *to* but *about* God, in the third person: "Who *has* sanctified us with *His* commandments . . . ," *asher kideshanu* and not *asher kidashtanu*. What we are taught, therefore, is that we ought to strain ourselves to experience the presence of God, especially in prayer, but that we cannot expect to remain on that lofty level in a sustained fashion. Inevitably we must revert to what the Kabbalah and Hasidism called "the periods of *Katnut*," of diminished spirituality.

The establishment of contact with God does not come to us effortlessly; it demands constant striving and initiative on our part, even if we know that we often fail. The failure, in fact, is part of the experience.

Secondly, this estrangement from God is a part of God's own plan, the inevitable consequence of breach of faith with Him. Man is endowed by his Maker with the freedom to turn *to* Him or away *from* Him. The climax of the *Tokhachah,* that list of dire Biblical punishments we read twice a year, is: "And I shall hide My face from thee." The Torah enumerates the many disasters to which Israel will be subject, the worst of which is: that God will hide His face from us, He will abandon us to the impersonal and inexorable forces of nature and history. *Hester Panim,* "the Hiding of the Face," is the inaccessibility of God to man who searches for Him. It means that man will find it much more difficult to contact his Creator. The punishment of *Hester Panim* is national-historical in nature; it may last for a period of centuries. Of course, individuals, with but one life to lead, are often impatient and interpret this inaccessability as the "absence" of God. But one must take the long view. The difficulty experienced in achieving the genuine inner religious life is in large measure the consequence of abandonment of God when it was much easier to be religious. Individual people, born, raised, and dying in this long and tragic period of alienation from God, this era of *Hester Panim,* are apt to conclude that God was never accessible, perhaps that He never was. They fail to appreciate that God is concealing his Presence. The Besht, founder of Hasidism, taught: the Biblical expression is, *Va'anokhi haster astir panai*—a repetition of the word "hiding" in the expression "and I will hide My face from thee." Even the very act of "hiding" will be hidden from man! Not only will man find God unavailable, but he will even find the concept of God's inaccessibility to be inscrutable.

THE THIRD EXPLANATION is that the alienation from God need not necessarily be the result of sin, as a subsequent punishment of "the hiding of the face," but may simply be a reflection of the quality of the times in which we live. There are ages when it is easier to be religious, and ages when it is more difficult. Naturally, greater virtue accrues to one born in the Twentieth Century and who is devout, than to one born in the Tenth Century who remains religious. Ours is an age of great complexity. We live in a society of science and technology in which man has been granted vast new powers. Most of the civilized world is, in effect, one large urban sprawl. In a large city, it is difficult to recapture the primitive sense of immediacy which is so important for a true religious experience. It is difficult not only to *act* religious, but to *be* truly religious in the sense of a deep, personal awareness of the presence of God.

There are times when the Divine Presence is withheld because of sin, and then we call it *Hester Panim*. But there are times when the presence of the experience of God's immediacy is a result of the nature of the times. Some periods of history are such that the reason for the absence of God is economic—too much affluence—or political or social or, as in our own times, a combination of all these and the cultural-scientific element. Whether our age is the one or the other is a matter of conjecture. But the fact remains that the loss of the awareness of God's presence is neither unprecedented nor unanticipated. Certainly, then, the problem is: How can man keep alive, and not: Is God alive?

In Search of Nearness

The question, is: what can we do about it? How can man, in this [20th] 21st Century, once again become alive to his Creator? How can we rediscover our relationship with God and experience His nearness? How may we overcome this cosmic estrangement?

It must first of all be clear that, important as subjective feelings are, Judaism does not stand or fall by how deeply we think we experience religious stirrings. Neither theology nor emotions will, in the long run, determine the quality of our lives; our conduct and behavior will.

Judaism has always valued objective observance over subjective experience. It is more important to *act lovingly* to our neighbor than to *feel* warmth and tenderness for him in our hearts. It is more important to feed the poor man and alleviate his suffering than to melt in compassion and commiseration—and do nothing. In a statement of surprising boldness, the Rabbis of the Talmud put into the mouth of God the following words: "Would that they abandon Me so long as they observe My Torah!" God is willing that He Himself be forgotten provided that His will, His Torah, be carried out. It is more important to *be* Godly, than to *believe* in God.

Yet, having said this, it would be a mistake to assume that the matter ends here, that inner religious experience is of no concern to us. The Jewish heart and soul still crave the loving attention of "Gottenyu." How, then, can we achieve in our times the reconciliation between God and man, when the two have moved ever further apart? How can we make Judaism and God personally meaningful in our lives?

Some have suggested that we search for the answer in Hasidism, which emphasizes the element of personality and relationship. Some two hundred years ago, Hasidism too faced a problem of the distance between God and Man, and, in response, emphasized the great principle of God's immanence. "The whole world is filled with His glory"; "There is no place in which God is not." In other words, we may look for God any place and every place. We therefore might just as well direct our attention to Nature and Man, and we will find God there too.

Now, that is a valid answer—but not for many people today. Of course God reveals Himself in Nature; but most of us cannot find Him there, precisely because we know too much about the minor details of Nature. The moon can no longer inspire us to poetry as it did before we saw television closeups of the surface, when a space-ship crashed into it, or when the Russian camera sent back pictures of its terrain. As we tighten our control over Nature, we are less prone to find God in it. Our vision of the heavens has become befuddled by formulae and equations. Our primal reaction to the wonders of the world has been blunted by slide-rule and spectroscope and computer. What we have gained in analytic knowledge we have lost in the responsiveness of the whole man. In the contemporary scientific age, we cannot see the forest because of the trees; we are so enamored of the wonders of God's work, that we forget that God is there. Perhaps, too that is why we recite only on the Sabbath the Psalm that begins *Ha-shamayim mesaprim kevod El*—" the heavens declare the glory of God." Only on the day of rest, when we withdraw from our involvement in Nature, when we attain the proper perspective towards man and world, do we suddenly realize that these heavens that we have examined so minutely and that we have probed so powerfully, that they themselves declare the glory of God!

———

THE MOST SIGNIFICANT contribution to our problem, telling us how to attain a personal encounter with God in this terribly impersonal world, is offered by Rabbi Hayyim of Volozhin.

In viewing his approach, it is important to know how Jewish tradition formulates its faith in God. Briefly, this holds that there are two aspects of man's understanding of the Creator. The first is known to us from the Bible and Jewish history. It is the belief in a personal God, One who reacts to man, who seeks man out, and who wants man to seek Him out. When we are happy, we experience His love and compassion and call Him "Father"; when He punishes us, we detect the qualities of severity and justice and call Him our "Judge." This belief in God as possessing personality is a fundamental of Judaism.

At the same time, the great sages of Judaism, in both the Kabbalistic and philosophic traditions, have taught that God is also more than personal. It is true that God relates to us personally; but God's existence is not exhausted by His relationship with man. In fact it is not exhausted by "relationships" at all. God is also beyond man, beyond all the universe. In His Essence, His infinity, God is totally unknowable, even nameless. In His absoluteness, the Kabbalists taught, the world does not even exist for Him. In this respect God is the "great mystery," and man must forever despair of being able to understand Him.

God, then, is both personal and trans-personal, both related to man and totally unconcerned with him. Granting that all analogies are at best faulty, the best simile is that of the relation of a good but limited student to a brilliant, world-renowned teacher. The teacher pays attention to the student, answers his questions, offers him instruction, and relates to him in many ways. But the teacher's interests are far beyond the student: intellectual, personal, cultural, social. The student cannot even begin to imagine how far and wide the mind and the intellect of the teacher range. He is unaware even of the areas of interest in which the teacher distinguishes himself. For the student, this teacher is both personal and trans-personal, both related and utterly separate.

Multiply that analogy a million-fold, and we may have some idea of this dual nature of the relationship between God and man. God is infinitely personal, closer to man than his own mother and father—and yet infinitely absolute, terribly distant and incomprehensible. God is related and withdrawn, involved and aloof, exceedingly close and immensely remote.

What Can We Do About It?

What does this mean for man?

If he succeeds in feeling God's closeness, in—as it were—getting God to be close to him, to be personal with him, then his life is fulfilled, it has purpose, and man achieves happiness.

But if man lives so that his God is distant, impersonal and aloof, then man despairs, he shrivels in cosmic loneliness and universal solitude. Man cannot survive the terror of God's remoteness. If God is not alive for man, then man must die spiritually.

The stakes, then, are monumental. Life or death, meaningfulness or aimlessness, fulfillment or frustration, all depend on whether God is personal or impersonal, related or absolute.

What can we do about it? Can we, indeed, do anything about it?

The answer of Rabbi Hayyim of Volozhin is: Yes, we certainly can. Whether God is personal or impersonal to us—depends upon us: If we are personal to Him, He will be personal to us. Whether God concerns Himself with us or ignores us depends on whether we concern ourselves with Him or ignore Him.

But how can man become personal with God? All of Judaism, all of Torah and Mitzvot is the answer to this question. Judaism, in its totality, is the way in which man makes the great gesture of turning his own personality and humanity to God. The purpose of all Judaism is to make God personal by making a man a human, a person, a "mentch." If we are just machines who devour the raw products of experience and disgorge jobs and profits and pleasures and waste, then God has nothing to do with us; He turns us over to the giant, cold, ruthless machine called Nature and its impersonal laws. If we are human—warm, concerned with God—then He emerges from His infinitely mysterious depths and turns to us. The degree to which God emerges from His absoluteness into warm, life-giving personality, depends squarely upon man and his exercise of *his* spiritual potential. The greatest blessing is: *yisa ha-Shem panav elekha*—"May the Lord turn His face unto thee," may God turn to you and emerge into a personal relationship with you. It is this *nesiat panim*, "the turning of the face," which is the direct opposite of *hester panim*, "the hiding of the face." It is this richness of Divine personality that is implied in the Yiddish "Gottenyu," a word which is untranslatable because of the wealth of its spiritual and psychological implications.

A TRULY OBSERVANT Jew knows that his God is *Elohim chayyim*, "a living God." In the Psalms David tells us: *Ha-shem tzilkha al yad yeminekha*, "The Lord is thy shadow on thy right hand." A sage of two centuries ago comments: As a shadow follows the body when the hand is raised, so does the shadow rise, and when the hand is lowered, so does the shadow descend. So is the relation of God with man: the way man acts to God, is the way God acts to man—just like his shadow.

God lives for man, only as man lives for God. If God is to be alive for us, we must get personal with, and be alive and alert to Him.

Man cannot simply sit back, and challenge God and Judaism, the Rabbi, and the synagogue to make God real for him. God will not be brought out of His mysterious aloofness by arguments or logic, by science or philosophy, even by sermons or lectures or articles. There is only one way out of the dilemma for the modern Jew: he must make the first gesture to God. He must make this gesture of personality by *Torah,* for by studying Torah he shows that he takes the words of God seriously. He must do so through *prayer*—addressing God feelingly, directly, imploring Him to descend out of His mysterious depths to a relationship with man. He must do so through the *Mitzvot*, by performing the will of God, for actions speak louder than words. The "aliveness" of God is reciprocal to that of man.

This view of the Divine-human encounter is symbolized, I believe in the first revelation by God to Moses. Moses is attracted by the strange phenomenon of the desert bush which is aflame and yet not consumed. This burning bush is a symbol of God's paradoxical relationship with man. On the one hand the flame is attached to the bush—"the bush is burning in fire." On the other hand, the flame is separated from the bush—"and the bush is not consumed." What a strange relationship—attached, yet separate; close, yet far. It is indeed a symbol of the mystery of God's relation with the world and with man. Moses is, of course, fascinated by this marvelous sight. Yet the Divine command stops him from approaching the bush. Even Moses is mortal, and hence may not pursue his fascination with this mystery beyond his human limits.

Moses acknowledges the superior wisdom of his Creator: "and Moses hid his face for he was afraid to look at God." He recognized that he may not and cannot probe too deeply into this marvelous mystery of God's dual relationship with the world. If God does not "hide His face," Moses must soon hide his! Furthermore, there is a more compelling task before him than satisfying his theological curiosity: leading his people out of Egypt. Performing the Divine will takes priority over probing the Divine nature. Moses is satisfied—yet disturbed. What, he asks, if my people will ask the same question: *Mah Shemo* "what is His Name?" They will want to know something about You. The Divine response is, *Eh'yeh asher Eh'yeh*, "I am what I am," or "I will be what I shall be." The Midrash explains this as: "What you will be with me, I will be with you"; as you act toward Me, I will act towards you.

––––––

THIS IS THE ANSWER of Judaism: If we want God to be close to us, we must first get ourselves close to Him. If we want God to be personal with us, we must get personal with Him.

That indeed is the over-arching purpose of Judaism—its prayer, its laws, its way of life, its study of Torah.

God is not dead for us unless we are first dead to Him. He is very much alive to those who are alive to Him. As we will be to Him, so will He be to us.

~ 8 ~

THE *COMMENTARY* SYMPOSIUM—1966

I have always felt that Shammai's policy was wiser than Hillel's in their respective reactions to the Gentile who challenged them to teach him the whole Torah while standing on one foot. It is probably better not to try at all than to risk all the ambiguities that must necessarily attend a condensation of one's religious outlook to a couple thousand words. Nevertheless, out of deference to the preference of the Jewish tradition for Hillel, I am willing to take my chances and come armed with naught but naive trust in the reader's fairness, no matter what his convictions.

(1) I believe the Torah is divine revelation in two ways: in that it is God-given and in that it is godly. By "God-given," I mean that He willed that man abide by His commandments and that that will was communicated in discrete words and letters. Man apprehends in many ways: by intuition, inspiration, experience, deduction—and by direct instruction. The divine will, if it is to be made known, is sufficiently important for it to be revealed in as direct, unequivocal, and unambiguous a manner as possible, so that it will be understood by the largest number of the people to whom this will is addressed. Language, though somewhat faulty an instrument, is still the best means of communication to most human beings.

Hence, I accept unapologetically the idea of the verbal revelation of the Torah. I do not take seriously the caricature of this idea which reduces Moses to a secretary taking dictation. Any competing notion of revelation, such as the various "inspiration" theories, can similarly be made to sound absurd by anthropomorphic parallels. Exactly how this communication took place no one can say; it is no less mysterious than the nature of the One who spoke. The divine-human encounter is not a meeting of equals, and the *kerygma* that ensues from this event must therefore be articulated in human terms without reflecting on the mode and form of the divine *logos*. *How* God spoke is a mys-

---

My contribution to the famous symposium by Commentary *in 1966 on matters of Jewish faith and belief. The questions are evident from my replies.*

tery; how *Moses* received this message is irrelevant. *That* God spoke is of the utmost significance, and *what* He said must therefore be intelligible to humans in a human context, even if one insists upon an endlessly profound mystical over-plus of meaning in the text. To deny that God can make His will clearly known is to impose upon Him a limitation of dumbness that would insult the least of His human creatures.

Literary criticism of the Bible is a problem, but not a crucial one. Judaism has successfully met greater challenges in the past. Higher Criticism is far indeed from an exact science. The startling lack of agreement among scholars on any one critical view; the radical changes in general orientation in more recent years; the many revisions that archeology has forced upon literary critics; and the unfortunate neglect even by Bible scholars of much first-rate scholarship in modern Hebrew supporting the traditional claim of Mosaic authorship—all these reduce the question of Higher Criticism from the massive proportions it has often assumed to a relatively minor and manageable problem that is chiefly a nuisance but not a threat to the enlightened believer.

Torah is not only God-given; it is also Godly. The divine word is not only uttered by God, it is also an aspect of God Himself. All of the Torah—its ideas, its laws, its narratives, its aspirations for the human community—lives and breathes Godliness. Hillel Zeitlin described the Hasidic interpretation of revelation (actually it was even more true of their opponents, the Mitnagdim, and ultimately derived from a common Kabbalistic source) as not only *Torah min ha-shamayim* (Torah *from* Heaven) but *Torah she'hi shamayim* (Torah that *is* Heaven). It is in Torah that God is most immediately immanent and accessible, and the study of Torah is therefore not only a religious commandment *per se*, but the most exquisite and the most characteristically Jewish form of religious experience and communion. For the same reason, Torah is not only legislation, *halakha*, but in its broadest meaning, *Torah*—teaching, a term that includes the full spectrum of spiritual edification: theological and ethical, mystical and rhapsodic.

Given the above, it is clear that I regard all of the Torah as binding on the Jew. To submit the *mitzvot* to any extraneous test—whether rational or ethical or nationalistic—is to reject the supremacy of God, and hence in effect to deny Him as God. The classification of the *mitzvot* into rational and revelational, or ethical and ritual, has descriptive-methodological but not substantive religious significance. Saadia Gaon, who a thousand years ago proposed the dichotomy between rational and non-rational commandments as the cornerstone of his philosophy of law, maintained that even the apparently pure revelational laws were fundamentally rational, although man might not, now or ever, be able to grasp their inner rationality. At the same time, far greater and more genuine spirituality inheres in the acceptance of those laws that apparently lack ethical, rational, or doctrinal content. It is only these performances, according to R. Hai Gaon, that are prefaced by the blessing, "Blessed art Thou . . . who has sanctified us with His commandments and commanded us to . . ." Holiness, the supreme religious category, contains an essential non-rational core; and this state of the "numinous" can be attained only when man bows his head and submits the totality of his existence to the will of God by performing His *mitzvah* for no reason other than that this is the will of the Creator. R. Nachman of Bratzlav recommended to his followers that they observe the "ethical" laws as though they were "ritual" commandments. In this manner, the ethical performance is transformed from a pale humanistic act into a profound spiritual gesture. I do not, therefore, by any means accord to ceremonial laws any lesser status than to the others. One the contrary, while confident that these *mitzvot shimiyot* are more than divine whim in that they are ultimately of benefit to man and society, I prefer to accept even the *sikhliyot*, the rational and ethical, as "ritual" in an effort to attain holiness, the ultimate desideratum of religious life.

(2) It should be unnecessary to have to clarify to sophisticated readers, at this late date, that the Jewish doctrine of the election of Israel is not one of racial or ethnic superiority. The chosenness of Israel relates exclusively to its spiritual vocation embodied in the Torah; the doctrine, indeed, was announced at Sinai. Wherever it is mentioned in our liturgy—such as the blessing immediately preceding the *Shema*, or the benediction over the Torah-reading—it is always related to Torah or *mitzvot*. This spiritual vocation consists of two complementary functions, described as *goy kadosh*, that of a holy nation, and *mamlekhet kohanim*, that of a kingdom of priests. The first term denotes the development of communal separateness or differentness in order to achieve a collective self-transcendence. The *Halakha* is the

method *par excellence* for the attainment of this goal. The second term implies the obligation of this brotherhood of the spiritual elite toward the rest of mankind; priesthood is defined by the prophets as fundamentally a teaching vocation. The election of Israel "because all the earth is Mine" was understood by Seforno (to Ex. 19:5) to mean, "because I love all the peoples of My world, I have elected you to teach all mankind to call upon the Name of the Lord and serve Him in unison."

These two functions, the tension between which is inherent in the concept of chosenness, are not antonyms, mutually exclusive, but supplementary ideas. In a study of how this doctrine was treated in Tannaitic times, a contemporary scholar has discovered that the greater the emphasis by an individual sage on chosenness and its inescapable particularism, the greater the breadth of his universalism. This separateness of Israel, its "holiness" function, may both result in and be fostered by a sense of alienation. But to assert, as some have done, that it is *exhausted* by the experience of alienation, is to misread the whole meaning of election by eliminating its clear *telos*, that of holiness. There is no virtue in alienation, or particularism, or an inclination for dissent, for their own sake. They may be characteristic, respectively, of modern man's psychological condition, or the aspirations of Jewish secular nationalism, or the liberal credo; but they are not Judaism. And, ultimately, they cannot nourish the soul or provide an answer for the spiritual yearnings of men and women.

Can the idea of chosenness give birth to the wild *Herrenvolk* theories that have proved so catastrophic in our times? Of course it can, and possibly has (although it never has with Jews). But such noxious notions are not legitimate children of the biblical doctrine of election; they are monsters, genetic mutations. Any idea contains the risk of distortion; and the nobler the idea, the greater the danger and the uglier the perversion. The concept of government can be reduced to tyranny; must we, therefore, all be anarchists in order to avoid such dangers? Religion can become superstition; democracy, mobocracy; liberty, libertinism; respect, subservience; love, lechery. Shall we abandon the former because they can and often do degenerate into the latter?

The same holds true for the chosenness of Israel. It is a teaching of service and a service of teaching. It is concerned with the attainment of spirituality. Its particularistic aspect, while essential and indispensable, is propaedeutic; its universalist element remains the ultimate *telos*. Israel may be a reluctant teacher, and the world an unwilling pupil. But the methodology of divine pedagogics is rarely directly didactic. The teaching occurs on many levels and is expressed in many ways: by word, by sublime example, and most notably by the very mystery of Jewish history. That Israel is the chosen agent for this education of mankind does not reflect either on the superiority or inferiority of this people—although intimations of both may be found in Jewish literature. The nearest that any major Jewish thinker has come to a biological interpretation of this spiritual elitism is the highly ethnocentric historiosophy of Judah Halevi. But only a deliberate misreading of the *Kuzari*, the work in which this idea is proposed, can mistake it for a precursor of modern racism. The whole of the argument is addressed by the rabbi in the book to the pagan king of the Khazars in an endeavor to convince him of the truth of Judaism. At the end of the book, the king converts to Judaism—surely an astonishing conclusion to a tract supposedly elaborating an exclusive doctrine of Jewish racism!

(3) The nature of Israel's priesthood, its teaching to all of mankind, can be divided into two: the social-ethical and the spiritual-metaphysical (the two, of course, are ultimately interrelated). The *Halakha* articulated the first in the form of the "Seven Noahide Laws" which, in effect, mean civilized behavior. (Nachmanides considers these as seven categories of law, rather than as individual commandments.) These are essentially negative: the rejection of immorality and brutality and lawlessness. The only "religious" one of the seven laws is also negative: the proscription of idolatry. To this the prophetic tradition adds a second element—the spiritual-metaphysical content of priesthood, positively formulated: the recognition and service of God. This is the vision of a day when "the Lord will be King over all the earth," and the redemptive future when "the knowledge of the Lord" will fill the earth as the waters cover the seas. This acceptance of God, of course, comprehends the good life. Maimonides distinguished between the first and the second of these two elements— the humanitarian-humanistic and the profoundly theistic ethos—by referring to the practitioners of the first as *wise* Gentiles, and to the second by the more honorific term, *pious* Gentiles.

That a number of these ideas are shared by the major religions, some as a result of Jewish influence and some independently, cannot and ought not be denied. But this by no means relieves Israel of the obligation to pursue its vocation without relaxation. Surely this post-Auschwitz era needs education in civilized conduct as much as did the Canaanites of antiquity; and contemporary man—whose avant-garde theologians have killed what he had of God and directed his religious concerns solely to the worship of a man—needs, no less than the fetishistic primitive, the constant reminder that "the Lord [and not an apotheosized human] is God" and that the Lord is One. And perhaps the most significant teaching, the uniqueness of Judaism, is the coalescence of these very elements—the spiritual and the practical, the theological and the ethical, *aggada* and *Halakha*. Judaism has always resisted the effort to foist on it—as metaphysical truth rather than as a merely analytical device—the bifurcation of body and soul, of letter and spirit, of ritual and social, of cults and ethos. The restriction of religion to worship and cult was accepted quite naturally by the ancient pagans, and the confinement of the spirit to cult in modern times, despite all gallant attempts at developing a "social gospel," is one of the sad triumphs of secularism. We have cornered God, locked Him up in little sanctuaries, and now complain that we cannot find Him in "the real world." Judaism's unique contribution to modern man may well lie in its insistence that God is very much alive, that He is *not* absent from society (even "secular" society) for those who invite Him in, and that the best way to achieve this goal is to release Him from His incarceration in our barren and dessicated temples. In a word: *Halakha!* Through a sanctifying of all of life, meaning and purpose return to man, God is once again accessible, and human spirit can be affirmed in the very midst of life in all its existential tensions and the wealth of its variegated phenomena. It is through *Halakha* that a new relationship is established between the sacred and the secular (Rabbi Kook referred to them as the holy and the not-yet-holy), and that man can reorient himself toward nature in a manner that affirms the development of technology joyously.

(4) I do not believe that Judaism commits us to any specific social, political, or ideological system, but I do believe that it may negate certain viewpoints. Fascism and Communism, for instance, insofar as they offend human dignity and strip us of cer-

tain human rights, are obviously in violation of the principles of Judaism. Just as Judaism allows, within certain limits, a latitude for various philosophical tenets, and does not bind us to any one comprehensive metaphysical outlook, so there exists an area of freedom for different social and political philosophies. Much work remains to be done in elucidating the limiting principles beyond which a political theory is considered offensive to Judaism. It should also be emphasized that not all contemporary political issues can be resolved by immediate reference to Jewish sources. The attempts to align Judaism as a religion with either side of the Vietnamese question is a case in point. The naiveté in proposing simplistic solutions to enormously complex international issues, and the almost incredible *chutzpah* in labeling one's prejudices as official "Judaism," point to the danger in making religion *too* relevant. Judaism certainly has something to say about every significant issue in life, but this judgment can be meaningful only if it is applied to a problem that has been properly defined. Neither world political and social matters nor individual halakhic questions can be decided when they are enshrouded in an impenetrable vagueness. Appeals to sentiment and good intentions cannot substitute for the intellectual exertion that is the task of man in clearly formulating the problem for which guidance is sought in divine revelation. The giants of *Halakha* have always emphasized that enlightenment cannot be acquired cheaply. Judaism may be neglected if it is too remote from the issues that agitate contemporary men; it will surely be held in contempt if it presumes to offer snap judgments in the form of pronunciamentos by self-proclaimed spokesmen on every issue that journalists and politicians consider of abiding importance.

(5) Space does not permit me to dwell upon what I believe is an authentic Jewish reaction to the current "God is dead" controversy. I have commented on that in a recent article in *Jewish Life*.

I feel quite differently about the exciting talk of the relation of religion to the secular world, as propounded by Cox and others. Here I think that Judaism has a great deal to say, if we are willing to liberate ourselves from the defensive, apologetic positions that we have taken *vis-à-vis* Jewish secularists in the last hundred years. I suspect that research into the philosophy of *Halakha*, the thinking of the founders of Hasidism, and the writings of Rabbi

Kook will offer a great deal of enlightenment on this problem.

The real challenge to Jewish belief in our day will come, I believe, from the cyberneticians who have been developing a metaphysics of cybernetics in which they attempt to use theories of communication and control to establish criteria for a materialistic conception of meaning and purpose. If the source of human purpose is in the neuronic feedback circuits of our nervous system, then we have snuffed out freedom and established a new and imposing deterministic materialism.

But challenging though it may well be, I do not fear it. The computer is an extension of the human brain even as the scissors is an extension of the hand and the automobile of the foot. Just as we need our limbs to operate our instruments, so will we need our minds to ask the right questions of our omniscient answer-machines. I have faith that mindlessness will not prevail, and that human dignity—the divine image—will not be proven obsolete. And after all, it is that historic and personal Jewish faith, that *ani maamin*, that has prevailed and kept us alive to this day.

~ 9 ~
THE *COMMENTARY* SYMPOSIUM—1996

It goes without saying that I believe in God. But my big and terrifying question is whether *He* believes in *me*. . . . More than a cute answer, this is a religious as opposed to a theological response. Theology, a monologue by man about God, has its place on the periphery of the consciousness of a believing Jew. In the center, however, stands God, and man must not merely *think about* Him, but *respond to* Him as part of the dialogue between man and his Creator. The creation of the human race was an act of faith by God in man, and the response of man determines whether that confidence was vindicated or misplaced.

In Judaism, the will of God is made known to man in the Torah, mostly in the form of *mitzvot*, commandments. These commandments are, by their very nature, binding. They summon man to obey, and the human reaction comes on many levels and is accompanied by a variety of emotions. It is this interplay between summons and response, and their almost infinite variety of nuances and subtleties, that determines the quality of one's religious experience. But underlying all is the conception of the *mitzvot* as theonomous rather than autonomous: we may understand or not understand a commandment, prefer one *mitzvah* to another, but God's will must be obeyed.

Israel was chosen at Sinai as "a holy nation and a kingdom of priests." A "holy nation" is a mission for the polity in and for itself: to grow in sanctity as a Godly people. A "kingdom of priests" is the outward reach of the Jewish enterprise in the world: to be a priest-teacher to all of humanity, inviting it by both word and example to fulfill the "image of God" in which every human being was created. The two are linked: Israel cannot teach if it is not itself informed, and therefore it must always strive to be a "holy nation." And its own inner mission is unfulfilled if it fails to communicate holiness—in its numinousness and its ethical consequences—as "a kingdom of priests" to the rest of the world.

Thirty years later, the world was different, and Commentary *was different!*

The Torah makes it quite clear that we were chosen neither because of our intrinsic merit nor in order to lord it over others, but by virtue of the patriarchs, especially Abraham, whose heart was "found" by God to be faithful and who was promised a posterity which would carry on his work of "proclaiming the name of God" to the world.

The distinctive role of the Jewish people in today's world is blurred, because our people is hopelessly fragmented, with most Jews as unacquainted with their own history as they are ignorant of the fundamentals of their traditions and its texts. I regard as an aberration the notion that the "liberal agenda" so favored by most American Jews is the true mission of world Jewry. Transforming politics, no matter how high-minded, into a religion is a species of contemporary idolatry and is particularly peculiar when espoused by people for whom the separation of piety from politics is an unassailable dogma. The message of Torah must become clear to Jewry before it is propounded to the rest of mankind.

It is therefore incumbent upon that segment of the people which is genuinely and wholeheartedly committed to Torah, whatever the differences in interpretation that divide them, to become the surrogates of all Israel as the "kingdom of priests." That mission must be expressed in universal rather than in parochial terms, and in a manner that is both true to the sources and comprehensible to contemporary men and women who have gone through the experience of modernity. In its broadest terms, that means the teaching of the dignity of humankind (the "image of God"), the unity of all His creatures ("for have we not all one father?"), the concern for the well-being of society (*tikkun olam*), the sanctity of life ("he who saves one life, is as if he saved the entire world"), the ultimate redemption of mankind (the belief in Messiah—too much to elaborate in a short statement!), etc. More specifically, it means the seven Noahide laws as prescribed by the Halakhah.

Such a program, whether conceived of narrowly or broadly, incorporates much of the more generous sentiments of modern Jews at the same time as it rejects the hedonism and relativism that have been adopted by secularist Jews as fundamental to their outlook.

The Holocaust, incomprehensibly cruel, has shaken my faith—

but not destroyed it. The emergence of Jewish independence, especially after the Holocaust, has reinforced my faith—but not convinced me that we necessarily live in Messianic times. The confluence of both in my consciousness has stretched the perimeters and deepened the quality of my faith, and made me more tolerant of both those who lost their faith and those who clearly perceive the footsteps of Messiah in the State of Israel. Most of all, it has made me more consciously Jewish and, at the same time, less tolerant of pat answers and simplistic formulations about the truly overarching questions of life and destiny.

To the extent that political views reflect broad cultural orientations, the political center to right-of-center provides the most accommodating environment for the growth of Jewish religious life and, hence, Jewish continuity. If the Left is the home of secularism, materialism, permissiveness, etc., and the Right of a repressive conformity and religious fundamentalism (both descriptions are exaggerated), Jewish life in America will not flourish; the former encourages values that are thoroughly inimical to Judaism, and the latter is threatening to Jews who live in a country with a Christian majority.

Jewish tradition has suffered enormously under the cultural hegemony of the elitists of the Left. The academy and the media, among others, have not proved hospitable to religion in general and to Jewish religion in particular. A right-of-center orientation—inclining to traditional values in such matters as sexual morality—which also respects differences in our multicultural society, and which steers clear of dogmatic extremisms of both Right and Left, will foster Jewish commitment more than either end of the political-cultural spectrum.

Jewish "unity" is a theme guaranteed to evoke an industrial-size yawn. It is a chimerical nostrum regularly invoked by organizational drum-beaters, not an idea capable of real expression. It is best to give up the ghost and speak not of unity, but of civility, respect, and cooperation—where possible. It is inconceivable for me, as an Orthodox Jew, to think of genuine Jewish religious unity when Reform, currently the largest movement, has embraced patrilinealism, ordained gays and lesbians as Reform rabbis, and otherwise given enthusiastic ecclesiastical approval to almost every avant-garde liberal movement in the general society. Extremes beget extremes, and significant segments of Or-

thodoxy are moving in the opposite direction, demanding conformity, and associating almost automatically with the more (or
even most) right-wing political movements both in America and
Israel.

It is a moot question as to which side began the process of estrangement. The fact is that real unity is impossible and even unthinkable today, and the best and most advisable policy is for all
to seek enough common ground to devise an agenda which will
benefit the entire people.

There can be no large-scale revival of *Judaism* as long as *Jews*
are vanishing. With out-marriage at an all-time high, the birth
rate below replacement, and assimilation rampant, it is hard to
conceive of a broad revival of Judaism in this country. But this
pessimism applies only to the near future. Looking further
ahead, I see a rearrangement of forces in a shrunken American
Jewish community—one that is far more committed to Torah,
with a much higher birth rate, paying real attention to Jewish
education, that holds the promise of growing into a more populous, self-confident, and religiously committed community—all
this, of course, depending upon the nature of the environing society and developments within the State of Israel. The great question at that time will be whether a modicum of cohesiveness can
develop between the then much larger religious segment and the
smaller but still significant secularist/liberal groups. That is
what worried and enlightened Jewish leadership must address
itself to—now, not later, when it may well be too late.

~ 10 ~

THE GOD
I BELIEVE IN

Q: What religious or Jewish upbringing did you have? Did you come from a very traditional home?

LAMM: Yes, I grew up in a community that once was famous, some might say infamous, and that is Williamsburg, Brooklyn, which later became the center of Satmarer Hasidim. But when I was growing up, Williamsburg was a lower- to- middle-class Jewish neighborhood; very fine, and not at all wealthy—but we didn't know that as children. We thought we were just normal people and had no sense of disappointment in our lot. It was a very rich Jewish life. My father came from observant Jews in Lemberg [Lvov], Poland, now the Ukraine. His father, as my father often said, made a living out of not making a living. My mother came from a rabbinical family that traces itself way, way back up to Rashi. My maternal grandfather, was a *gaon* [eminent Talmudic authority] whom I recognize as one of my two major *rebbeim* [rabbis]. He passed away when I was twenty-one, but from the time I started Gemara [Talmud] when I was about nine years old or so, he was my teacher.

Q: Where did your family come from?

LAMM: In Europe, my mother's family was from small towns, rabbis in places like Szczawnica, Kroscienko, etc.

Q: Anywhere near Lemberg?

LAMM: My father was from Lemberg.

Q: My mother came from Rava Rsuka and my father from Sambor.

LAMM: Galitzianer! Most of the Viennese Jews after World War I were Galitzianer. I grew up in what to me was a normal Jewish way. I went to Yeshivah Torah Vodaath, which then was considerably less extreme than it is today. My grandfather impressed

A conversation with Rabbi Joshua O. Haberman in the book of the same name by the author, published by The Free Press, in 1994.

upon me the need to continue "learning" before going to college. He wanted me to go to college. He was a *Rav* [rabbi]. He was a great *Talmid Chakham* [scholar]. There are *teshuvot* [responsa] of his that are world famous, collected in his two-volume *Emek Ha-lakhah*.

Q: Was he a follower of *Torah im Derekh Eretz* [combination of Torah and secular education]?

LAMM: Oh, no; he was a *heimisher* [warmly familiar] Rav.

Q: He just wanted you to have a good education.

LAMM: Right. He wanted me to go to Yeshiva University and study under Rabbi Soloveitchik. So for one year, I took off from high school to spend half a day in Torah Vodaath and the other half a day "learning" with him and his brother. At night, after it was done, I did a little bit of autodidactic work. I read through a good deal of philosophy and all of Freud, Jung, and Adler. It was a great year, my greatest year so far as study is concerned.

Q: So you ventured into psychological and philosophical studies?

LAMM: Yes, early on. From there I went on to Yeshiva University and got my Semichah [ordination] and my doctorate.

Q: Did you ever experience what some people call a major turning point, religiously or theologically, in your life, or has it been an ongoing, steady development?

LAMM: It was an ongoing development and maturation. There were points, of course, at which I probably regressed and then progressed.

Q: The normal crises of doubt?

LAMM: Precisely. I experienced that, as I suppose every intelligent or sensitive person always does. You have your feelings of distance and feelings of closeness and probably it accounts for the fact that I've been thinking about these issues all my life.

Q: If you were to trace your way to God, your faith in God, which sources would play the major role? Books, or people, or events, or ideas?

LAMM: I think all of that. I'm not particularly linked to any one of these. Personalities, of course, had a profound influence on me. Intellectually, my grandfather, and *le'havdil beyin chayim Le'chayim* [let us distinguish the living from the dead], Rabbi Soloveitchik had a very strong influence. I'm just finishing my first year of mourning for both my parents, people of no great intellectual attainments, yet they had a tremendous effect on me. They set an example by way of elemental human decency. I was very fortunate to have come from a home where love was never talked about, but always practiced; very little demonstrative, but ever-present. It predisposed me to think that the kind of life they were leading, this kind of supportive, happy atmosphere between parents and children was only natural. Also, that may account for the fact that I'm so traditionally inclined. I'm not ready to overturn tradition at mere whim. I prefer to examine things very carefully because tradition has a *chazakah* [a prior claim or hold] in my own intellectual life, and it requires a lot to overturn a *chazakah*. It can be done, but it requires very strong proof.

Q: Is there some kind of mystical or intuitional side to your faith in God?

LAMM: Oh sure, I find it very difficult to see how one can separate clearly between the purely intellectual, rational approach and an intuitive, and if you will, a somewhat mystical approach, too.

Q: To what extent would you say your faith in God was shaped by one side or the other?

LAMM: It's hard to say. We think rationally. But what I think is very much akin to what Judah Halevi says about prophecy. He agrees with the *Rambam* [Maimonides], whom he didn't know, that you have to prepare yourself intellectually for it, but then the last spark is an intuitive one. God has to choose you, but you must prepare yourself intellectually. I would apply that not only to prophecy, but even to my own religious development. I strongly believe that one must spell it out intellectually to be able to handle it with a certain degree of discrimination, but the ultimate acceptance, the ultimate commitment, requires that final, but very decisive, leap of faith that we call "intuition."

Q: Do words like "encounter" or "dialogue" with God mean anything to you?

LAMM: Yes, they do. I think, of course, that they become buzz words and after a while they become emptied of all content. I think it is always necessary for every generation, maybe for every thinking person, to develop his own neologisms, because the old words sometimes carry baggage which no longer is real. Now when Buber started to talk about it, he used the special terms of "encounter" and "dialogue." I think they were fresh, they meant something, even if not exactly defined. But it meant something. But after a while, it became so overused that if I say "Hello" to you, we're "dialoguing." If I meet you in the street, it's an "encounter." The word loses its special quality.

Q: Can we define a little more clearly what is meant by an "encounter" with God?

LAMM: I try to encounter God three times a day. To me, *tefillah* [prayer] if done with *kavanah* [devotion], is an encounter. Is it a dialogue? I don't know. Dialogue means that the other side answers, and while I'm always sure that God is a *shome'a tefillah* [one who hears prayer], I'm not always sure that He is an *oneh tefillah* [one who answers prayer], the way I'd like it. Of course as someone once said, No is also an answer. But I do feel that He is listening.

Q: You incline toward a concept of God that is personal?

LAMM: Oh, sure.

Q: You favor a personal divine being as against an impersonal force or power?

LAMM: Yes, but let me define that a little better. I believe both are true. I don't believe we can *onchappen dem Ribbon-shel-olam beim bord* [grab God by His beard]. I don't think we can pigeonhole Him quite that way. Perhaps the best way to express it is a kabalistic way, that there is a core aspect of God which is *ein sof* [infinity], and then there is the revelational aspect of the *esser sefirot* [ten aspects of divinity]. I believe that it may be contrary to the way we think of divinity. We think that the personal is a higher degree than the impersonal. It may be that for God, looking down *mem'eon kodsho* [from His holy abode], it is the reverse, i.e., the highest level is the impersonal one, but then He relates to us through His personal aspect. So, it is a personal God I believe in, but the personal God is more than personal. Personality is an aspect of God. If the *chitzoni* [external aspect of God] is represented, as it were, by the *esser sefirot*, then the essence of God is far beyond personality. As a human being I cannot relate to it. But I can assert it.

Q: One of the most troubling articles of faith has to do with the element of revelation in the Bible. In what way do you sense the Bible to be God's word?

LAMM: The word "word" is wisely chosen, because that's the term the Chumash [Pentateuch] uses and the *nevi'im* [prophets] use: *ne'um ha'Shem, devar ha-Shem* [utterance of God, word of God] for which the term "logos" was used by the Greek translators. I do believe that there was revelation, that the revelations are authentic, that God speaks in one voice, but it is heard in many ways. We can say that with regard to the *aseret ha-dibrot* [ten commandments]: *shamor vezakhor be'dibbur echad.* ["Keep" and "remember" in one expression, i.e., the two versions of the Sabbath Commandments in the Decalogue, Exodus ch. 20 and Deuteronomy ch. 5, were simultaneously uttered.] It comes as if it were not a physical voice, of course, but as one message, and each person hears it in his own way—each man or woman, to whomever the *nevuah* [prophecy] comes. *Ein shnei neviim mitnabe'im be'signon echad* [no two prophets prophesy in the same manner] is also a reference to the ways they perceive it. One symphony is heard in many ways by many listeners. I believe that there was a period in human history when God's revelation was direct.

Q: As an external event or as something felt from within?

LAMM: I think it was felt within, but objective nonetheless.

Q: Historical?

LAMM: Yes, I believe that, let's say that when Moses says *vayomer ha-Shem el mosheh lemor* [and God spoke to Moses, saying] or when one prophet says *vayehi devar ha-Shem elai* [and the word of God came to me], I don't think that an acoustically sensitive instrument could have measured the decibels in which God spoke. That would be far too literal. It is simply the only way one can express it. I believe that revelation occupied a major, very significant part of human history until that part of religious history faded away to be replaced by the intellectual and behavioral medium and God, as it were, left the Torah in the hands of man and said "I've given you My speech, now go ahead. Maybe someday I'll speak to you again"; but right now that more direct form of revelation is done and we remain with the fruits of that revelation. Now, God reveals Himself in events as well as in words. Events, therefore, have the same importance today that direct revelation had at one time.

I think what is happening to us has meaning in the same way as with the earlier revelation. In the period of the *tekufat ha-nevuah* [era of prophecy] from Moses until the *anshei haknesset hagedolah* [men of the Great Assembly], God spoke and the prophets heard Him. It was essentially the same message, but with certain nuances that were different; some people refused to hear Him. There is a *hakovesh nevuato* [the prophet who willfully suppresses his prophecy]. There is *nevuat sheker* or *navi sheker* [false prophecy or a false prophet]. Once prophecy is real, then other forms of *avodat ha-Shem* [worship of God] expressions, including the most spurious forms, cluster around it, which becomes a question of which is authentic, and which is inauthentic, a matter which the Torah itself discusses. Now the same thing is true of revelation, not through word but through event: the *Shoah*, the *gerush sefarad* [the Holocaust, the expulsion from Spain], a pogrom, *medinat Yisrael* [State of Israel]. These are events which are the contemporary form of the divine word. And they, too, can be understood differently by different people and they, too, can be misunderstood, even as was the original word.

Q: Are you suggesting that divine *hashgachah* [providence] is in some way fulfilled through events? That God participates in events?

LAMM: Yes, He does participate especially in the great historical events and it is His way of addressing us in a contemporary form, but it all depends on how we're going to understand, perceive, and react. And I think we've fluffed many of them in the course of our history.

Q: I hear you say that you do believe in the historicity of revelation. That God reaches us through a message, whether it is in writing or whether it is oral; but you are struggling, as all of us must, with the limitations of speech to understand and describe what ultimately is a mystery.

LAMM: Of course!

Q: Those messages which guide us, which are perceived as mitzvot, commands, how do you relate those to morality? Is morality the outgrowth of the mitzvot or are the mitzvot the outgrowth of morality?

LAMM: I do not have a definitive answer for that. I'm struggling with it, I'm still struggling with it and have not come to a conclusion. I know that they must be tied into each other. I do not accept that the mitzvot are a pure form of *avodat ha-Shem* [service of God] that has nothing to do with morality. This kind of thing is popularized by Yeshayahu Leibowitz.

Q: Then you obviously do not favor Kierkegaard's interpretation of the *akeda* [binding of Isaac]?*

LAMM: No, I don't accept it. To me there is a relation. Does it mean, therefore, that mitzvot are all subservient to a moral test? Since morality or conceptions of morality change in every generation, do I believe that the mitzvot rise or fall? No, because then my performance of a mitzvah is no longer obedience to God but

---

*In fierce opposition to what Kierkegaard considered a shallow moralizing rationalism fashionable in the mid-nineteenth century liberal Protestantism, the Danish existentialist philosopher cited the story of Abraham's test (Genesis 22) in which the patriarch proved willing to sacrifice his son Isaac at God's command. Kierkegaard, pointing to the immorality of God's command and Abraham's obedience, underscored the rationally incomprehensible, even demonic aspects of God's ways. In Kierkegaard's view, religion and morality represent separate concerns.

to my own fallible sense of what is moral, and that I don't think I can trust. The history of mankind does not inspire much confidence in man's moral judgment in and of itself. I would say, likewise, that we have no right to be so terribly confident in man's religious judgment in and of itself. Incidentally, in the classical sources there is *yesh dorshim lekhan ve'vesh dorshim le'khan* [one can interpret either way], one can look at it both ways. On the one hand, for instance, the famous statement that *mah li shechita min ha-tzavar mah li shechita min ha-oref—lo nitnu mitzvot le'Yisrael ela litzrof bahen et ha-beriot* [whether you slaughter the animal this way or that, the commandments were given only for Israel's refinement].

So the mitzvot are there for a moral purpose, to purify man's character. At the same time the mitzvot are beyond morality. I do not believe they conflict with morality in essence. In certain special cases they can. I refer now especially to (this may be irrelevant to a theological discussion, but to me it is not irrelevant because Halakhah has a great deal to say about it) the halakhic discussion mainly in the *tekufat ha-geonim*, e.g., Rav Hai Gaon. He asks why you make the benediction *"asher kideshanu be'mitzvotav, ve'tzivanu"* [who has sanctified us by His commandments and commanded us] only for certain mitzvot and not for others. For instance, why not for *tzedakah* [charitable deeds]? Why not for *leket, shikecha, u'peah* [the sheaf or corner of field left for the poor]? He says that any mitzvah that is morally rational, does not require the *berakhah* [benediction]. Only mitzvot which do not have any obvious rational or moral basis and which are neutral and which otherwise I would not do, require the *berakhah*. Why? Because total obedience, submission of man with his whole being including his intellect to God, leads to *kedushah* [holiness]. So, therefore, in performing a mitzvah like Shabbat or *tefillin* [phylacteries], etc. which have no moral dimension or no obvious moral dimension, I achieve *kedushah*, because I am going beyond myself, beyond my own concern. Whereas a mitzvah like *tzedakah* [charity], which I would understand even without the Torah, is something very important, but not because God told me.

Q: So in other words, by obeying the mitzvot, you feel you are rising to a higher level?

LAMM: A higher level than morality—that of holiness.

Q: But your moral tenets or principles are not all exclusively derived from the mitzvot?

LAMM: No!

Q: And what would be the other source?

LAMM: The other source, I believe, with all apologies to Judge Clarence Thomas's critics, is a form of natural law and I think the Torah itself alludes to it. Why was Cain punished?

Q: Because he offended.

LAMM: Of course; he offended natural law.

Q: Can you conceive of God caring one way or the other how you and I behave?

LAMM: I would be dismayed with the kind of God who didn't give a damn about how we behaved. All He could do would be to create a physical world, then, let all of man's spiritual achievements be just unforeseen accidents of the creation of the physical universe. I don't believe that.

Q: What would you answer a person who has studied a little astronomy, knows a little physics, knows a little chemistry and tells you, Professor Lamm, do you realize what you are saying? In this vast cosmos, I, as a human being, am a speck of dust; my time in life is so short as not to count measured against astronomical time. There are millions and billions of creatures like myself; could God really be concerned about my being?

LAMM: I would tell this astronomer, astrophysicist, chemist, biologist or what you will, it all depends on how big a God you believe in. Somehow a small computer has only a certain number of bytes but a very big computer can process a great deal more information. I believe in a very big God who can be concerned with everything, even a speck as apparently insignificant as my own life in this vast universe.

Q: Turning to the Holocaust and the immense amount of suffering which afflicts the innocent, even the just, can we still uphold belief in retribution for evil, reward for good, or must we fall in with the despairing judgment of Kohelet [Book of Ecclesiastes] that there is no evidence that the good is favored or rewarded as against the evil doer?

LAMM: Well, that problem is as old as religion itself. It probably is the oldest and the most excruciating problem with which any religion, particularly a monotheistic religion, must deal. The problem was stated long ago as *tzaddik ve'ra lo, rasha, ve'tov lo* [righteous, yet badly off; evil, yet prosperous]. The whole Shoah experience is different only because it is so different in number, when quantity affects quality.

Q: We can raise the question about innocent suffering, even in the case of a single child who is run over by a drunken driver.

LAMM: You see, the fundamental question remains. It becomes a somewhat different question on a national, universal basis. But the fundamental question is there. How can a good God abide such cruelty and such suffering of apparently innocent people? I don't have an answer any more than Job did. All I know is that when God appeared out of the whirlwind to Job, Job retracted not his questions, but the poignancy of his questions. I think that what Job retracted was his expectation of an answer, because the problem remains a problem. But when he demands of God an answer, that part is blunted at the very end. To ask the question not only is permissible, I think it is inevitable. Any moral human being, any moral religious person, must ask the question. But there comes a point when you bow your head and you say, *af al pi khen*, nevertheless, I accept. I don't know why. All I know is that I am mortal and my mortality not only makes me vulnerable to pain and suffering, it makes me vulnerable to not understanding why I am suffering.

Q: In the light of history, the Shoah as well as the establishment of the State of Israel, can you believe that the people Israel is the chosen people?

LAMM: Oh, if I ever have any doubts, I believe it now. What a small country Israel is, a tiny state, a small, tiny country! Consider that the Jews of that country are one-tenth of one percent of mankind and whatever happens in that tiny little country, called Israel, is trumpeted throughout the world. I think there are more people of the world press in Tel Aviv and Jerusalem than there are in Moscow or Washington or anyplace else. Why, what's going on? Is it all because of "Real-Politik"? Not so. There is mystery there that is so evident that you overlook it. We seem to have been the subject of fascination by mankind ever since Sinai. Yes, of course, I believe we are a chosen people. I don't believe "chosen" in a sense of "superior." I believe we are just a different kind of people and it goes back to belief in revelation. I believe we were meant to do something and be something in the world. Have we succeeded? No we have not. Not yet. Do we seem to be succeeding right now? No, I don't think so. But it doesn't mean we don't have that mission. History goes on, it goes on beyond our lifetime. I think the obligation of every Jew is to see to it that the Jewish people, Israel, does fulfill its mission as we were charged at Sinai.

Q: You base the idea of election on the *berit*, the covenant?

LAMM: Yes.

Q: Why would God need a special people to fulfill His will or His plan?

LAMM: He tried twice without it and the alternatives failed. This is Buber's way of reading and I agree with him there. He tried it universally, without anyone special, and that was the end of it. A flood came. He tried it with Noah and again the experiment failed and the knowledge, the awareness, and the service of the one God simply did not take hold. So God decided to make a nation, the people of Abraham, and we are still around and now some of us are trying hard to convince ourselves that we are "unchosen." What other people has expended so much effort to prove that it is not special?

Q: With regard to the idea of a mission, a special role, are we not promised help in the form of the Messiah? What do you think of the expectation of a redeemer? Do you think there is a need for the Messiah?

LAMM: Yes I do. That the concept, or the belief in the coming of the Messiah, has caused us grief such as in the days of Shabbatai Zvi, or, for that matter Christianity itself, I have no doubt. But two things have to be said. First, you have to make a cost-benefit analysis, to use crass managerial terms, of the whole belief in Messiah. It has cost us. And what has it given us? It has given us a sense of hope to know that despite two thousand years in *galut* [diaspora] we are going to make it, and if we won't, my great, great grandchildren will. Only because of a belief that there will be a *ge'ulah* [redemption], there will be a Messiah. As much as it has cost us, it has given us much more. I think in purely empirical terms what the concept of Messiah has meant for the people of Israel. Second, I believe that any great concept has negative features and the greater the concept, the more negative the features. The Zohar teaches that God, the *ein sof* [the Infinite], revealed Himself in the *esser sefirot*, and these were the *esser sefirot d'kedushah* [ten aspects of holiness]. But, simultaneously there were also revealed or emanated what the Zohar calls the ten aspects of contamination, of evil. Every idea has an equal and opposite coordinate that is negative. You show me an idea that has no possibility of negative results and I will show you an idea that is insignificant. You take any idea—love, peace, any of the great ideas that inspire mankind—they all can be corrupted, and the more inspiring they are, the more potentially positive they are, the more potentially negative they can become.

Q: The *Rambam* (Maimonides) was leery about specifying a Messianic concept. Did he not try to distance himself from it?

LAMM: I don't think he tried to keep a distance; after all, he did write about the Messiah extensively in his *Iggeret Teman* [letter to Yemen]. But he took a much more rational view which, I think, fits in with his whole outlook and probably is much closer to us about what is going to happen some day. But without the poetry behind it, people would not have been inspired by it. If Isaiah, the prophet, had said there will come a day when we Jews are not going to be bothered by the rest of mankind, when we're going to have time to sit and study Torah and philosophize about the nature of God, how would that have affected his contemporaries as compared to his vision of "the wolf shall dwell with the lamb and the leopard shall lie down with the kid" (Is. 11.6)? There is no comparison. Poetry has the ability to ignite a fire in the soul. Ideas can make it go up only very slowly.

Q: Is the Messiah as a person merely symbolic? Would you say that we are to hope for a development of mankind, of history, toward the kind of reconciliation and peace that is expressed by Isaiah and other visionaries? Should we speak of a Messianic Age rather than a Messiah (as a person)?

LAMM: I take the more naive view, perhaps more primitive view, in the eyes of some, which I think ultimately may be more sophisticated psychologically. Yes, there is a tendency that we have to sort of depersonify the Messiah and read him as a concept, an age, a feeling—but that is part of the whole tendency to depersonalize religion, isn't it? God is an idea within; He's a concept; Messiah is an age; the next thing you'll know is that man is a concept too so that you can go around killing individual men because only man as a concept matters.

I'm rather personalistic in my approach, keeping in mind what I said originally, that there is "something beyond personality" as I referred originally to the nature of God. The same thing holds true of the Messiah. If you read what *chazal* [the Sages] said, you see there is a pre-Messianic age which has nothing to do with individuals, but is the gathering storm which cleanses, as it were, the world for a different kind of era or epoch. The preparation for Messiah and the era itself which is ushered in or symbolized by a personality is far more than a personality. Don't forget that the Messiah in classical Jewish sources was never looked upon as a magician, as a miracle worker, or as someone who could rival the prophets, let's say Moses. He was always a human being. As *Rambam*, believing in a Messianic King, said, he will rise and die after he has accomplished his mission. If the concept is altogether woven into the personality of Messiah, into the glorification of a person, it becomes the cult of a personality, and all else is forgotten. When that person dies or leaves the people disappointed, the sense of frustration is crushing. Jesus came and some of his Jewish followers saw him as Messiah. Then, he died or was killed, and the promises that Messiah should have brought to the world never were fulfilled. But they were so convinced of the importance of a personality that they followed the Guru and ignored the realities. Now look at all the other false Messiahs.

Q: Bar Kokhba?

LAMM:Bar Kokhba was not a false Messiah. Rabbi Akiba thought he was the Messiah, but most of the sages never accepted him, nor am I acquainted with anything in the historical record which speaks of a personality cult. I think that Rabbi Akiba came to regard him as the Messiah, because Rabbi Akiba saw the beginnings of Jewish liberation and redemption and since Bar Kokhba was the general leading it, he said, "You are the Messiah." Akiba's designation of Bar Kokhba as the Messiah was proof that it is not a personality cult.

Q: Do you see in the readiness today of hundreds of thousands, if not millions of Jews, to once again follow a cult figure, a Messianic undercurrent that could erupt anytime? Does that trouble you?

LAMM: It troubles me very much. But it points to a psychological fact which I may not like but which is very real, and that is something in which all modernist forms of Judaism sin, including what I stand for. We always underestimate the power of personality. We are so inebriated with the power of ideas, we fail to realize that people respond more to people than they do to concepts.

And that is why I said that my belief in the Messiah, and in a personal Messiah, may sound more primitive, but ultimately is more sophisticated because it recognizes the power of personal relationship. If you have a charismatic figure or a figure that is attractive, magnetic, and has influence, his ideas will win. The best ideas can flounder if there is no one to symbolize them or personify them.

Q: The two are logically inseparable because there will never be a Messianic age unless there are fitting personalities for it.

LAMM: And there will never be a Messiah without an age which will reflect his influence.

Q: Let me get to the last point, one vastly underrated or neglected in current Jewish thought and particularly in contemporary rabbinic teaching and preaching. It has to do with the life of the soul, the hereafter, and the resurrection of the dead. We say too little, and tradition perhaps too much, for us to accept this idea today. How do you see this? Does that cluster of ideas play a role in your own religious, spiritual life?

LAMM: In my intellectual religious life, no. In my personal, spiritual religious life, yes. Judaism tells us about the resurrection, but it tells us so remarkably little, that it should be easy to accept. Consider what Judaism tells us about the "other world" and about the resurrection of the dead: It is far less than what we get in Islam, for instance, which is also a monotheistic religion. The Sages deemphasized the "other world," simply asserting its existence, but being mostly concerned with this world. Sometimes I sit back and wonder at it. Look at our entire literature. How much of this is devoted to the hereafter, to the resurrection of the dead? It's a tiny portion, a drop in the ocean. It's nothing compared to the overwhelming amount that Torah tells you about your diet, about your sex life, about your cycle of leisure and work, or your clothing. It's a fantastic emphasis on how to live in this world, as if to say, listen, we can't know very much about that other world. We believe it exists because the spiritual is simply beyond the physical.

To get back to what I originally said, I think there is a pattern there, the physical is the underside of the spiritual, and therefore there is a kind of movement between one and the other. But we don't know very much about the total, extracorporeal or noncorporeal existence. So, all we can do is say it's there and it's the scene of the rectification of the ills of this world in an ultimate sense. But it is no longer a place of active participation. This is the world—what did someone call it?—the vale of soul making. This is the realm where we make and recreate ourselves.

Q: Can you conceive of continued identity as a soul in a hereafter?

LAMM: I just don't know. I should like to think that there is. Why shouldn't there be? Why is it so easy to believe about separate identity here and not separate identities in another realm? Once you accept that there is another realm, you are over your major hurdle.

Q: But you do not become obsessed with it?

LAMM: No, I'm not obsessed with it at all. Because I do believe that transcendent realm, beyond the physical universe, is the realm of the Holy One, blessed be He. And listen, if I won't have a separate identity, I'll be identified with Him.

Q: A final question. What do you see ahead for the Jewish people or for Israel?

LAMM: I'll tell you a story about the two Israelis who were talking and one said to the other, "Are you an optimist or a pessimist? He said, "I'm an optimist." The first says, "If you're such an optimist, why do you look so terrible?" The other answers, "You think it's so easy to be an optimist today?"

Chapter 3

THE
COMMUNITY

Judaism as a faith and Jewish history revolve around the community. Both in a real sociological sense and as a hypostatic essence, Kelal Yisrael *plays a great if not dominant role.*

The first of the five entries in this chapter discusses the possible conflict between the love of Torah and the love of Israel—another way of posing the question of the religious ideal vs. the historical reality, or Religion vs. State in another context. The second of these, "Seventy Faces," poses the question of the extent to which, if any, diversity is welcome in traditional Jewish thought, and this deals with the question of denominationalism from the point of view of Orthodox Judaism.

The next two items treat of several aspects of the unity of Israel and the various challenges faced by the wish and need for Jewish unity.

The last entry goes from the question of the Jewish community to the world at large: is there such a thing as the World Community—and, if there is, is it desirable and in what form?

~ 11 ~

A STORY OF TWO LOVES

*Creating Jewish leadership
and Jewish Community*

If one sees large numbers of Jews before him, the Talmudic
Sages taught (*Ber.* 58a), he should recite a blessing: "Blessed is
He who in His wisdom discerns secrets." What are these "secrets"? The Talmud explains: no two Jews look alike and no two
think alike. It is a divine "secret" how such fiercely independent
individuals can pull together as one people.

I am moved to recite the same blessing, *Barukh Chakham ha-
Razim,* as I address this distinguished gathering this evening—
some two thousand or more Jews and Jewesses who neither
look alike nor share identical opinions, and yet labor together, in
unison, for the welfare of our people. That certainly deserves a
blessing!

My theme this evening is both general and specific. I shall try
to trace some of our current problems to a conceptual dichotomy
that has been latent for centuries. I shall seek, thereby, to identify
two constants that are prerequisite for Jewish leadership and for
a viable Jewish community as we move into the closing decades
of this century.

In his *The Great Chain of Being,* a pioneering work on the history of ideas published almost 50 years ago, Prof. Arthur O.
Lovejoy showed how two ideas conjoined in the philosophy of
Plato lived side by side peacefully for about two millennia, only
to come into violent conflict with each other as their implications
were spelled out over the generations. Even in the realm of ideas,
friends can become foes. Compatible ideas can break out into
open opposition, and apparently differing concepts can later
merge into one.

I detect a similar process taking place in the thought and experience of the Jewish people. Two great precepts that lived harmoniously with each other have now become sharpened into

---

*Delivered at the 50th General Assembly of the Council of Jewish Federations in
St. Louis Missouri in November 1981*

two antagonistic forces that threaten to rip apart the fabric of our people. Only a deliberate and conscious effort on the part of Jewish leaders and opinion-molders to establish peace between these ideas—to embrace both of them harmoniously—can restore the wholeness of the House of Israel in our time.

Ahavat Yisrael and Ahavat Ha-Torah

These two ideas are: *ahavat Yisrael*, the love of Israel, the feeling of profound kinship with all Jews everywhere, the sense of identity and sympathy with all Jews whatever their disposition; and *ahavat ha-Torah*, the love of Torah, the esteem for learning the divine Word, the immersion in Jewish law and lore, the appreciation and pursuit of Jewish education.

These two principles of love of Israel and love of Torah appear to be thoroughly compatible, indeed complementary to each other. What can be more natural than the love of one's people and the love of that which gives it its meaning, its mission, its culture, its way, its distinctiveness?

Yet, early on there began a testing of these two ideas against each other—only in a theoretical way, of course, and without any clear awareness that this opposition could have real and even disastrous consequences.

Clearly, these two are foundations of Jewish existence and experience. They represent the body and soul of our people, its physical identity and metaphysical dimension. Yet, which is more important? Which must give way before the other? We have here a classical *machloket rishonim*, a disagreement between two of our most eminent authorities.

The spokesman for one opinion is the Egyptian-born giant of Jewish law and philosophy, the tenth century Babylonian Saadia Gaon, who wrote that "our people is a people only by virtue of the Torah." Our peoplehood is meaningless without the Torah which gives us purpose and direction, and hence the love of Torah is clearly superior to the love of Israel.

The opposing point of view is advocated by the immortal poet-philosopher of twelfth century Spain, Yehudah Halevi, who taught that the special qualities of Israel existed before the giving of the Torah; that we are not Jews because of the Torah but rather the Torah was given to us because we are Jews. The matter is put beautifully in an anonymous Midrash, *Tanna de'vei Eliyahu*, composed some time between the third and ninth centuries. The author meets a semi-literate man who says, "Rabbi, there are two things in the world which I love with all my heart, and they are Torah and Israel, but I do not know which comes first." The Rabbi responds, "My son, most people think that Torah comes first, but *I* tell you that Israel comes first" (Chap. 14).

I know of no real consequences of this difference of opinion between Saadia and Halevi in the Middle Ages. At the beginning of the modern period, we do begin to notice a practical turn to this controversy. There emerge certain movements which are Israel-centered rather than Torah-centered—Zionism, Auto-Emancipation, and the like. Others base everything on Torah, on religion, and relegate Israel or Jewish peoplehood to second rank: it is more important that Torah prevail, even if in the process large numbers of Jews have to be written off. Yet even then the split between the two was not catastrophic. Even the most extreme nationalistic Jews were immersed in Jewish culture and learning to some degree, and the most separatist Jews lived in Jewish communities where they were linked with all other Jews.

It is in our days and our times that this bifurcation of the two loves becomes downright sinister and a threat to our survival. Gentle preferences tend to become exclusive choices—with tragic consequences.

The Dangers of Exclusivity

To concentrate solely on our physical survival with no thought to our cultural and religious tradition or, conversely, to focus our loyalties exclusively on our spiritual legacy even if it means alienating vast numbers of Jews who may be indifferent to it— this is the primal sin of our times. Jews without Judaism, Judaism without Jews—either one is treason, because each of these is a prescription for the end of the story of both Israel and Torah.

More than that: each is self-defeating and counter-productive in its own terms. The preoccupation with Torah and Jewish learning to the point where we ignore or distance those many

Jews who do not subscribe to it—this can only result in a narrowing of the circle so that before long there is only a tiny remnant of loyalists left, too few to regenerate a whole people, too few to carry on the Torah tradition. Such love of Torah without love of Israel results in no Torah as well as in no Israel. Saadia never intended this.

Similarly, the exclusive concern with Jews as a people—with the State of Israel, with anti-defamation, with Jewish charities, with Jewish self-defense, with the Jewish poor and aged and sick and underprivileged—all this, with no care and no concern for the legacy of learning and culture and Jewishness, is a tested formula for national cataclysm. In an open, democratic, pluralistic society, Jews have to know *why* they should be Jewish, and without Jewish learning they will never know the answer. And if they have no answer they will stop being Jewish, and the Jewish people will cease to be. H.G. Wells was right when he said that the future is a race between education and catastrophe. Love of Israel without love of Torah therefore results in neither Torah nor Israel. Halevi would have been aghast at this.

If we yield on either principle—Israel or Torah, Jewish welfare or Jewish education—we are doomed. Despite the inevitable tensions between them in ordering the priorities on the agenda of North American and world Jewry, we must avoid their total contradiction. The Jewish community must be rebuilt on both these foundations. The contest between Saadia and Halevi must be declared a draw: both are right and both are wrong, because Jewish leadership—and this distinguished assembly represents nothing if not Jewish leadership—stands under the sacred imperative to advance both great loves, to embrace both historic concerns, to abandon neither one.

It is immoral to neglect the human needs of Jews, or to use the love of Torah as an excuse for functionally regarding whole parts of the Jewish people as out of the fold. It is blasphemous to ignore and denigrate and alienate Jews in the name of the Torah. To criticize Jews, to reprimand them, to upbraid them—that is legitimate if it is done with love and compassion. That was the way of the Prophets. But to do so without love, without friendship, without making every effort to achieve Jewish unity, that is by no means the way of Torah. After what we Jews have been through, we dare not give the impression of lightly excluding whole segments of the Jewish people from the fraternity of the House of Israel. I have many reasons for saying that. Millions of reasons. Six million reasons.

However, this is hardly the kind of audience that has to be reminded of its obligations to the Jewish people, whether in North America or Israel or the Soviet Union or Ethiopia or anyplace else in the world. You are wise enough and benevolent enough to seek to heal rifts and work for unity and not react with rancor to statements that displease you and positions that may appear offensive. Wisdom usually thrives best in an atmosphere of calm deliberation. I know you will not color your rhetoric purple.

But really, it is not necessary for me to preach to the converted. The majority of the Jewish people of our time, and especially its leadership, needs to be reminded of the other half of the story, the other principle that is in danger of being forgotten.

Will Our Leaders Be Jewish Enough?

Your President last night reported to you the happy news that you have made substantial gains in your annual campaign, and that you can expect spectacular increases in your endowment funds—more than $1 billion of endowment in this decade! All this is a tribute to your effectiveness as fund-raisers. Your leadership here is uncontested. But I wish to re-echo a question he asked that is not only important but fateful: "Will our leaders be Jewish enough?" To me, that is the question of questions.

What you have achieved so far is a glorious testament to your love of Israel, to your sense of American voluntarism, to your human capacity for compassion for the needy. I have no doubt that in the process of exercising communal leadership you have had to put up with much criticism, some of it patently unfair, with much anguish, with considerable sacrifice, and with a degree of insomnia. (Incidentally, it has always been thus. When the immortal Rabbi Akiva was approached to become the *parnas* of the community—the equivalent of today's president of Federation—he said that he would have to consult his wife and family. When he did, the Jerusalem Talmud reports, someone in the family was overheard saying to him: Take it—on condition that you know in advance that some will curse you, some will humiliate you [*Pe'ah* 8:6].) But it is all worth it, because you have succeeded magnificently in providing for the State of Israel, for Soviet immigrants, for the poor and the aged and the young and the widowed and the orphans and the sick.

But the question that should gnaw at our vitals, that we must expose relentlessly to our own consciousness and conscience, is this: does all this have a future? Will all this be a record of past accomplishments without continuity? This General Assembly is the fiftieth such of the Council of Jewish Federations. Half a century from now will our grandchildren be assembling to celebrate the centenary of this Council or its successor, and carry on the business of advancing the cause of a thriving Jewish community; or will we become the moribund subject of dry scholarly papers by historians debating how and why this once great community came to an end?

A Community in Crisis

You know it as well as I do. We are a community in crisis—internal chaos and disarray, beset by problems of identity and survival. The implications of the Emancipation are still being played out, and we have not yet begun to emerge from the trauma of the Holocaust. The figures for mixed marriages are horrendous, and no amount of preposterous self-delusion about marrying out adding strength to our ranks can make the ugly fact go away. The number of our children receiving any kind of Jewish education is depressingly low. Indeed, the number of children, with or without Jewish education, is depressingly low. Assimilation continues unabated.

Now, I do not mean to despair. Jews do not despair. But I am genuinely frightened. It is not too late. But it is very late. It is time to turn, with a new sense of urgency, to the spiritual legacy, the Jewish culture, the tradition of learning and heritage of wisdom, that alone can stem the tide and assure us of a future. For the first 50 years of Council's existence as an organized community of Jewish communities we have proven our *ahavat Yisrael*, our love of Jews. Now, if we really love Jews and want to see them escape the threat of extinction, we must reenforce our *ahavat ha-Torah*—

the love and devotion to Jewish learning and living, the transmission of Jewish teaching and tradition.

By "love of learning" I mean not only the geriatric concern that so many of our grandparents shared—that study of Torah is for the old or retired folks; not only the pediatric preoccupation that was pressed by so many of our predecessors—give it to the kids to prepare them for Bar or Bat Mitzvah; not even, as so many of us have finally come to accept—and I shall return to this presently—the philanthropic commitment of the community to Jewish education. I intend, in addition, a deeply personal, lifelong commitment to Jewish learning—*our* learning, *our* study of Jewish texts and courses, *our* Jewishness, *our* Jewish education, *our* intelligent awareness of what being a Jew is all about. The Jewish condition can abide skeptics. Non-believers too can be Jewish lay leaders. But what is unthinkable is *am haaratzut*, ignorance of Jewishness by those who purport to lead Jews.

Just as you cannot ask for money until you yourself have given—a cardinal rule of communal leadership—so you cannot effectively plead and work for a more Jewishly-informed community until you yourself have exposed yourself to Jewish learning. You cannot be a general unless you are a soldier, you cannot be a leader unless you are a participant.

Becoming Jewishly Knowledgeable

Besides, why *should* you deny yourself the pleasure of being Jewishly knowledgable? Why forego the exquisite delight of a new insight into a passage in Exodus, of mastering a Rashi, of understanding a Mishnah? Why forfeit the thrill and excitement of analyzing a simple text of Talmud, whether in the original Aramaic or in English translation, of appreciating the towering genius of a Maimonides? Why not be selfish and let the sheer wonder of Yehudah Halevi's poetry, even in English, move your heart as you share his longings and his loves? Why not try to decipher the symbolic meaning of a Midrash, its parables and legends and interpretations? Why not follow the twists and turns of Jewish history as this tiny, often pained, but always magnificently different people winds its way through the corridors of time? All that is required is intelligence, with which you are abundantly blessed, a little time, and some ingenuity. Notice that I am not pleading for a faith-commitment.* That will come or it will not come. I am speaking of Jewish literacy and knowledgeability.

Our own study of Torah will not only challenge us intellectually and spiritually; it will also do more for us *as community leaders*. It will invest all our activities with new significance. It will impart to us a sense of *mitzvah*, of mission and ennoblement and contentment, as we go about our otherwise mundane business of allocating and administering, of deciding on budgets and personnel, on agency turf and on campaign progress, on visits to Congressmen for Israel and on absorbing new immigrants.

It will provide for us a scale of values, reminding us that each human being entrusted to us is unique, as unique as the "image of God" in which he or she was created; that tending to the sick and lonely is more than just social ethics, it is the "Way of God" who clothed Adam and Eve, healed Abraham, buried Moses; that the State of Israel is not just another politico-ethnic national entity that happens to be Jewish, but is a state built on the land of *our* fathers and mothers, a land that longs for us, its children, and whose prophets and seers wanted it to become a center of peace and justice and instruction for all peoples; that how we exercise our leadership in the 1980's is not an evanescent concern of an ephemeral community but part of an overarching history and a crucial act in the drama of the covenant between the Creator and this people called Israel; that we are not Jews just because we are not non-Jews or because so much of the world is against us, but because through our veins there courses the blood of prophets and philosophers, of sages and

---

Indeed, one may ask: What of the love for God which plays such a significant role in Jewish religious thought? A seminal Hasidic thinker of the last century, R. Zadok Hakohen of Lublin (in his Tzidkat ha-Tzaddik, 196) has written of three loves: of God, Torah, and Israel. The latter two, which are "revealed," stem from the first which is "concealed." By this he means to say that the pursuits of knowledge ("love of Torah") and human fraternity ("love of Israel'") fundamentally derive from religious faith, even if it be unconscious. Passages in the Talmud speak of the study of Torah, even in a "secular" manner, ultimately leading back to religious affirmation. Elsewhere in Jewish literature we find similar statements about human love leading back to love of God. In an age of such religious diversity in the Jewish community, therefore, it seems to me more fruitful to concentrate on the two derivative loves, of Israel and Torah, as the conscious foundations of the Jewish community, and allow the element of religious faith to remain "concealed" as a matter of both confidence and prudence.

jurists and poets, of God-seekers and teachers of human fellowship, because we carry and pass on to our children the genes and chromosomes of Abraham and Moses, of Hillel and Akiva, of Rashi and Maimonides; that not only great historical decisions are of importance, but also how we deal with wife and husband and parents and children, how we comport ourselves with friends, how we go about the daily business of living, even what we think in the depths of our hearts when no one is looking and no one is listening and there is no one in front of whom to posture and pose.

All of us are in search of something transcendent, something nobler, something exalting, to touch our lives, grab us, uplift us, fill the emptiness within us with new meaning and new insight. Well, that is what the study of Torah was meant to achieve, in any language and form. It really is, as Proverbs teaches, a "tree of life for all who take hold of it and it gives happiness to whose who support it."

Communal Obligations

But I return to our communal obligations as leaders. If indeed there can be no Jewish people without Jewish learning, then the future development of *Jewish* leaders and a *Jewish* community demands of us a resolute effort of unprecedented proportions to inculcate and implement the teaching of Torah on all levels, from primary grades through higher education, in all groups, and as widely as possible. I know that Federations across the country have made remarkable progress in appreciating the significance of Jewish education. The last two decades have seen an astonishing change of attitude—a tribute to Federation's openness to changing conditions and perceptions and its willingness to learn. But meanwhile conditions have worsened and yesterday's dosage of medicine is inadequate for today's disease. Half measures and tokens will not—will no longer—do.

Franz Grillparzer, the Austrian playwright and poet of the early part of the last century, wrote of the Hapsburgs,

It is the curse of our proud dynasty
To move half-heartedly, to stop half-way,
To adopt half measures hesitantly.

The Hapsburgs fell because of their half-heartedness. We will prevail only if we pursue our goals with "all our heart and all our soul and all our might." Our communities will survive these dark days only if our young people are given much more intensive Jewish education, formal and informal. Federations must consult anew on how to solve the problem of underpaid and undertrained teachers, and tuition too high for young families. They will have to be carefully selective in differentiating between Sunday School tokenism and real education. They will have to encourage innovation and shun faddism. They will have to demand performance from Jewish schools. They will have to appreciate that the real decisions as to whether or not to remain Jewish are made by young people of high school and college age, and therefore turn their attention to *higher* Jewish education. At the schools I head some of our very best and most Jewishly-dedicated students, young men and women motivated to serve the community, are those who came to us at age eighteen, on their own, searching for something more intensively and authentically Jewish.

The resolve not to allow the learning of Torah to be eclipsed will require special courage and even heroism, especially in these trying days when the Federal government has reduced its own subsidies and passed on its responsibilities to the private sector, while at the same time enacting tax laws that make life more difficult for philanthropy. Your tasks are exceedingly difficult. But real leadership, authentic Jewish leadership, must not flinch before hard decisions. We will be confronted by instances of communal triage: who gets the vital dollar and who does not? It will test our values, our principles, our ideals, our priorities. Many good causes will have to suffer so that better or more important causes can survive.

One More Generation May Be Too Late

But remember this: One more generation without massive help to Jewish education—one more *half*-generation—and it may be too late. And if that happens, no amount of hand-wringing and breast-beating and finger-pointing will restore vitality and viability to the fatally sick body wilting of malnutrition of the Jewish mind and heart.

I know—your tasks are unenviable. Decision-making in such an environment is grueling. It will win you enemies. It may well disturb your peace of mind. But I recommend to you the closing sentence in *The Tragic Sense of Life* by the Spanish philosopher, Miguel de Unamuno: "May God deny you peace but give you glory."

The trade-off is worth it. No peace of mind and no freedom from criticism are a small price to pay for the prize of glory—the glory of preserving and enhancing for Jews throughout the world their most precious possession, the worlds' most priceless heritage; the glory of resolving the contradiction between two fundamental principles that nurtured our people from the beginning of our history, and of embracing once again, equally, both our sublime loves: of Israel and of Torah.

The clock of history is ticking away. Choices must be made. We shall have to decide between different courses. We can allow the aging of the North American Jewish community to continue on its path as before, while we routinely tend to its concerns as best we can but effectively allowing the process of disintegration of a once great Jewish community to be played out until its bitter and sorry end. Or we can take a new turn, tap within ourselves heretofore unexplored resources of human spirit and Jewish creativity, and transform this affluent but threatened and diffident Jewish community into one of the most vigorous, constructive, and promising in all of the history of the Diaspora. And of course, what happens to American Jewry will profoundly affect the destiny of the State of Israel.

Let me conclude with the metaphor of the clock by telling you a Hasidic story.

When the great Hasidic "rebbe" known as the Seer of Lublin died, one of his sons came from some distance to claim his share of the inheritance. He took his father's *bekesha* (rabbinic cloak) and his clock that chimed the hour. On his way home, he stopped at an inn. He had to stay there for several days longer than he had planned because of heavy rains. As a result, he did not have enough money to pay the innkeeper, and so left him the clock in lieu of payment for his lodgings.

Many years later, a famous rabbi travelled and stopped at the same inn and noticed the clock. "Where did you get it?" he asked the innkeeper. The innkeeper told him of the rebbe's son and why he left it there. The rabbi told the innkeeper that he recognized the clock as having belonged to the Seer of Lublin.

"How did you recognize it?" asked the innkeeper.

The rabbi replied: "Every other clock, when it strikes the hour, has its own peculiar and characteristic message. The chime calls out, 'one hour closer to death.' But the clock of the Seer of Lublin has a message different from any other clock in the world. Its chime sings out, 'one hour closer to Redemption.' "

Inspired by the two great loves, of Israel and of Torah, in concert with each other, and fortified with the high resolve to commit our time and intelligence and strength and resources unhesitatingly and whole-heartedly to the tasks before us, *this* Jewish leadership will lead *our* Jewish communities not one hour closer to decay and demise, but one hour closer to triumph and redemption.

~ 12 ~

SEVENTY
FACES

It is with a troubled heart that, as an Orthodox Jew, I address a concern that unites us, namely, those issues that *disunite* us from each other.

The predictions of an unbridgeable and cataclysmic rupture within the Jewish community agitate all of us who love and care for and worry about our Jewish people and its future. The twin issues of conversion and of Jewish marital legitimacy—proper *gittin* (divorces) and, in their absence, subsequent adultery and the blemish of *mamzerut* (bastardy)—should give us no rest. The non-marriageability of a significant portion of the Jewish people with the rest of *am Yisrael* is too horrendous to contemplate—and yet we are forced to do just that lest our fragile unity, such as it is, be shattered beyond repair.

We have to try our very best, within the limits of our integrity, to promote unity and to oppose the seemingly inevitable disaster that looms before us.

The critical phrase is "within the limits of our integrity." I am an advocate of enhanced Jewish unity. But no honorable person can afford to dispense with his or her integrity even in the pursuit of unity.

The issues are too critical to permit us to indulge in a Jewish equivalent of the old "interfaith" meetings in which warmth substituted for light and good fellowship for genuine understanding. It is too late for that kind of goodwill posturing. It is a given that we must relate to each other in friendship and fraternity. Now we must also be honest and truthful with each other. The great Rabbi Saadia Gaon in the Introduction to his *Emunot Ve'deot*, while analyzing the causes of skepticism and disbelief, pointed out 1,000 years ago that the truth is bitter and distressing and it is more convenient to ignore it. But without it we are wasting our time; more—without it we are lost. So, if my thesis proves disappointing and unpopular to some, or even to all, it is

Published in Moment *June 1986, based upon an address at a CLAL conference*

because I am trying to be honest in keeping to the truth as I see it, even while attempting to be as accommodating as I can.

It is in this spirit of searching for unity within the limits of integrity that I address first the issue of pluralism.

———

I ONCE THOUGHT I knew what the word meant. I have a passing acquaintance with pluralism, in contrast to monism, as a metaphysical concept. I believe I understand what cultural and political pluralism are about. I have written in favor of pluralism within the halakhic context. But I confess to being confused by all the current talk of "religious pluralism" within the Jewish community. The term has been used in a variety of ways, both with regard to Israel and the diaspora, so that I am at a loss really to understand it. Moreover, my perplexity is deepened by the elevation of "pluralism" to the rank of a sacred principle. It has become a symbol, and whenever an idea is transformed into a symbol, it becomes so enmeshed in emotions and so entangled in mass psychology that it is exceedingly difficult to treat it analytically and critically. Sacred cows, like golden calves, inevitably lead one astray.

The way "pluralism" has been used in recent months and years makes it sound suspiciously like relativism, reducing all differences in principle and value to questions of taste.

Relativism is the proposition that because there are many kinds of "things" or points of view, and each has an equal right to be heard and advocated in a democratic society, they are therefore necessarily equally valid. If pluralism is just the newest name for that kind of discredited ethical or religious relativism, it is not deserving of our attention.

My conception of pluralism in the Jewish religious community can best be summed up by reference to a famous dictum in the Jewish tradition—that there are *shivim panim laTorah*, there are 70 faces or facets to Torah. No one is more valuable or significant or legitimate than the other 69. Judaism is not monolithic. However—there are only 70 (the number, of course, is arbitrary) and not an infinite number of such faces or facets. A pluralism that accepts everything as co-legitimate is not pluralism, but the kind of relativism that leads to spiritual nihilism. If everything is kosher, nothing is kosher. If "Torah" has an infinite number of faces, then it is faceless and without value or significance.

Orthodox Jews are fully aware of the Talmud's comment on the disputes between the House of Hillel and the House of Shammai, that "both these and these are the words of the living God." Unfortunately, this profound statement has been abused and turned into a slogan by ignoring the fact that the controversialists were at one in their commitment to the *Halakha* and its divine origin, and disagreed only on its interpretation with regard to very specific matters. The dictum implies a pluralism *within* the halakhic context—only. It simply cannot be stretched to cover all "interpretations of Judaism" as co-legitimate.

———

THERE IS ANOTHER and similar issue that has the capacity to befuddle rather than clarify. This deals with the terms "recognition" and "delegitimation." "Recognition" has become a red herring in the Orthodox camp, and "delegitimation" is the newest member in the semantic rogue's gallery of the other groups.

There has been a great deal of talk over the past several years about Orthodox rabbis granting or withholding "recognition" from non-Orthodox rabbis, and the latter, in turn, angrily demanding to know who authorized the former to grant or withhold recognition. So heated has the debate become, so inflamed the personal and political passions, that cool and disinterested analysis has become virtually impossible. But we are not going to make any headway unless we stop simmering for a while, separate our collective egos from the issues, and try to listen to each other and then argue calmly and dispassionately.

First, let it be understood that *no* Orthodox Jews, if they are true to their faith, refuse to recognize fellow Jews as Jews just because they are nonobservant. It is sad that such a denial is at all necessary, but one must give the lie to a canard that has been gaining wide currency, even in an editorial in a recent issue of an "official" Jewish weekly. A Jew is a Jew even if he sins, as the Talmud teaches, whether or not he thinks he is sinning. Those who deny this teaching are not Orthodox.

Second, should non-Orthodox rabbis want to know, out of curiosity, whether I, as a centrist Orthodox Jew, "recognize" their credentials as rabbis, I will gladly oblige them. It is helpful for each of us to know where the other stands, if we are to make progress on the truly critical issues of the day.

Where I stand: My premise is that Orthodox Judaism is, by its very nature, tied to a transcendent vision, to a Being who is beyond us; that vision includes the revelation of Torah and of *Halakha*—a way of life, formulated in terms of legal norms and discourse—that we accept as authoritative. It is the word of God, transmitted from Sinai down through the ages, and it is the backbone of the Jewish tradition. This *Halakha* is given over to humans to apply to their daily lives, but they are not authorized to dispose of it according to personal taste or whim. The *Halakha*, like any formal legal system, has rules that govern its change, amendment and application; all the more so because its claim is to divine rather than human origin. The central point is this: The *Halakha* is heteronomous, it obligates us, it is above us; we are bound by it and must live within its perimeters even if doing so proves personally, politically and even spiritually uncomfortable. It is, after all, the Word of God. Where the *Halakha* has spoken, therefore, we cannot negotiate, trade or barter.

THREE CATEGORIES to consider in the "recognition" or "legitimation/delegitimation" issue are: (a) functional validity, (b) spiritual dignity and (c) Jewish or rabbinic legitimacy.

Because Orthodox rabbis consider those movements not bound by the traditional *Halakha* as heretical, many refuse to accord non-Orthodox rabbis any credibility as leaders of Jewish religious communities.

I consider this an egregious error. Facts cannot be wished away by theories, no matter how cherished. And the facts are that Reform, Conservative, and Reconstructionist communities are not only more numerous in their official memberships than the Orthodox communities, but they are also vital, powerful, and dynamic; they are committed to Jewish survival, each according to its own lights; they are a part of *Klal Yisrael*; and they consider their rabbis their leaders. From a *functional* point of view, therefore, non-Orthodox rabbis are *valid* leaders of Jewish religious communities, and it is both fatuous and self-defeating not to acknowledge this openly and draw the necessary consequences—for example, establishing friendly and harmonious and respectful relationships and working together, all of us, towards those Jewish communal and global goals that we share and that unite us inextricably and indissolubly.

As an Orthodox Jew, I not only have no trouble in acknowledging the functional validity of non-Orthodox rabbinic leadership, but also in granting that non-Orthodox rabbis and laypeople may possess *spiritual dignity*. If they are sincere, if they believe in God, if they are motivated by principle and not by convenience or trendiness, if they endeavor to carry out the consequences of their faith in a consistent manner—then they are *religious* people. In this sense, they are no different from Orthodox Jews who may attain such spiritual dignity—or may not, if their faith is not genuinely felt and if they do not struggle to have their conduct conform with their principles. Phonies abound in all camps, and should be respected by no one, no matter what their labels. And sincerely devout people exist everywhere, and deserve the admiration of all.

But neither functional *validity* nor spiritual *dignity* are identical with Jewish *legitimacy*. "Validity" derives from the Latin *validus*, strong. It is a factual, descriptive term. "Legitimacy" derives from the Latin *lex*, law. It is a normative and evaluative term.

Validity describes the *fact* of one's religious existence. *Dignity* refers to the *quality* of one's religious posture, not its *content*. It is the latter which, to my eyes, determines what we are calling *legitimacy*. Here I have no choice but to judge such legitimacy by my own understanding of what constitutes Judaism and what does not. The criterion of such legitimacy is the Jewish *lex*—the *Halakha*: not a specific interpretation of an individual *halakha*; not a general tendency to be strict or lenient; but the fundamental acceptance of *Halakha*'s divine origin, of *Torah min hashamayim*. And if we become bogged down in definitions of these terms, then let us extricate ourselves from the theological morass by saying that the criterion is acceptance of *Halakha* as transcendentally obligatory, as the holy and normative "way" for Jews, as decisive law, and not just something to "consult" in the process of developing policy.

Hence, I consider myself a brother to all Jews, in love and respect, and together with them I seek the unity of all our people.

But I cannot, in the name of such unity, assent to a legitimation of what every fiber of my being tells me is in violation of the most sacred precepts of the Torah.

———

AT BOTTOM, any vision of the truth excludes certain competing visions. So it is with the Torah commitment. Under no circumstances can an Orthodox Jew, for instance, consider as Jewishly authentic a view of Judaism that excludes faith in God—such as "humanistic Judaism"; or one that condones marriage of Jew with non-Jew; or one that rejects the halakhic structure of Sabbath observance or the laws of divorce or the institution of kashrut. To ask that, in the name of pluralism, Orthodox Jews accept such interpretations as Jewishly legitimate is to ask that we stop being Orthodox. If that is what pluralism and mutual legitimation mean, the price is too high.

Harold Schulweis, a distinguished Conservative/Reconstructionist rabbi, writing in MOMENT ("Jewish Apartheid," December 1985), stated the following:

> In the name of the unity and continuity of my people, I acknowledge the right and privilege of Jews of diverse schools of thought to build their own institutions of learning, to support the rabbis they elect to follow, to entrust their children to these rabbis for instruction.

Agreed. I too acknowledge such right and privilege, and I have no argument with that statement in praise of unity. But the rest of the paragraph is one with which, unfortunately, I simply cannot go along. It reads as follows:

> For the sake of Zion, I may criticize their methods of conversion or their interpretations of the law, but I am pledged to recognize their authority, to accept their marriages, their divorces, their conversions. . . .

No, I am afraid that one cannot remain a halakhic Jew and make such a blanket statement. Nor, indeed, do I see how a Conservative rabbi can make such a statement. Neither can some Reform rabbis. Are traditional Reform rabbis ready to accept the authority of fellow Reform rabbis when and if they marry Jews and unconverted gentiles? Are Conservative rabbis ready to accept the authority of, and legitimate, a Reform remarriage when there was no divorce other than a civil document? Are they ready to accept those Reform conversions, which I take to be a majority, in which there was no circumcision, no immersion in a *mikveh* (ritual bath), no *kabbalat hamitzvot* (formal acceptance of the commandments)? If Conservative rabbis are not ready to accept such acts, Orthodox rabbis certainly should not be asked to do so.

Coherent and coordinated action to secure a decent Jewish future for our children and grandchildren, therefore, requires that we do away with slogans and buzz-words and reject vain hopes for the kind of "mutual legitimation" that cannot happen without doing violence to integrity.

In a positive vein, it calls upon us to accord to each other what I have called "functional validity" and, where deserved, "spiritual dignity."

ORTHODOX JEWS have not always been as forthcoming in this respect as one might have hoped. We have not always been models of tolerance and openness. For too long we have substituted invective for argument, and have often evoked an equal and opposite reaction. Indeed, in recent months the counter-invective has been very opposite and even more than equal. But Orthodox Jews will have to learn to be more civil in their rhetoric, more respectful in their approach, more conscious of their responsibility towards the *mitzvah* of "thou shalt love thy neighbor as thyself," and of Kohelet's admonition that "words spoken softly by wise men are heeded more readily than the foolish shouting by an official" (Ecclesiastes 9:17). Conservative and Reform Jewish leaders too must learn the same lesson and not adopt the stridency that they have learned from some Orthodox extremists. Neither abusive rhetoric nor blackmail nor financial pressure is the proper way to conduct Jewish fraternal discourse.

Moreover, Orthodox Jewish leaders should not have to be dragged kicking and screaming to meetings with their non-Orthodox confrères in order to develop common policy where possible, or at least mutual understanding. In addition to whatever formal communal structures now exist, there is a need for all major religious leadership to consult personally and unofficially, so that we know what we are about without the need to vote, lobby, or issue public statements.

A further point: In facing the future together we must reduce the *Kulturkampf* taking place in Israel and, to a somewhat lesser degree, taking place here as well. We should adopt a hands-off policy on all issues that do not constitute an immediate danger to the wholeness of *Klal Yisrael*, as defined by the ability of any one segment of Jewry to accept as Jewish or as marriageable members of any other segment. Hence, I may, as I do, disapprove of non-Orthodox sanctioning of women rabbis or abortion-on-demand or general permissiveness on a hundred other issues. And Conservative and Reform Jews may look askance at what they regard as Orthodox sexism or our rigidity on this or that matter. But even while being critical of each other, we must not interfere or allow such differences to break us apart. Let us argue with each other—but not fight. Let us be critical—but never obstructive. Each side needs to give the other the space to "do its own thing."

Factually, this is the situation that, to a large extent, now prevails. Except for certain pockets of population, there is *de facto* communication in most areas. There may not be sufficient inter-denominational relationship, but neither is there sufficient *intra*denominational communication—at least not in Orthodoxy.

Yeshiva University is, in many ways, a microcosm of the Jewish world. Who better than Rabbi Soloveitchik represents the meeting of Jewish learning and Western culture at their highest levels? Our students spend the first half of the day plumbing the depths of the Talmud, no less intensively than at any other good yeshiva, and in the afternoon they study the sciences and humanities and business no differently from that at any quality university. In my own work, I relate daily to the most committed Orthodox who consider me, as a centrist, much too much to the left; and with the most Reform of the Reform, for whom I am much too much to the right. Yeshiva University is a galaxy that contains several *kollelim* (post-graduate institutes of Talmud and talmudic research) along with a medical school and law school and their supporting boards. Yes, there are problems, but they are solvable. There are challenges, but challenges are made to be met and overcome. We are in effect a marvelous bridge, indeed a network of bridges, connecting many worlds—Jewish and non-

Jewish, religious and secular, Orthodox and non-Orthodox—in the academic, ideological and communal spheres.

So, the general situation obtaining in the Jewish community is sometimes taut and tense, but it is not terrible. I do not see the need for radical solutions or apocalyptic fervor. But I do see the need for more concerted efforts than have been made heretofore.

———

THE TWO AREAS that do warrant major concern are those that affect the future oneness of our people—the question of conversion or "Who is a Jew?" and that of *get*, the Jewish divorce, without which remarriage is considered *arayot* (adulterous) and the progeny as *mamzerim*, illegitimate and hence unmarriageable except to proselytes or other *mamzerim*.

The conversion/identity issue is the lesser of the two evils because it is not irrevocable. If Orthodox and Conservative Jews, say, cannot recognize a non-halakhic conversion by a Reform rabbi, at least the person involved can later undergo a halakhic conversion. It may be a blow to one's sense of identity and to the Reform rabbi's authority, but it is reversible. The second, *mamzerut*, is far more grave. It is, as our tradition puts it, a *bekhiyah le'dorot*, a tragedy for generations. The remedies are few and difficult.

Let me address the first of these matters. The issue in Israel has become transformed into a symbol and hence is seemingly impervious to a political solution.

But I am far more concerned about the problem in the diaspora. In Israel, despite the brouhaha over the "Who is a Jew?" legislation, perhaps a half dozen or dozen questionable conversions per year are at issue. In America, the number is probably more on the order of a hundred thousand. And it is here that the Reform patrilineal resolution of just three years ago becomes so critical and grave.

———

IT IS HARD TO BE dispassionate about the issue, but out of respect to our fellow Jews we must try to be. Responsible people do not undertake lightly, without powerful need and motivation, steps of such enormous consequence. Yet, even without considering the effects on the rest of world Jewry, I believe the patrilineal decision was not thought through properly, and that Reform groups would be well advised to take another look at it and reconsider it.

Truth to tell, from a halakhic point of view, patrilinealism makes almost no difference in the operative reality. Most Reform conversions do not require *tevilah* (immersion in a *mikveh*), circumcision or symbolic circumcision, and an acceptable minimum form of *kabbalat hamitzvot*. Hence, whether children of Jewish fathers and gentile mothers are declared Jewish en masse by a CCAR resolution, or are "converted" individually, the *Halakha* does not recognize such people as Jews.

Furthermore, a distinguished Reform rabbi (David Polish) has stated that "this resolution is a *de jure* formulation of what has long been a *de facto* practice in Reform congregations." Thus, both from the point of view of *Halakha* and that of Reform practice, the resolution does not really change reality to any great extent.

Its importance lies mostly in the area of psychology and symbol. It is painfully reminiscent of an ancient schism that became a turning point in the history of Western civilization. I refer to the attitude of the Tannaim, the Fathers of the Talmud, to Christianity. As long as Christians were Jews who went astray after one they regarded as the Messiah, but otherwise kept their *yichus* (genealogy) inviolable, they were regarded as *minnim*—heretics, apostates— but still Jews. It was when Christianity decided to abandon the halakhic standards for determining Jewish status and declared that effectively one could join the religion by self-declaration that it was regarded by the Tannaim as a separate religion.

Professor Lawrence H. Schiffman of NYU, in his *Who Was a Jew?* (Ktav: 1985), reaches the following conclusion:

> Had the rabbis relaxed these [halakhic] standards . . . Christians would quickly have become the majority within the expanded community of 'Israel.' Judaism as we know it would have ceased to exist. . . . Christianity would have been the sole heir to the traditions of biblical antiquity and observance of the commandments of the Torah would have disappeared within just a few centuries. In short, it was the *Halakha* and its definition of Jewish identity which saved the Jewish people and its heritage from extinction as a result of the newly emerging Christian ideology.

The ultimate parting of the ways for Judaism and Christianity took place when the adherence to Christianity no longer conformed to the halakhic definitions of a Jew. . . . The rabbis ceased to regard the Christians as a group of Jews with heretical views and Christianity as a Jewish sect. Rather, the rabbis began to regard the Christians as members of a separate community. . . .

The patrilineal resolution has thus touched a raw nerve in Jewish historical memory. And it has "resolved" nothing.

Furthermore, an often overlooked element in this resolution is one that requires that *all* "half-Jews," whether the mother or the father is the Jewish parent, have their Jewish status confirmed "through appropriate and timely public and formal acts of identification with the Jewish faith and people." Thus, the child of a Jewish mother and non-Jewish father will *not* be presumed to be Jewish by Reform standards if that child shows no signs of such "public formal acts," but *will* be Jewish according to the *Halakha*. Paradoxically, Orthodoxy—which has been falsely accused of "reading Jews out"—will accept the Jewishness of such a child, whereas Reform will indeed be excluding him or her from the Jewish people.

Clearly, this matter must be rethought by the Reform group for its own sake.

———

WITH REGARD to the second issue—*gittin* and *mamzerut*—the problem is more resistant to resolution and far more catastrophic in its consequences.

The only solution I can see—and it is only a partial solution—is to revive the stalled efforts of the 1950s at establishing a national *beit din*, court of Jewish law. The two leading personalities at that time were Rabbi Saul Lieberman, of blessed memory, and "the Rav," Rabbi Joseph B. Soloveitchik *(lehavdil bein chaim lechaim)*. I ask myself: If two such giants failed, how shall we succeed?

The first answer is that we have no choice. Immanuel Kant once said, *"Du kanst weil du must"*—"You can because you must." The sheer number of potential *mamzerim* and quasi-Jews is so much greater today that it was 30 years ago that we do not have the right to desist from a major effort—no matter how much we will be criticized by extremist elements in all camps. We can because we must.

Second, their efforts came to grief because, I believe, they tried for too much, and because they tied their plan too tightly to institutions and organizations. Thus, the insistence on organizational discipline caused the plan to fail when the Rabbinical Assembly felt it would not be able to get all of its members to agree to the authority of the *beit din*.

What we must now do, I submit, is try for "half a loaf" in the belief that partial cures are better than none. We must reach out for *nechamah purta*, at least some consolation, some relief.

I do not believe that, given the aggravated situation that prevails today, it is possible for the various groups to obtain the kind of consensus that can result in universal agreement and discipline.

What is possible, I suggest, is a more voluntaristic National Beit Din (NBD) that all groups will recognize as authorized to deal with personal status. The NBD will, in turn, set up branches throughout the country. All rabbinic and synagogue organizations will not only accept its rulings but will support it and actively urge all their constituents to have recourse to it.

The rabbis of all groups who subscribe to it will refer all cases to it or its deputized *batei din*. Hence, such cases will enjoy universal or near-universal acceptance, both here and in Israel. Those who do not subscribe to it will deprive their "clients"—prospective converts or marriage partners with halakhic problems—of such wide approbation.

I also endorse a suggestion by Dr. David Berger, a colleague on Yeshiva University's faculty, that all groups undertake an ad campaign, distasteful as it may seem, encouraging *gittin*—halakhic divorce—where a marriage is being dissolved, and perhaps making all *gittin* gratis.

All groups, however, will have to inform those people who do not apply to the NBD that their status and that of their progeny may be in jeopardy in the eyes of a major segment of organized religious Jewry. This is the honorable thing to do anyway; anything less is a violation of the moral and halakhic norm of *lifnei iver lo titen mikhshol*, not ensnaring one who is unaware of the consequences of his actions.

The critical problem of who will serve on such an NBD or on local *batei din* is not insoluble. The three *dayyanim*, judges, that form the quorum of a court should be chosen on the basis of scholarship and personal halakhic observance, not institutional affiliation. Rabbis who are experts and personally observant, no matter what group they formally belong to, may be authorized to serve. In addition, a broader-based committee may serve with the *beit din*, including the referring rabbi or his deputy, provided it is understood that the halakhic act is enforced by the *beit din* alone.

Now, it is true that such *dayyanim* will be found mostly in the Orthodox community. But three things should be borne in mind:

a) They will be serving as individuals, not as representatives of organized Orthodoxy.

b) They may well include non-Orthodox-affiliated experts. The late Conservative Rabbi Boaz Cohen comes to mind. His *gittin* were accepted by the Rav and the RCA. I too accepted them without question. No doubt, some such observant members of a non-Orthodox Talmud faculty, trained in these areas of halakhic law, can be found.

c) There is no special pleading here: By no means would all Orthodox rabbis automatically be qualified to serve on the *beit din*. Indeed, *most* would *not* be qualified.

I, for one, have never written a *get* or officiated at a divorce proceeding, nor do I ever expect to. The reason is not taste; it is competence. My training has not been in this area, and therefore I consider myself incompetent to preside at a *get*. There are perhaps a dozen or two dozen individuals in this country whose *gittin* I would accept as valid.

There are significant details that have yet to be elucidated. But if the idea is found attractive, the specifics can be worked out. Again, I caution that this is only a partial solution and by no means a panacea.

It will not be easy to set up such an NBD. Many of my Orthodox colleagues will not go along with it because of the implied "recognition" of non-Orthodox rabbis. But surely, with all respect to their qualms, such considerations ought to yield to the need to alleviate untold personal suffering by accepting purely halakhic standards and not being distracted by organizational/denominational considerations. The "Orthodox-Conservative-Reform" rubric is, after all, not a halakhic category. And Conservative and Reform rabbis, in turn, will have to surrender some of their professional and communal autonomy for the same sacred cause—

the wholeness of *Klal Yisrael* and the integrity of the lives of countless thousands of Jews living and unborn.

There are several contributions that can be made by the non-Orthodox groups. One, Reform and Reconstructionist rabbis should undertake explicitly to inform the people they are marrying that they do so according to *their* understanding of marriage law, and that this is *their* interpretation of the operative phrase *"ke'dat Mosheh ve'Yisrael"*—"according to the law of Moses and Israel"—and that, by clear implication, they are not acting in accord with Orthodox law, i.e., *Halakha*. By these means, those Orthodox Jews who follow the ruling of the late and much lamented Rabbi Moshe Feinstein (which disqualifies certain specific types of heterodox marriage ceremonies) will then be able to accept the progeny of the remarriage of people so married without fear of *mamzerut*.

Second, again in order to spare grief for future generations, and therefore as an act of moral probity, Reform and Reconstructionist rabbis should insist, when remarrying one who was married at an Orthodox ceremony (or, for that matter, a Conservative ceremony), that he or she obtain a valid *get*—bill of divorce—first. Consistency requires that a status assumed under a specific legal system be abolished by the norms of that same system before a new status is achieved under a different system.

Third, our American non-Orthodox groups might well adopt the practices of the Liberal Jews in England. All Liberal converts sign a document that confirms their knowledge that their conversion will not be accepted by the Orthodox, and that the children of female converts will not be considered Jewish according to *Halakha*. Appropriate advice regarding Orthodox law is given to all those who marry without a *get*. Divorcees are encouraged to obtain Orthodox *gittin*. (This information is taken almost verbatim from a letter in the London *Jewish Chronicle* of February 21, 1986, by Rabbi Sidney Brichto, Executive Vice President of England's Progressive Synagogue.)

———

IF MY IDEAS for an accommodation find enough resonance to allow for their further development, then the proper forum—a private one, shielded from publicity and posturing—must be found soon, in order to stop the unraveling of the fabric of Jewish unity. If there is enough ground to warrant further work on this or other ideas in this vein, it would be best to call a halt, insofar as it is within our power to do so, to the cycle of mutual recriminations and, even more, to any "new directions" or actions by rabbinic bodies that might aggravate the situation and add oil to the flames. This is not the time for further "innovations" that will bedevil our efforts and strike further blows at what is left of Jewish unity.

The Talmud tells us that just as we don the *tefillin* so, as it were, does the Almighty. And whereas in our *tefillin* we bear a scroll that reads, *Shema Yisrael*—"Hear O Israel, the Lord is our God, the Lord is *Echad*—One," His *tefillin* bear the words, "Who is like unto Your people, *goy echad baaretz*, one nation in the world."

Neither unity has yet been sufficiently achieved or acknowledged. Just as we conclude our prayers with the verse from Zechariah, "And the Lord will be King over all the world, on that day the Lord will be One and His Name will be One," so I suspect, does God Himself offer the prayer, "May Your people Israel again be one people; may the day come soon when Israel will be *goy echad*, one unified people in the world."

It is a prayer worth hearing—and answering with all our might.

———

NOTE: The plan here offered was later presented to Prime Minister Yitzhak Shamir who sent an emissary to the United States to organize and establish it. Unfortunately, it came to grief because of opposition by both ends of the spectrum. Thereafter it formed the basis of the Knesset's "Neeman Commission," headed by the then minister Yaakov Neeman.

~ 13 ~

INTEGRITY OR UNITY:
WHICH?

There is a problem that has long been the cause of deep distress to me. We stand today at a critical juncture in the history of our people. Our generation must make a fateful decision: will we remain one people, or will we be fragmented to two or more peoples unable to marry each other and therefore permanently divided from each other?

Since the beginning, it has been Torah, our ancestral faith, that has kept us as one, despite all the centrifugal forces threatening to pull us apart. With the weakening of Torah study and observance, we have tended to become unglued and atomized.

The fact of our disunity now looms over us like some giant, brooding, threatening presence, one that we deny at our own peril. What role does Torah play in this unfolding drama? Never before has Torah been accused of being the focus and the cause of our disunity, yet today that is precisely the charge leveled against it. There are those who use Torah as a weapon against Orthodoxy, saying that our rigidity is the cause of our woes. Others say that we never were united, that the unity of Israel is a myth, a fantasy, a legend, and therefore our present disunity should not worry us. And yet others act as if disunity was inevitable—and welcome.

Where do we, of the community represented by the Orthodox Union, stand? Are we blameless? Do we believe we were and should be One People? Can we persuade others—and ourselves—that Torah is a source of cohesiveness, that it is not a cause for divisiveness?

One thing is and should be clear to us: the approach of the non-Orthodox groups to conversion will lead to disaster. If there is more than one way to enter the Jewish fold, and any one of them is non-halakhic, it will lead not to the kind of disunity that now afflicts us, but to something infinitely worse: the break-up of our one people to two or more nations, officially unable to intermarry with each other. Consider this situation: we will not

An address at an Orthodox Union dinner in New York City 1998.

recognize most Conservative conversions (depending on the individual officiant). The Conservatives—if they are true to their own convictions—will not accept Reform conversions. Furthermore, the Israeli Reform group has said that it does not recognize American Reform actions such as patrilinealism and same-sex marriages. Thus, we so far can count *four different* groups that will not marry the other's converts. Is this what they want? Will the Israeli Supreme Court support such a situation in the name of civil rights?

Haredim are accommodating themselves to the idea that unity is impossible, that we are already broken up into two separate peoples. A lead article in the January 20, 1998, *Yediot Acharonot*, tells it all; it is entitled, *"Nipared ke'yedidim"*—"let us part as friends."

Let me record a personal note: A few years ago I met with one of the most prominent Hasidic rabbis. In the course of a pleasant conversation, I complained about an article by the editor of a newspaper published by this group, in which he wrote that he doesn't understand why there is such a tumult about *Kelal Yisrael* (a term denoting the totality of the Jewish people), when after all, "according to our calculation there are no more than about a million people who belong in this group." I asked the Rebbe if I and my parents and wife and children and grandchildren are or are not considered part of *Kelal Yisrael*. His painfully ambiguous and evasive answer was, "Rav Lamm, ihr fregt tzu harb a kashe" (Yiddish for: "Rabbi Lamm, you are posing too difficult a question.")

Unity vs. Halakhic Integrity

The struggle in Israel concerning conversions is beset by all kinds of arcane nuances, confounded by obscure currents and counter-currents, and permeated with political cabals and machinations. But if we break down the arguments on both sides to their constituent essences and seek out the fundamental values at issue, we will succeed in simplifying the issues without being overly simplistic.

The heart of the matter, to my mind, is this: which should prevail: the wholeness of Torah or the unity of the people? The Right holds that we must maintain the hegemony of Torah even at the expense of the oneness of Israel. The Left believes we must strive to effect the unity of Israel even if it means compromising the Halakha.

The conflict, as we have formulated it, is not completely new. According to the Gemara, Moses and Aaron are the archetypes of these two differing attitudes: "Moses would say, let the law prevail over all else; Aaron, however, loved peace and pursued peace, and made peace among people" (*Sanhedrin* 6a). Moses symbolized the preeminence of law and principle, Aaron—that of peace and unity. Another Talmudic work, the *Tanna de'vei Eliyahu*, maintains that in a contest between the love for Israel and the love for Torah, the former, prevails. In the Middle Ages, R. Saadia Gaon declared that, "our people is a people only by virtue of the Torah," while R. Yehuda Halevi considered Israel as the constant, unchangeable pole, the element without which Torah could not and would not have been given.

How, then, shall we decide our current issue? Which should predominate: the integrity of the Halakha or the unity of *Kelal Yisrael*? Do we insist upon a halakhic conversion with all its accumulated stringencies in order to keep it whole beyond challenge, even if we thereby alienate whole sections of American Jewry and hundreds of thousands of non-Jewish Russian immigrants to Israel? Or do we embrace all comers, within reason, even if that means undermining the essential Halakha?

My answer is clear: *In our present situation, we dare not ask such a question, because it is a prematurely forced and therefore false dichotomy!* When the Nazis were bored by ordinary torture of Jews and wanted to reach the zenith of sadism they resorted to psychological torture. So, for instance, they told a man that he would have to choose between having his father killed or his mother killed, and that if he refused to choose, both would be murdered. To force us to choose between our love for Torah and our love for Israel is a cruel, inhuman demand. Granted, under extreme and dreadful conditions, we may conceivably have to decide which to choose and which to abandon. But to ponder the question and choose sides for imminent application before every single solution has been examined and tested, is an act of gargantuan irresponsibility.

The presumption that the two values are locked in mortal combat is an abstraction that in the context of our own particular and peculiar predicament is utterly misleading. We can and we must hold on to both elements for dear life. No Jew may cavalierly despair of and abandon thousands upon thousands of his fellow Jews. And no Jew has the right to dispense with the integrity of the Halakha, the source of our spiritual and communal existence and the only guarantee that we and generations after us will remain Jewish.

Moreover, the problem is formulated in a way that assumes that Torah has no special place for the wholeness of *Kelal Yisrael*. But that is not so. When our ancestors left Egypt on the way to Sinai and the Revelation, we read (Exodus 19:1): "On this day they came to the wilderness of Sinai." Rashi comments: Should not Scripture have said "that day," not "this day?" Why "*this* day?" To teach us that the words of Torah should appear new to us as if they were given this very day.

Now, that is a beautiful sentiment, but there is an inaccuracy or anachronism lurking in the background. The Gerer Rebbe (author of *Sefat Emet*) asks: how can those two words apply to "the words of Torah" when the Torah was not yet given, for it would only be revealed several days later? In answering his own question, he points to the very next verse: "And there Israel (singular) encamped before the mount." Why the switch in number from plural to singular? Rashi here records the answer: Israel arrived at the mountain *ke'ish echad be'lev echad*, united as one person with one heart beating for all. The approach to Revelation was one of transcendental unity, a togetherness not known before or after. And here the Gerer Rebbe adds: *this very fact of utter Jewish unity—this in itself is an aspect of "Torah!"* The experience of *ke'ish echad be'lev echad* is not merely a psychological or sociological phenomenon; it is a spiritual value that in itself constitutes Torah, the Author of which is known by the name of *Shalom* (Peace), for that too is a Name of God. And since that is Torah, it is no longer an anachronism to say that "the words of Torah should appear new to us as if they were given this very day." Hence, if we recognize that the unity of *Kelal Yisrael* is a fundamental of Torah, that it has the value of Halakha, then we will not pose it as an antagonist of Torah.

Attitude to the Non-Orthodox—and to Ourselves

Before we go further on this theme, it is important to confirm the fundamental attitude that marks our community in its dealings with our non-Orthodox brethren—and amongst ourselves. And permit me to do so in the form of an insight I garnered from a recent publication of a manuscript in which the "Netziv" (R. Naftali Zvi Yehuda Berlin) quotes his predecessor, R. Isaac of Volozhin who, in turn, cites his father, R. Hayyim of Volozhin.

The second of the Ten Plagues that were visited upon Egypt was that of frogs. We read that Aaron stretched out his hand over the waters of Egypt *va-taal ha-tzefardeia*—literally, "the frog came up" (Exodus 8:2). Here again we chance upon a case where the Torah surprisingly uses the singular rather than the plural. Rashi comments: "Should it not be written, "the frogs came up? [The answer is that] there indeed was one frog, but they beat it and [as a result] it sprouted long streams of frogs." Upon which R. Isaac comments that had they but *spoken* to the frog instead of striking it, it would have remained alone, but once they came to strife and rained blows against it, it produced swarms of frogs covering the land. He continues, "So it is with regard to the struggle against the new sects and movements that have arisen in Israel (referring to the Haskalah movement): we ought conduct ourselves as our Master R. Hayyim taught us—never to follow the path of strife and open warfare, for the very act of confrontation gives strength to the opposition."

Everyone, it seems, is in an attack mode. Everyone wants to beat up on someone else. Every argument is extravagant—and loud. And the more we allow ourselves to descend into open confrontation, the more do we strengthen the opposition.

We must not be drawn into such shouting matches. We must, of course, remain firm in the battle of ideas, but never react with the kind of snide sneers and intemperate charges that have characterized our polemics for too long. Let us talk before we strike— lest all of us be overwhelmed by a plague the equivalent of a swarm of ugly reptiles . . .

Equally and even more important is how we view ourselves. It is about time that we grew up and achieved a degree of self-confidence in what we are and what we stand for. Let us stop fidgeting and hemming and hawing and let us say outright: we are fully committed to Torah; we unquestionably abide by Halakha; we cherish and strive to observe every mitzvah; we have deep respect for our *Gedolei Torah*, our eminent Torah personalities. At the same time, we hold that Torah Umadda is a principle and not a concession. We do not believe that our Orthodoxy requires of us to seal off our minds from the worlds of science and the best of contemporary culture. We affirm that *Medinat Yisrael* has special significance for us and is not the same as any other polity. The welfare of all of *Kelal Yisrael* is of major concern to us—and we do not advocate a narrow definition of the term *Kelal Yisrael*. Let us say these things with pride and, equally, without arrogance or apology.

I therefore congratulate the Orthodox Union for its forthright support of the recommendations of the Ne'eman Commission. Such advocacy will undoubtedly occasion controversy, but the Orthodox Union has thereby demonstrated moral courage. It has done what is right and proper.

If we stand for moderation it is not because, like little children, we are afraid of loud noises. We do not take the Mishnah's teaching, "Be moderate in judgment" (*Avot* 1:1), as a rule of etiquette for those aspiring to higher-class delicacy. It is, for us, a norm of judicial conduct that obligates every Jew and especially every *ben Torah*. Hence, while our manner of expression and quality of relationship is moderate, our basic commitment allows no softness, no yielding on principle for the sake of good fellowship. On the contrary, it is our firmness of conviction that allows us to be moderate and dignified towards those with whom we disagree on fundamentals. We should not by any means minimize our differences with the non-Orthodox. The fact that we prefer civility to shouting does not mean we should mute our profound unhappiness at some of the outrageous "innovations" they have visited upon us in recent years, from patrilinealism to same-sex marriages. A Polish poet, writing about the Shoah, said, "I would want to keep silent, but my silence would tell a lie." That kind of silence is not for us.

For those of faltering faith in this, our vision of *Yiddishkeit*, let me recall for you those whom we regard as our predecessors, those who inspire us and in whose reflected light we flourish: the Rambam (Maimonides); the Maharal; Rav Reines; Rav Kook; Rav Hirsch and Rav Hildesheimer; Rav Herzog; the Rav (our teacher, R. Joseph B. Soloveitchik), may the memory of the righteous be a blessing for us. It is their teachings that inform our *Weltanschauung*, in one way or another. And these are only a few of those whom we regard as our ideological ancestors, regardless of the marginal differences among these staunchly independent thinkers who were both sages and saints. They are our teachers and our guides.

And let us not be distracted and discouraged by opposition, even or especially when such opposition is not in the realm of thought and ideas, but is expressed with hostility and contempt and hatred—perhaps especially when their antagonism is formulated in the most scurrilous personal terms. Don't forget that the Rambam's *Guide for the Perplexed* was burnt on the altar of a Dominican church by the equivalent of today's militant zealots. Such opposition would never bother the Rambam—who wrote that he'd rather please one intelligent person even if it means displeasing ten thousand ignoramuses (*Guide*, ed. Pines, p. 16). Rav Kook was vilified mercilessly, and to this day a *sefer* that is *kulo kodesh*, totally non-objectionable, if published by Mosad Harav Kook, will not be permitted into certain yeshivot—not all of them, of course—simply because of the blot and stain of being associated with his name. And the Rav—need we be reminded of the shameful way he was treated by some of the very people who repeat his creative *hiddushim*, often in their own names? So, we are in good company if we suffer from similar assaults.

The Halakhic Contribution to Unity

Let us now return to the problem of unity and, especially, to its halakhic dimension.

The Rambam (Laws of Shabbat, 2:3), in discussing the *halakha* that the preservation of life takes precedence over Shabbat, says: "Hence you learn that the laws of the Torah are not [meant to be] a source of *nekamah*, vengeance, upon the world but of compassion and kindness and peace in the world."

Let us be open about it. It is easy enough to remain pat and unmovable, ignore the real needs of ordinary men and women, dismiss the consequences of halakhic decisions—and thus unintentionally prove that Halakha is indeed a form of *nekamah* against people.

But it should be clear that the alternative to such rigidity is not to play fast and loose with the Halakha. There are no "quick fixes" in the Halakha. The halakhic method works by precedent and proof, by citing sources and consulting colleagues. "Quickie" solutions become the quicksand of reputations, and should be studiously avoided. *Gedolei Torah* throughout the generations most certainly were sensitive to the needs of individuals and responded to them not *despite* but *through* the Halakha, and in accordance with its time-tested methods. And their decisions were not filtered through the lens of the media . . .

What we must demonstrate in our times is precisely this: that authentic Halakha is not an angry, wrathful, vindictive, malevolent system; that the Torah is not out to make life unbearable for us; that, on the contrary, properly interpreted and understood, it is the source of our life and our guarantee of peace—"Its ways are ways of pleasantness and all its paths are peace" (Proverbs 3:17).

Yet we are constantly criticized and told that Halakha is inadequate to deal with our stormy, complex age because of the stand-pat policy of our *posekim* and their lack of concern for the social consequences of their decisions. But that is simply not true. Thus, allow me to share with you the essence of a *teshuvah* from one of the greatest of all halakhists, R. Yaakov Reischer of late 17th century Prague, in his work of Responsa, the *Shevut Yaakov* (III:110). I offer it not for its own specifics but as an example of the halakhic method and as a *symbol* and *paradigm* for our times.

In certain cases where a man drowned in the ocean over a year earlier, and there is a question of ascertaining his death, the law is that the wife may not remarry, but if she did, she need not divorce the second husband. In other words, before the fact (*le'khatchila*), she is considered married, but after the fact (*bi'diavad*), if she remarried, we do not consider the second marriage adulterous and the progeny illegitimate. Now if the woman comes before us and we decide she is forbidden to marry, she will remain an *agunah,* chained to a missing husband, probably forever. Is there any way to release her from her *agunah* status and let her live a normal life? The *Shevut Yaakov* decided in her favor, based upon solid sources and the exercise of brilliance plus enormous courage. His reasoning? He cites the Talmudic principle that whatever is permitted only *bi'diavad* is permitted even *le'khatchila* in the case of an emergency or great need (*sha'at ha-dechak*). But does not every case of *agunah* qualify as a situation of great need? It depends, he replies. If the woman is elderly, and has or expects no suitors, her situation is not to be considered a *shaat ha-dechak.* But if she is young and has reasonably good opportunities to start life anew by accepting a marriage proposal and, as may often happen, if we do not grant her the right to re-marry she may leave the fold altogether, then her case should be considered as a *shaat ha-dechak,* and she should be permitted to marry *le'khatchila.*

This is the way true giants *(gedolim)* have acted throughout the ages. And so must we do today. By analogy, we are nationally—throughout the world—in a state of *shaat ha-dechak,* of true emergency and distress. If in all cases we refrain from treating the *bi'diavad* as a *le'khatchila,* or making bold use of other halakhic remedies, we will bear the responsibility of, Heaven forbid, an ir-reparable breach in the unity of Israel for generations without end. We will push masses of Jews to leave the fold, just as the *Shevut Yaakov* feared. In effect, there will be two parts of the people of Israel who will treat each other as a permanent *agunah*—outwardly indistinguishable from each other, yet unable to marry each other—forever . . . and therefore in a perpetual state of alienation, hostility, and hatred.

So, Orthodox leadership must, in certain situations, give way on the *le'chatkhila* in order to preserve the primacy of both the Halakha and the integrity of *Kelal Yisrael* which, as we said earlier, is itself a value of Torah. And at the same time, we must drive and drive hard to exact from the non-Orthodox that they do no less than we in sacrificing for *Kelal Yisrael* by yielding on their clerical autonomy, denominational equality, or institutional pride, and abandon those radical changes, such as patrilineal-ism, that have impeded any chance for national reconciliation—all for the sake of future interrelations of our people.

When such remedies are available to us, we must recognize the critical *sha'at ha-dechak* nature of our times and act accord-ingly—both responsibly and courageously.

We often recite and take comfort from the extremely important reassurance by the prophet Jeremiah (51:5) that *lo alman Yisrael,* "Israel is not widowed"—and indeed they are consoling words; we will not be abandoned by the Almighty, and we will always have leaders who will guide us properly.

But that is a task for the Almighty Himself; *our* task, the enor-mous burden that rests on *our* shoulders especially in this crucial *shaat ha-dechak* period of Jewish history, is not only to proclaim *lo alman Yisrael,* but also to declare and realize and emphasize with equal vigor and determination the promise that *we* make: *lo agu-*

nah Yisrael, we will not allow Israel to become a national *agunah*—and there is little doubt that the state of *agunah* may even be worse than that of widowhood!

We must not permit the dogmatists and exclusionists to preach that unity is not desirable. And we must not allow the cynics and the self-proclaimed realists to tell us that unity never existed and hence never will. Our Sages told us that the *tefillin* of the Almighty proclaim the unity of Israel, that inscribed in them are the words, "who is like unto Your people Israel, one nation upon the earth." And we should not "possel" or disqualify the *tefillin* of the Almighty!

Conclusion

With clear-eyed vision, with hearts dedicated to the Master of the World, with backbones to act courageously despite criticism and in defiance of the professional nay-sayers, and with stiff-necked insistence that we will not falter in advancing simultaneously the unity of *Kelal Yisrael* and the integrity of the Torah of Israel, we may turn to the Master of the World and pray for His divine aid in our efforts to advance His cause in the world. In the words of the daily *Amidah,*

"Bless us, our Father, all of us together, *as if* we were one."

Even though we suffer sharp differences with each other and sometimes act like enemies instead of family; notwithstanding our impatience with and impertinences towards each other; and despite our occasional outbursts of temper and use of intemperate language, bless us *ke'echad,* to act *as if* we were one, united in a common destiny, living with each other like brothers and sisters who may have radically different points of view but yet recognizing that we are related by blood and by fate, and—yes!—with friendship and fraternity and peace—and even with love.

For there can be no greater blessing than this.

~ 14 ~

JEWISH SOLIDARITY

The theme of Jewish solidarity (or unity) invariably evokes from the listener an industrial size yawn leading to a religious experience, namely, the recitation of the blessing, *Ha-mapil chevlei sheinah al einai, u-tenumah al afapai*—who causes sleep to descend upon on my eyes. So, I too rise before you with a large degree of trepidation.

The subject of Jewish unity is much more relevant now than it was before the onset of the recent Intifada #2, with all its attendant dangers. I am confident that world and American Jewry will not, indeed never, abandon Israel; that we are in the right; that our cause is just; that "The Guardian of Israel neither sleeps nor slumbers." (Psalms 121:4). What worries me more is the internal dissension within Israel and in the Diaspora—not differences of opinion or life-style, but the intolerance, the bitterness, the incivility, and the *sinat chinam*—baseless hatred—all at a time when unity is so vital to our future.

Jewish solidarity, according to the Talmud, has one of two sources:

> When the Torah was given to Israel, it was heard from one end of the earth to the other, and all the pagan kings began to tremble in their palaces . . . Whereupon they gathered together and came to Balaam and said to him, "What is this great noise we have heard?—is it another flood that is engulfing the world?" Said he to them, "Fools! The Holy One had already sworn never to engulf the world in a flood!" They replied, "Is it possible that He will not bring a flood of water upon us, but He will bring a flood of fire on the world?" . . . Said Balaam, "He promised never to destroy the world." "What then," they asked, "is the great noise that we heard?" He answered, "He has had a rare treasure in His private safe for 574 generations before the creation of the world, and now He is giving it to His children"
>
> —*Zevachim 116a*

Address at the Orthodox General Assembly in Jerusalem, and published in February 2001

The Gentile kings expected the Jews to be disunited. When they heard the theophany at Sinai and saw the sudden expressions of Jewish unity, they thought it was a new Noahide flood that would engulf the world, and they trembled in fear. Balaam reassured them: this time the unity is not because of an external cause, but internal: *Mattan Torah*.

Hence, there are two separate causes of unity amongst Jews: threats from without, and inspiration from within.

What unites us today in both Israel and the Diaspora? Both: the threats from without and the opportunities for renewal from within. The immediate reason for solidarity is the cloud of war and random violence that hovers over us, and the specter of endless and unresolvable guerilla warfare in Israel; and, in the Diaspora, the prospect of more than half of our Jewish population being defeated by success, suffocated by affluence, and crushed by easy acceptance by our environing culture. And the danger to Jerusalem concerns all Jews throughout the world. But our future remains dismal and dangerous unless we attain minimal unity in the face of the threats from without. And it is by no means certain that such unity will be attained . . .

Yet, we must make every effort to succeed in the quest for unity. In American history we find an impressive example of the terrible cost of disunity. Before the Civil War, the term "United States" was always used in the plural—as in "the United States are ready to sign the treaty." After the Civil War, however (and 620,000 dead) the name "United States" was and is always used in the singular—"the United States is ready to sign the treaty." Language reflects both the ordeals and the achievements of national self-identity.

But there is another kind solidarity we must affirm: we Orthodox Jews solemnly believe and declare that there is a greater if more elusive unifying element—one that issues from above and from within: *Mattan Torah*—the giving of the Torah. Our transcendent ambition is to unite all Israel by means of the spiritual power and under the banner of Torah. And Torah must become not a cause of dissension, but a mighty stimulus for the blessing of unity.

However, before we seek unity with other Jews, we must undertake to explore unity within our own ranks. During these fateful days for the State of Israel and all the House of Israel, we cannot hope to foster unity within all Israel unless we first learn to work together as Orthodox Jews. Those of us who presume to represent *Mattan Torah* must prove to the world—and to ourselves—that "unity" is not an empty phrase of no value other than propaganda. Let us be realistic: full-scale unity is neither doable nor necessarily desirable. But a minimum and effective degree of unity is both desirable and attainable.

We must try to attain the assent by a maximum number of Orthodox groups and individuals to a minimum number of principles. All who aspire to Orthodox unity must agree to abide by these major elements, and are free to disagree on all others. And those who do not join in these major elements remain outside the consensus. For if we do not work together we shall separately be overwhelmed by the "Secular Revolution!"

This is the time for the leadership of all Orthodox groups to meet to define and refine these principles—and meanwhile to restrain any overzealous and ubiquitous spokesmen and PR people from rushing to the media . . .

What are some of the principles that should be considered? I propose a list of Three Loves, the first of which is *ahavat ha-Torah*, the love of Torah.

We are all committed to the primacy of Torah, the inviolability of Halakha; this is a *sine qua non* for being Orthodox, whether we speak of an individual or a group. But there should be no identification of individual halakhic decisions that may be in dispute, and there should be no insistence upon particular halakhic authorities whose words are law.

On these we may differ, provided the method for arriving at decisions—whether of Halakha or policy—is authentic from the point of view of Halakha. Allow me to cite an example, or perhaps analogy, from a decision of the Rambam regarding heresy:

> There are five heretics in the category of *minnim* [the most severe] . . . (One of them is:): he who says there is but One God, but He possesses a body and is visible . . . each of these five is labeled a *min*.

> *Gloss of Raavad:* Why should he (Maimonides) refer to him as a *min*? There are those who were greater and better [than him] who advocated this idea based upon what they read in Scripture and, even more, what they gleaned from the *agadot* which lead to distorted opinions.

This gloss by the Raaved is elaborated in a somewhat revised passage as cited by R. Joseph Albo:

> Even though (divine incorporeality) is a foundation of the faith, one should not characterize as a *min* a person who advocates that He possesses a body as a result of the way he interpreted the language of Scripture and the *midrashim*

Thus, the conclusion may be erroneous, but the process is such that the person drawing the wrong result from the right premises cannot be considered heretical.

Similarly, if the method of any participant is halakhically legitimate, he is entitled to come to conclusions different from those of others.

The second of the three loves or principles is the love of Israel—*ahavat Yisrael*. We must agree to be exceedingly careful before reading anyone out of the membership of the Jewish people. An alacrity to restrict the fellowship of *kelal Yisrael* to those who think and act exactly as we do—or demand of them—does not make sense especially when we Orthodox Jews are a minority of our people. We may disagree with others vigorously, even condemn them, but as long as they are Jews (halakhically), they are entitled to our *ahavat Yisrael*.

The late saintly Kapishnitzer Rebbe o.b.m., put it beautifully when he said that if you love a fellow Jew because he is learned, that is an act of the love of scholars. If you love him because he supports the Torah, you have fulfilled the requirement of the love of Torah. If your love issues from admiration of his or her charitableness, that is a case of the love of *tzedakah*. But if you love a Jew who is neither scholarly nor a supporter of Torah nor a person of charity—that is *Ahavat Yisrael!* So, all Orthodox Jews must expand the boundaries of our *ahavah*, love, to the full limits permitted by Halakha. If the groups or individuals are not halakhically Jewish, but identify with the Jewish people and the State of Israel, and therefore there is no technical requirement for *Ahavat Yisrael*, then at least we are obligated to extend to them *Ahavat ha-beriyot*, the love we owe all of God's creatures created in His image.

Thus, we may disagree on the nature of our relationship to non-Orthodox groups, but no one group should refuse to work with another Orthodox group because of different approaches to the non-Orthodox. True, this is one of the things that divide us, but Orthodox unity will never be attained if we insist on controlling each other on this point.

The third of the three principles is the love of the Land of Israel. This commitment can lead to unity whether we accord historic significance to *Medinat Yisrael*, the State of Israel, or only for *Eretz Yisrael*, the land of Israel; whether we see it as *at'chalta di'geulah* or as a divine gift that is not necessarily an integral part of the Messianic redemption. But we can all affirm our commitment to the peace and welfare of our people in this holy land. And just as we may disagree on our theological conception of the State, so may we disagree on whether religious political parties are effective or desirable. In order to achieve this goal of unity based on the Three Loves, if indeed we can ever agree on them, we must bear in mind two extremely important prerequisites:

First, we must act and behave and speak and do business so that we incur a *Kiddush Hashem*—or at least avoid *chilul Hashem*. Thus, we must be exceedingly careful how we use language especially when we express disagreement with others—whether those within or without our camp. Recent events within the Orthodox world, especially in Israel, unfortunately, make it necessary to plead for the need to be less truculent towards our fellow Orthodox Jews. Remember: historically, *charamot* never worked; they mostly proved counter-productive. In our days and our times certainly, excommunication is a direct cause of *chilul Hashem*. It confirms the widespread contempt for Orthodoxy because it paints us as medieval, coercive, and exclusionary. We do not need excommunications; we need more communication amongst ourselves.

Indeed, *Kiddush Hashem* must be the very basis of our unity. One wise man once said that Hasidim and Mitnagdim are at odds as to whether we ought recite *Hodu* before or after *Barukh she'amar*, but both converge when it comes to *Yehi kevod*. In our schools and in our shuls, we must teach and preach and emphasize and insist on ethical conduct and sensitivity in the ways we disagree, without which no Jew has the right to the honorific "Orthodox." Perhaps a good working definition of an Orthodox Jew is one who contributes to *Yehi kevod Hashem le'olam*.

Finally, if this program is to succeed, leaders of all groups within Orthodoxy need a great measure of courage to stem the tide contributing to disunity rather than unity. There will be criticism and rebuke from both ends of the spectrum. Leadership, especially in our community and in our times, especially in the presence of hyperactive and overreaching media, cannot be effective without taking personal and professional risks. An Orthodox leader today must have the moral, psychic, and political courage to walk by himself, alone amongst those who disagree and deprecate and defame him (and even when his closest colleagues keep their silence while he is denounced). He must be ready to defy public opinion and do what is politically incorrect, guided only by his commitment to what he considers is right and true in the eyes of the Almighty.

The 85 letters of the two verses of the *Va-yehi bi'nesoa,* which we recite when the Ark is opened before the reading of the Torah, appear in the Torah surrounded by two strange symbols, one at the beginning of the passage and one at the end. They are the *nunin hafukhin,* the letters Nun inverted. The reason for this strange use of orthographic symbols is offered by the Kabbalistic work, *Midrash Ha-ne'elam*—and it is even stranger than the symbols themselves!

The Midrash Ha-ne'elam states:

> They are the actual glory of the Holy One, the foundation of the world, and by means of these nuns the Holy One will redeem Israel and bring the Messiah. It is by means of these nuns that Jacob blessed his grandchildren, [as it is written] *ve'yidgu la-rov be'kerev ha-aretz*

The last item refers to the root of *va'yigdu* which is *dag* or fish, meaning that Jacob blessed his grandchildren that they increase as profusely as the fish of the sea. (so the Aramaic translation by Onkelos).

I suggest that what this extravagant praise of the inverted Nuns means is this: In order to bring about the Redemption, to set the word aright and justify its continued existence, to bring the spirit of Divinity into the world, what is necessary is—the readiness to do what fish do, namely, to swim upstream, to go against the tide, to dare the raging currents of the foaming sea. It means the ability to hew to your vision even when the masses declare you blind or unfit, even when the powers of the world or community disparage you and isolate you.

Without the readiness to swim upstream when you are convinced it is the only right way to go, you will never get to the other side. That readiness is what we call courage.

So, whether it is the struggle against the implacable enemies of Israel, such as Arabs and fundamentalist Muslims, or the biased European Union and CNN, or maybe even an American administration; or the many detractors of Orthodoxy in all places high and low, or even within our own camp—we must be prepared to swim upstream. Government leaders need courage as Israel enters uncharted waters, but religious leaders need it as well.

Courage summons us to activity, to power, to protest, to a show of strength; but sometimes, depending upon the circumstances, the greatest expression of courage is in restraint—in knowing when and how to keep silent despite all provocations, to be patient when you are bursting with the need to shout, to restrain yourself for a greater good. Above all, courage demands that we be exceedingly careful about what we say and, even more, how we say it, especially when we feel compelled to be blunt when such bluntness can prove damaging and counterproductive.

In conclusion, the task is formidable. The shrillness of our disunity can lead one almost to despair. But we dare not despair; we do not have the luxury for that. Maybe we can't achieve that unity. But we may never refrain from trying for it. For that may well be our divine mission—to restore the unity of Israel, in the same way the Kabbalah urges us to restore the unity of the Creator.

We have no guarantees that we will achieve unity on any front. But we do know one thing: that God expects it of us. On the verse in *Haazinu*, we read *El emunah*, ordinarily translated that He is a God of faith—whatever that means. The *Yalkut*, however, gives that expression profound and dramatic meaning: *she'maamin bi'veruav*, He believes in us. He has faith in us that we will be kinder and more loving towards each other. We must never disappoint Him.

It is our task to vindicate His faith in us. The mission is daunting, but it is also ennobling. May we never fail Him.

~ 15 ~

THE QUEST
FOR WORLD COMMUNITY

1. The effort to achieve world community, as a voluntary plural-istic entity rather than as an imposed uniformity, raises a partic-ularly sensitive question—one amongst many—to which each participant in the endeavour must essay his own answer. That question is: How can we understand and work together with communities of other religions and ideologies in their quest for a world community based on their own resources? This paper is an effort to formulate a Jewish response to this challenge.

2. It is a truism that Judaism has often interacted with contem-porary civilizations, and cultural borrowing is a fact of history which requires no documentation. Yet with Judaism, such bor-rowing as did occur was largely unconscious. Deliberate imita-tion was explicitly proscribed. "Neither shall ye walk in their statutes" (Lev. 18:3) was taken as a general prohibition of pagan practices and became a major source of Judaism's strictures against non-Jewish ritual and mores. To speak, therefore, of co-operation with other faith communities on the basis of their own resources, poses an immediate dilemma.

3. There is an inherent danger in the whole enterprise that we have labelled "the quest for world community." It may, if we are not on our guard, result in committing one of three fundamental errors.

The first of these is the possibility that "world community" will become a euphemism for what can only be called religious and ideological imperialism, whether conscious or uncon-scious. If our goals are largely identical, why not adopt my methods?

The second is the imposition of a kind of apologetic straitjacket on individual philosophies, frequently distorting them in the course of striving for preconceived conclusions acceptable to

---

Delivered as part of an interreligious dialogue in Geneva in 1972, this was subse-quently published in Jewish-Christian Dialogue *in 1975*

others. Jewish thought has too often suffered from this wilful if well-intentioned distortion.

Third, one must beware of falling into the trap of a theological indifferentism which regards theological and cultic exclusiveness as retrograde and reactionary. If, according to this doctrine, all that counts is the ultimate desideratum—whether that be a moral principle or ethical conduct or belief in a supernatural god or religious experience—and all the various methods of reaching that goal are of little import, then our problem is no problem; but then too, our Judaism is no Judaism, and we have no right to speak in its name.

4. However, the biblical prohibition against cultic promiscuity, especially as it was expanded by the Rabbis, cannot and need not be taken as an assertion of the total self-containment of Jewish teaching and a denial of validity to any and all non-Jewish wisdom. That there have been such introversionist, centripetal, and exclusivist tendencies in the history of Jewish religious thought and life cannot be denied; but the tradition speaks with other voices as well.

One finds, in general, a more open attitude in the earlier sources of the Rabbinic tradition than in the later ones. We may accept as normative, I believe, the Midrashic dictum: "If someone tells you that the nations of the world possess wisdom, you may believe him; that they possess Torah (read: religious truth), do not believe him" (Lam. R.2:13).

One can cite a whole roster of examples from the medieval Sephardic authorities to illustrate the receptivity of Judaism to the insights of others when such insights are not in conflict with basic Jewish thought. Maimonides, whose name is the first to come to mind in this respect, explicitly taught, "accept the truth, no matter what its source" (introduction to his "Eight Chapters"). And Don Isaac Abravanel, somewhat later, was not averse to quoting Christian exegetes and sometimes preferring their interpretations of Scripture over those of the Jewish commentaries.

5. One must, of course, make a clear distinction between cultic practices and intellectual insights. Whatever else the terms *chokhmah* (wisdom) and *Torah* may mean (in the Midrashic passage cited above), they do differentiate between the realm of par-

ticularistic cult and universal knowledge. Jewish ritual practice is "private," normative, and specific, and hence should be guarded against infusion of non-Jewish religious forms. But cult and culture are by no means identical. Human culture and civilization have broad universal aspects in which all human beings share by virtue of their very humanity; hence, the Noahide laws as the common heritage of all mankind. The Sages of the Talmud were not averse to holding up certain contemporary pagan nations as exemplars of particular moral behavior which they considered worthy of imitation (see BT, *Ber.* 8b).

6. Judaism imposes on its members a normative code of conduct, yet it cannot be considered monolithic in its insights and values. It exhibits paradoxes and, often, opposing principles. The Halakhah itself, the very expression of Judaism's quest for essential uniformity in moral and ritual behavior, is often arrived at as a result of the clash of and interplay between conflicting rules, principles, and values. One may thus find elements in Judaism which articulate well with insights of other faiths or secular ideologies. To cite but one example, Judaism knows of both quietistic and activistic streams in its tradition. It may find resonance for its quietistic dimensions in certain Eastern religions, and its activism certainly corresponds to that of modern, secular technological culture. The presence of such polarities and ambivalences within the Jewish tradition allows us, as committed Jews, to work cooperatively towards world community with others who espouse any one side of such views and are seized of one aspect of such polarities, without our necessarily adopting the whole context of these insights or subscribing even to that one particular view for ourselves.

7. Our further caveat is in order in formulating a Jewish response to this challenge of working towards world community with others on the basis of their own particular resources. The attempt to assign to other religions an anticipatory messianic role in the redemptive conception of history (e.g., Jewish versions of the concept of *preparatio evangelica*) should not serve as a legitimation of our goals. Judaism can no more use Christianity than Christianity can use Judaism by virtue of this argument. Furthermore, this argument is confined to one or two historical reli-

gions—Christianity and Islam—and says nothing about all others, especially non-Western religions.

8. In view of what has been said thus far, we must now formulate the *modus operandi* for such a cooperative quest for world community, and here two points need to be made.

First, a guiding principle should be that while every religion and ideology draws upon its own indigenous resources in order to formulate its insights, attitudes, and doctrines on world community; and while these resources should be respected and peculiar modes of hermeneutics and exegesis accepted as valid for that group; the other religions and ideologies joining in the quest for world community should consider only the conclusions, and not the resources and methods, in devising means for working cooperatively towards world community.

An example of the above may be cited from resources of Judaism. A law or a generally sanctioned approach to non-Jews may be a basic *halakhah* with pronounced universalistic and humanistic emphasis, or it may turn out to be of sufficiently broad scope only as a result of certain correctives that the halakhic method supplies, such as the principle of *kiddush hashem* ("the sanctification of God's name") or *darkei shalom* ("For the sake of communal peace"). How we arrive at such conclusions is irrelevant to other groups; *which* resources we use is only of academic interest to them. Of real and effective significance are only the specific *conclusions* at which we arrive.

9. The second point is far more difficult to attain, because it obligates all participants to a form of collective self-restraint. Many religions, especially Western religions and certain ideologies possess, to varying degrees, dreams of universal acceptance, whether by force or by conviction. The utopian views of Christianity and Islam have traditionally envisioned the ideal state of mankind as the embracing by all humans of their respective prophets or dogma. Judaism, at the very least, looks forward to the obliteration of idolatry, and the universal acceptance of the One God. Marxism strives for domination by the proletariat and the establishment of a classless society based on its dialectical materialism. If such ultimate aims are denied, we are false to these individual outlooks.

How, then, can Christianity achieve a genuine world community with Jews, when it desires all Jews eventually to accept Jesus? How shall Moslems work with Christians when the goal of Islam is the universal acknowledgment of Mohammed? How shall Jews cooperate in one world community with religions which they traditionally consider idolatrous? And how shall the materialistic Marxist achieve genuine cooperation with any of the above, when he sees them as obstacles to the realization of his utopian vision?

It is here, perhaps, that all religions and ideologies may have to be called upon to make a clear decision, in common, in order to proceed both honestly and honourably on the quest for world community. That is, that having openly acknowledged its eschatological goals, each group must affirm that our contemporary mutual quest for world community is non-eschatological or, at worst, pre-eschatological. Allied with this must come a resolve that even if world community represents, according to one's insights and orientation, a pre-eschatological state, such world community must never become the instrumentality for activistic eschatological realization, and the proselytization that it implies.

That is admittedly asking a great deal from those communities for whom the achievement of the *eschaton* is an essential doctrine and effective motivation of conduct. But unless such self-restraint is forthcoming, and unless it is forthcoming in a manner that will inspire trust by others, the quest for world community will be bedevilled by mutual suspicion and will die while being born.

Chapter 4

MORALITY
AND THE FAMILY

Society, Eleanor Roosevelt once wrote, is the family writ large. So is the Jewish community ultimately tied in with the Jewish family. The various serious problems that plague the Jewish community today are the direct outgrowths of the changing Jewish family.

The destiny of the family cannot be separated from the state of morality, because the family is the major arena in which morality grows—or is eclipsed. In turn, morality, in the Jewish tradition, is intimately connected to Jewish law. My first article in this chapter discusses the relation of Love and Jewish Law. The next contains some remarks about courtship and marriage, and the final item discusses an important element in Jewish morality, that of modesty (tzeniut), but in a broader sense than that which the term usually evokes.

~ 16 ~

LOVE
AND LAW

Jews who have not been brought up in the full Jewish tradition
are often taken aback at the way in which Judaism expresses
its concerns about marriage and married life. Even when predisposed to a sympathetic appreciation of the Torah tradition, such
people cannot understand the severely legal manner of the Jewish doctrine of marriage. When discussing the relationship between husband and wife, the Talmud speaks of *mitzvah* and *din*,
of *halakhah* and *issur*, of rights and duties—exactly, it seems, in
the same terms of its discourses on civil and commercial law. Is
there no difference, people ask, between the area of domestic relationships and these others? Is not the derogatory charge of
"legalism," so often pressed against us, justified in the light of Judaism's treatment of marriage in the language of commandments and prohibitions, laws and duties? The modern mentality
cannot understand that these laws referring to family life should
constitute as much as one fourth of the entire *Shulchan Arukh*, the
Code of Jewish Law; that married life should be based on any
factor other than love.

Of course, husband and wife, parents and children, cannot
think only of their rights and their demands upon each other. For
a family to be successful there must be love and patience and tenderness and a willingness to forgive and forget and forego. The
Talmud *(Kiddushin* 41a) teaches that the famous commandment,
ve'ahavta le'reiakha kamokha, "You shall love your neighbor as
yourself," refers, in the first instance, to one's wife. And Maimonides codifies as Jewish law *(Hilkhot Ishut* 15:19) the statement
of the Sages that a man should honor his wife more than himself—in the manner in which he provides for her—and love her
as much as himself.

Having said this—it is a self-evident principle—we must add
another truism: love itself is an insufficient basis for life.
Solomon proclaimed that *Azah ka-mavet ahavah*, "Love is as

strong as death." Love is powerful, one of the most powerful forces in the universe; but, unregulated and undirected, it can also be deadly and destructive.

Why is this so?

———

FIRST, WITHOUT LAW we cannot distinguish between licit and illicit love; the limits of love's expression are gone, and one does not know where it will lead. That "love is the only law" is an ancient Christian teaching with disastrous implications; some of them are being spelled out in our own times, as Christian antinomianism is being wedded to the permissiveness of the New Morality. Thus, the scandalous effort by certain clerical groups to legitimize homosexual "marriages" provided both partners truly love each other. Once love is set up in opposition to law (and the tension between them is always resolved in favor of love), love itself can become a menace to all other values cherished by civilized man. This is an insight anticipated in the Torah's use of the term *chesed* (love) for a particular form of incest: the same quality of God's redemptive relationship to man, and man's outgoing goodness to his fellow man, is deemed ugly and repulsive, an abomination, when it is uncontrolled and undisciplined.

———

SECOND, HUMAN LOVE, for all its eminence in life and in doctrine, does not remain the highest value of all. Judaism teaches man that he must submit his entire life and his most cherished commitments to the higher authority of God Himself. There is a love that transcends our love for parents and wife and children—and that is love for God. There is a judgment that surpasses any human judgment no matter how ethical, and that is the divine judgment. This, indeed, is the teaching of the *Akedah*: Abraham, despite his passionate and deathless love for his only son, bows his head and submits to the divine decree to offer up his only son as a sacrifice. The Law of God takes precedence over the love of man.

This is the only authentically religious position open to believers. The subordination of *Ahavat Hashem* to human love characterizes, essentially, a secularist-humanist view.

———

THIRD, WITHOUT LAW, love "conquers all," but it also *destroys* all—including itself. Law is that which allows love to endure within the context of life. The *mitzvot* provide the framework in which true and authentic love can flourish; otherwise it may spend itself prematurely.

Observing our own society confirms this unhappy assertion: rarely before has the word "love" been as popular. Despite some recent assertions that "love is dead," it remains the cheapest commodity on the market today. It fills the scrapbooks of countless teenagers; it is the chief attraction of all popular magazines; it is sentimentally blared forth on television and peddled in the cinema. Oversized buttons and signs implore us: MAKE LOVE, NOT WAR; and in the name of love, war is declared against the Establishment. Society in general—not only the avant-garde—is successively discarding all traditional laws and religious and moral restraints. Yet who is it who will maintain that human relations nowadays are usually characterized by an excess of love?

The Hippies recognize the cynicism and cant and hypocrisy that lie at the heart of modern society. They are sensitive to this corruption and this rot, this lack of genuine love. Yet they make the disease worse by giving unrestrained expression to what they consider love while at the same time abandoning all laws and restraints which alone can make it meaningful by channeling it properly. Their life is amoral, uncreative, and astoundingly self-centered—and egocentricity and authentic love do not go well together. Any sane person—especially one over thirty!—can see that this is a caricature of love and life. Like a living cartoon, it does expose the ludicrous bluff and bluster in our society; but it has no solutions to offer, no cures for the ills it protests against. It cannot therefore be taken as a serious social movement. The trouble with "Flower Power" is that it has no roots and therefore must wither. This is not meant to challenge the sincerity of the New Moralists or Hippies and Yippies or college radicals. Their

178 | SEVENTY FACES

sincerity is entirely irrelevant. But we have no proof whatever that genuine love is more characteristic of these circles and their much vaunted "honesty," than of the "hypocritical" establishment. Indeed, the more love becomes a doctrine that is preached, the less is it available as a reality that is experienced.

———

So JUDAISM APPRECIATES the importance of love as a basic ingredient in successful and meaningful human relations. But it knows that love cannot flourish if we do not place it in the context of justice. The Kabbalah teaches that *Chesed* (love) alone is overwhelming and destructive, but when it is dialectically joined to *Gevurah* (law and justice), it yields *Tiferet*—harmony and beauty and truth. Love must have the protection of laws and duties and restraints. Those fortunate enough to experience love, must direct it and orient it properly, and must always consider its effects on others—on old and young, on contemporaries—even on the unborn.

Finally, we must not ignore those (and they constitute a large segment of humanity) who cannot or do not experience love. Their inner life is emptier than those who are capable of feeling love, their emotional life is attenuated and poor. But such people are no less decent or moral or valuable than those who do love. They have every right to a decent life, and to the protection of their emotions, of their families, of their children—no less so than those fortunate enough to be endowed with the capacity for love. The Erich Fromms, who consider the absence of the capacity for love an instance of mental illness, may be right. But as long as a large number—perhaps a majority—of human beings are so afflicted, there is no warrant for basing all of social ethics on love alone.

Jewish law creates the conditions under which love can flourish in human relationships, and under which people can live humanly with each other even if they do *not* attain love. If one examines the consistent manner in which the Talmudic Sages applied the commandment *Ve'ahavta le'reiakha kamokha*, he will discover that its correct translation ought to be not "*Love* your neighbor as yourself," but "*Act lovingly* towards your neighbor as you would act towards yourself." (See the commentary of *Ramban* on this verse.)

———

IT IS PRECISELY because of Judaism's concern for the integrity of marriage and home that it legislates on such matters. In fact, the more important the subject, the more does Judaism hedge it about with laws. It is *because* marriage is so sacred and sexuality so sensitive that Torah prefers to protect it by *law* rather than wax poetic about it romantically. Torah considers marriage and family and *yichus* (the legitimacy of lineage) so significant, that it will not leave it to the whim of sudden passion and instantaneous infatuation.

That is why *Gittin* and *Kiddushin* (divorce and marriage) abound in such complex technicalities. Marriage is a lifelong relationship of the most significant and far-reaching consequences, and is initiated by a single ceremony or contract. Therefore, we must make sure that both parties know exactly what they are doing, that both offer their free and untrammelled consent, in order that no avoidable errors be perpetrated. Hence, the Halakha's insistence upon the formality of the ring, of the witnesses, of the proposal formula, of the proper quorum, and so forth, so that there be no misinterpretation or misunderstanding of what is occurring.

For this reason, the Halakhah places even greater emphasis upon the technicalities of *gittin* than upon *kiddushin,* because the former has such a massive impact upon the lives of two people— usually more than the latter. Every detail therefore becomes exceedingly important. To undo a relationship is even more difficult than creating it in the first place. With all the difficulties imposed by Halakhah in divorce, these laws have been the safeguard of Jewish morality throughout the ages.

These considerations explain the very special care that the Halakhah insists must be taken in any matter relating to marriage or any situation where there exists the possibility of *mamzerut* (illegitimacy.) Too much depends upon this and so every precaution must be taken.

It is deeply distressing that some Jews, through no fault of their own other than ignorance, are often caught up in tragic situations. Unfortunately, people are sometimes innocently misled and later discover that they face horrendous problems. Hence, knowledgeable Jews have a duty to inform others that if, as often happens in the course of life, they are ever beset by a problem in this area, they ought always inquire of competent rabbinical authority—and the emphasis is on the word "competent." Every Jew must remember that rabbis who function in marital matters must be fully Orthodox, experts in the field, and ethical individuals. When we disqualify those who do not fully accept the authority of Jewish Law, it is not a matter of pique or institutional rivalry, but of principle and law as well as common sense. Unfortunately, there are some few Orthodox rabbis whose credentials are questionable, and one must therefore always check carefully in advance—no less than one solicits opinions about the reputation of a physician or a surgeon.

These matters, about which extreme caution should be exercised, include marriage and divorce; remarriage of any person who has previously been married; proselytization or marrying a proselyte or a descendant of a proselyte; the adoption of children, whether Jewish or non-Jewish. *The problems that exist in such cases can be enormous; most of the unhappy consequences are avoidable if we are wise enough to inquire before proceeding impulsively or thoughtlessly.*

———

THE TORAH IS the center of our lives as individuals and as a people. Its *mitzvot* guide our conduct, its ideals define our destiny. It has served us well throughout our long history. We are naturally as flawed as others, subject to the constant blandishments of the *yetzer ha-ra* no less than others, and prone to the same corruptions that afflict other human beings. Yet the Torah has made possible for us a family life as moral and as stable as any people has ever known. At the very least it has given us a guilt feeling which acts as a marvelous restraint on further degeneration. The Jewish tradition does not often speak overtly of love; yet its legal restraints and the duties it imposes have given it the greatest opportunity for expression.

No matter how much an Orthodox Rabbi wants to maintain good relations with all Jews, whatever their convictions, he can only view with the deepest sorrow the havoc wrought by Reform when it abandoned Jewish marriage law. *This was probably the most irresponsible act in the recent annals of the Jewish people.* Based on a piece of spurious scholarship, Reform proclaimed that a civil divorce is adequate, and that a *get* is unnecessary for remarriage. It overlooked the glaring inconsistency of insisting that marriage should be a religious ceremony, while divorce may be a civil ceremony. As a result, it cavalierly dismissed the fact that the Halakhah considers the previous marital bond still in full force. Therefore, the person who remarries without a proper religious divorce is living in adultery, and the children of such a union are illegitimate.

Now, illegitimacy, *mamzerut,* imposes a terrible burden on such children: they are forbidden to marry any others save those in the same category. Too much human tragedy has resulted from this irresponsibility for us to remain silent. That is why, whatever anyone may believe about religious freedom in Israel, we must draw the line at matters of *Gittin* and *Kiddushin*. It is bad enough that Reform has destroyed the happiness of so many men and women in this country, often forcing a young couple to make a tragic choice between love for each other or loyalty to the basic tenets and laws of their faith. We dare not acquiesce by our silence in the destruction of the unity of the Jewish community of the State of Israel as well. One can only hope that enlightened Reform leaders will themselves come to this realization and attempt to correct the situation—or at least not endeavor to impose it on Israeli Jews. Israeli secularists and American Reform spokesmen—and some editorialists in the Anglo-Jewish press who are, as is well known, the ultimate authorities in all matters affecting Judaism from marriage law to culinary fashion—have knowingly or unknowingly misrepresented the position of American Orthodoxy. They have asserted that the introduction of civil marriage and divorce in the State of Israel would not be divisive and would create no insuperable difficulties, appealing to the example of American Jewry where co-existence reigns supreme. While it is true that in general communal matters, many Orthodox Jews and a number of Orthodox Jewish institutions have co-operated with Reform and Conservative groups, it is simply not true that such accommodation has extended to halakhic issues, and it is certainly untrue that no serious complications have arisen. Orthodox Rabbis now must inquire, as a matter of course, of every prospective bride and groom about divorces and conversions of their parents and grandparents. When we discover anything of this nature in the lineage of the couple, sanctioned by Reform, we know that in most cases we cannot condone the marriage. Usually, the situation is incorrigible: *me'uvat she'lo yukhal li'tkon,* as the Talmud calls it. Such couples often go "shopping" for Reform or Conservative dispensations—imposing on their progeny the prospect of the same heartbreak in years to come.

————

THESE MATTERS are not at all pleasant to discuss. Denouncing those who do not share our convictions is not always the criterion of *yirat shamayim,* nor is it always the best way to bring such people closer to Torah. But these threats to our peoplehood are too important and too menacing to pass over them in polite silence. It is our duty as responsible Jews to let our fellow Jews know the facts lest, by default, we share in the guilt of creating human misery. It is bad enough that so many Jews have chosen to live outside the pale of Jewish law. But to impose the burden of illegitimacy upon an innocent child who may one day choose to reclaim his Jewish heritage, is to be guilty of an act of unspeakable cruelty. Our zeal in making all Jews aware of these facts derives from the deepest feelings of human compassion.

The prophet Isaiah proclaims, *Ki mei No'ach zot li,* "For this is as the waters of Noah to me." Just as I have sworn, says God, not to bring another Flood to the world, so will I not punish My people again. But the Zohar (*Lev.* 14b) asks: Is this not a strange expression? Should the waters of the flood not be referred to as such, *mei mabbul,* "the waters of the Flood," rather than as *mei No'ach,* "the waters of Noah?"

The answer of the Zohar provides us with a pertinent insight: when the Almighty wishes to bring destruction upon a world deserving of such cataclysm, He first informs the pious of that generation, hoping that they will intercede before God for their fellow men, and that they will inspire their contemporaries to righteousness so that, having changed their ways, God may feel free to change His decree. Thus Moses pleaded before God and preached to his fellow men, and thus did the prophets after him. Noah, however, failed to do this—he was concerned only for himself. When God told him that a flood would destroy every existing thing, he built an ark for himself and his family; he worried about Noah and no one else. Because of this spiritual self-centeredness and his indifference to the religious well-being of his fellow men, he carries the eternal stigma of having the Flood known as *mei No'ach,* "the waters of Noah." The devastation, the destruction, the calamity bear his name as he bears some of the blame.

We Orthodox Jews must not be guilty of the same kind of spiritual egotism under the pious guise of not wanting to interfere in the lives of others. We are not *interfering* when we bring to our fellow-Jews, who have abandoned Jewish marriage law, the message of Torah. We are *discharging our responsibility to them* and to their children, and to their children's children, and to generations yet unborn, informing them and cautioning them about the Torah's law of marriage and legitimacy and its implications for them.

———

HAVING DONE THAT, we shall discover that just as the punishment for irresponsibility comes in the form of water—the *mei No'ach*—so the reward for the proper responsibility is also "water," but of a different kind, and also spoken of by the prophet Isaiah: *"And the entire world will be filled with the knowledge of the Lord, even as the waters fill the sea."*

~ 17 ~

GREAT
EXPECTATIONS

My remarks will be divided into two parts—"great expectations" with regard to love and marriage, and the often difficult and conflicting realities of marriage and career in our own
days.

At services yesterday, one of my fellow-congregants said, "I
see that your brother wrote a book about love and marriage.
Well, tell me: which one are you going to favor?" That question is
not really as cynical as it sounds when we view "love" against its
cultural and historical background.

When we speak of love in our context, we usually speak about
romantic love—an ideology which emerged only at the end of
the twelfth century and quickly became the "in-thing" in Europe.
The troubadours and their message of chivalry even penetrated
the Jewish world.

One of the great classics of European Jewry, *Sefer ha-Hasidim*,
contains many references to romantic love. When I first read this
volume, I was non-plussed, even outraged. Thus, a question
(*she'elah*) is asked about a man who loved a woman whom he
had never met. This sounded to me like a case of mental distur-
bance. I was wrong; such phenomena were prevalent because
this was the nature of romantic love at that time. It exalted "pure
love"—a love that was never fulfilled carnally and where very
often the object of love was not known to the lover. This was the
era of Romeo and Juliet, of Tristan and Isolde.

Usually this kind of love existed outside of marriage. That is
why the question of which, love or marriage, will be favored is
not necessarily cynical or funny. A man can be married to one
woman and in love with another woman who may not even
know about it.

In the Western world since the sixteenth century, romance and
marriage have been joined. It became expected that one find romance with one's own wife. This became the new ideal. It was

*Presented at a symposium on "Love and Marriage" and published under that name by
the sponsors, Stern College for Women and American Mizrachi Women, March 1981*

this that everyone strived for—the fulfillment of romantic love within the confines of marriage. Thus, courtship rituals began to replace the arranged marriage and the date took the place of the *shadkhan*. Everyone had to find the woman he loved, or the man she loved, and that could be done only by personal initiative and not by pre-arrangement. Supposedly, according to the dating myths by which we now live, the relationship is predetermined, and this attracts the two lovers to each other.

In fact, of course, this hit-and-miss method cannot by any means guarantee success. It is questionable whether the dating system has produced better results than the *shadkhan* system. Are marriages happier? Does love last longer, if it comes at all, after the first burst of infatuation? I can't answer that.

I would hazard the guess that there has been no real improvement in marital love since the demise of the *shadkhan* and the advent of romantic love. Charles Darwin pointed out that men often pay more attention to the pedigrees of their horses than to the qualifications of the women they marry. No one would go to buy an expensive house without any preparation other than the expectation that I'll just happen to meet the right house. When it comes to marriage however, we expect merely to meet the girl or boy of our dreams and everything will turn out right.

Horse-trading, house-hunting, insurance-buying—these are approached rationally and without the encumbrances of myth. The search for a mate, however, finds reason conveniently put aside in favor of a heightened expectation that we will "hear bells ringing," that the spine will tingle and the heart will know and the head will turn. The dating process, in our current mythology, is not a creative, reasoned process in which I make autonomous decisions, but a search for a preordained relationship that, for its fulfillment, merely awaits the chance meeting between the two lovers.

Romantic love, therefore, is the stuff of songs, of poems, of dramas. But it sets up expectations that, especially with the immature (75% of the population?) can only lead to grief. These are expectations that cannot be realized most of the time, and certainly not on a sustained level. I recall the story about the display in a store window. It featured four kinds of perfume—Passionate Love, Hedonistic Delight, Ecstasy, and Reasonable Expectations . . . Romantic love does not lend itself to reasonable expectations.

My (previous) professional experience confirmed this for me. I used to do a great deal of family counseling, and time and again certain patterns of cases came to my attention that taught me a great deal about society, about life, about myself, about the people amongst whom I lived. A man would come to consult me, a year or two after marriage. What a wonderful relationship it had been, a great love story, a fabulous wedding. He would appear in my office distraught, and would say to me, "Something is terribly wrong. I have got to get out of it, I no longer hear bells." (My immediate reaction the first time I heard this cliché, was to send him to an audiologist.) Twenty-five years ago I would smile, put my arm around him, and teach him some of the existential and emotional facts of life—what life is really all about, and how such expectations were foolish and immature. He would go back, and quite often, they would work things out. (Today, unfortunately, the divorce would follow almost immediately because, as restraints and inhibition have been attenuated by society, people do not give themselves a chance and every marital problem is considered as having an immediate solution—divorce.)

I do not mean to say, of course, that love is a "goyish" invention. Certainly love is important. R. Akiva declared that one who marries a woman who is not suitable for him violates five commandments, amongst them: "Thou shalt love thy neighbor as thyself." Rav taught that a man should not marry a woman until he has seen her. (In those days of prearranged marriage, he might have come to the *chuppah* without ever having seen her. Hence, he had to lift her veil and look at her and she at him. This is the origin of the "badeken" or veiling ceremony prior to the actual wedding.) The reason for this is to make sure that they do not find each other obnoxious or repulsive. Such a marriage would be forbidden because the Torah says that you must love your neighbor as yourself, and your closest neighbor and friend is your own husband or wife. Similarly, Maharik ruled that despite the great emphasis that Judaism lays upon respect for parents, nevertheless, if a man wants to marry a woman, provided that she is suitable for him in other ways, and his parents disagree, he need not obey his parents if they cannot give a reasonable explanation for their refusal.

Certainly, then, love is a critical element in Jewish marriage, but it is not the only criterion. Love must be seen within a value-context in which consideration is given as well to character, loyalty to Torah, and compatibility. The emphasis in Judaism is more on love after (that is, during) marriage than it is on love before marriage. Romantic love alone cannot be the cement which binds the marriage. The binder must be a sustained rather than ecstatic love, and has to be learned and nurtured. That may or may not begin with infatuation but it must go on to affection and respect and then mellow and mature into responsible love.

We said that the marital relationship derives from the principle of neighborly love, "Thou shalt love thy neighbor as thyself." Now, Ramban notes that it is often impossible to feel real love for your neighbor. He concludes that the verse means that you must *act lovingly* towards your neighbor, even if there is no significant emotional component. That practical lesson must not be lost upon us with regard to marriage. When married, whether or not it was ushered in by a great love affair, we are commanded to act lovingly to each other. If I *act* lovingly, then a true love relationship will be built up, and after a while it will not be mere role-playing, but genuine.

That is the kind of love that you climb up to, not "fall into"; the kind that two people build by trial and error, by exposing their own vulnerabilities to each other, by shared values, by owning up to mistakes, and by a willingness to learn to appreciate each other, to act civilly when upset and affectionately even when not aroused, to miss each other when apart, to enjoy each other's company, to protect each other, to find that each brings out the best in the other. When you have that you have attained love.

Let me now comment briefly on the theme of Marriage and Career. We cannot accept the extreme feminist argument that denigrates family, marriage, home. I believe very few people take that seriously—although, unfortunately, those few are far too many. Children and home can never yield their primacy in the value structure of Jewish life for women or for men. For me that is so obvious it does not require elaboration. The race dies without children. We cannot continue as a people without reproduction and wise child raising. The Jewish family is the core of the Jewish community.

We are here at Stern College for Women, so I will allow the comment that I am not shaken by the widespread, snide remark,—"So you are going to Stern! Are you working for an MRS.

Degree?" My answer would be: and if so, why not? In addition to receiving an education whether humanistic or pre-professional (in addition to Jewish), what is wrong about aspiring to marriage? What is less valuable about marriage than chemistry or French? Is it less worthy or dignified than the extracurricular ambitions, such as overnight entertaining in mixed dormitories, that are prevalent in other universities? I am proud of the fact that here in Yeshiva University young men and young women who share traditional Jewish values can meet each other. I think it is beautiful and I encourage it.

Yet it is also unJewish to teach that reproduction and childrearing preempt all other values in a woman's life. To say that a woman should receive no advanced education because her job is to be a wife or a mother or a homemaker, is to commit a terrible wrong to the woman who accepts such doctrines.

Five hundred years ago, R. Isaac Arama offered an insight that is fresh and relevant today. Jacob, in the Biblical tale, married two sisters, Leah and Rachel. Rachel was his favorite wife, but she was unable to bear any children. She said to her husband, "Give me children, for if not I am as good as dead." Jacob lost his temper and said: "what do you want from me, am I God?"

Now, why was Jacob's response so uncharacteristically harsh, and apparently insensitive? It seems Jacob detected in Rachel some of her father's paganism. In the Torah, we learn that at creation, the woman is given two names. The first name is *Ishah,* woman, because she is the same as man (*Ish*). The other name is *Chavah* (Eve) because she is the mother of all humans. The difference between them is this: *Chavah* implies that a woman is created for motherhood, she is given a role as a functionary. *Ishah* goes beyond this. Over and above all functions, she is a human being in her own right. She has worth and value in and of herself, independent of what she achieves or what functions she performs. She is an individual of value no less than a man. Hence, when Rachel said that if she cannot have any children she is as good as dead, Jacob could hear his pagan father-in-law Laban speaking through her. A human being has been reduced to a functionary. By means of his irate rebuke, Jacob wanted to teach Rachel Abraham's view—that even if you don't have any children, your personality remains sacred.

To say that a woman's goals are exhausted by motherhood is

simply not true. We must seek to develop the whole array of talents in our daughters and in ourselves. If we affirm *ishah* the same as *ish*, then whether one is an *ish* or *Ishah* it means that the divine image within is waiting to be expressed. Women must be educated out of respect to that innate worth and, additionally, to fill in creatively the empty time after their children grow up. Boredom and idleness are dangerous to one's psyche and one's mental health—and one's family.

Permit me to make one more point. I do not believe that a Jewish woman's talents must necessarily be expressed in a manner that appeals to the market place. A woman, in order to be true to herself, must not necessarily get a job. She should be able, if she so wishes, to devote her time to community work, to organizational work, and to charity. Voluntarism requires no less talent than banging away at a typewriter or even looking up cases in a law book. It requires certain kinds of interpersonal relationships, certain qualities of heart and mind, that are in many ways greater than those valued by the market place.

Yet for the contemporary Jewish woman and family, despite all this, a special effort must be to reestablish that priority of family and children. It is disheartening to read the statistics about Jewish population decrease. Larger families must be encouraged. Without such a reordering of values, women who feel that their major commitment is to family and children rather than to a career that demands total commitment will feel put upon. We have to be very careful about overdoing the contemporary emphasis on self-realization. Valuable as it is, it has been exaggerated. We are living in a frighteningly narcissistic society. But we will not fall prey to that narcissism, whether as men or women, as long as we retain some element of Jewish dignity. We are called upon to establish a difficult balance, within marriage, of responsibility and self-interest, one which will involve us neither in punitive self-sacrifice nor in egocentric, pathological disregard of our obligations to family. It means that the *ishah-chavah* equilibrium must be maintained with the awareness that it is different for each individual.

It is a difficult challenge to achieve that proper balance, but if the marriage is secure, and indeed if there is love in marriage, we will find the proper formula for marriage and career as well.

~ 18 ~

TZENIUT:
A UNIVERSAL CONCEPT

One of the defining characteristics of the Jewish religious personality is *tzeniut*, which may approximately be translated as modesty. Normally, the concept of *tzeniut* is discussed in rather technical terms: how low or how high a hemline, the length of sleeves, the form of dress, the number of square millimeters of skin that may be exposed, and so on. Indeed, these are important issues, but they are aspects or details of *tzeniut*, not its heart. It would be a pity to limit our understanding of *tzeniut* to that which can be measured by a ruler, while ignoring its conceptual matrix. What should concern us is the worldview of Judaism that informs the concept and the practice of *tzeniut*, an exceedingly important Jewish principle and value which touches the fundamentals of our faith. In seeking the broader implications of *tzeniut* and its universal context, we must explore three dimensions of *tzeniut*.

The first of these is the principle of *kedushah*, holiness. The Torah says, "You shall be holy." The Sages of the Talmud comment: *hevu perushim min ha-arayot*, you shall separate yourselves from immorality. The commandment therefore concerns immorality in its strictly sexual significance. The more one distances himself or herself from expressions of illegitimate sensuality, the more one is able to achieve personal sanctity or *kedushah*.

How does *tzeniut* relate to *kedushah*? The most fruitful way to begin is by citing an explanation I heard from my illustrious late teacher and mentor, Rabbi Joseph. B. Soloveitchik, *zekher tzaddik li'vrakhah*. The "Rav," as he was known, offers a very trenchant insight: *kedushah* thrives in *he'elem*, in hiddenness, in obscurity, not *be'giluy*, openness. (Indeed, the Torah's euphemism for illicit sexual intercourse is *giluy arayot*, the exposure or baring to public view of nakedness.) These two concepts of hiddenness and openness are most relevant to *kedushah*, which flourishes only in the hidden.

Published in the Haham Solomon Gaon Memorial Volume *ed. Rabbi Marc Angel*, *1997*

The holiest place in the world for Judaism is the *Kodesh Hako-doshim*, the Holy of Holies in the *Beit Hamikdash*, the Temple in Jerusalem. The holiest person during the service in the Temple was the *Kohen Hagadol*, the High Priest. And the holiest day of the year is Yom Kippur. No one may enter the inner sanctum of the Holy of Holies, except the *Kohen Hagadol*, on Yom Kippur. Here we have a converging of three forms of *kedushah*: the *kedushah* of place, the *kedushah* of time, and the *kedushah* of personality—in one place, only once a year, by one person. If *kedushah* is so important, we might have expected masses of Jews crowding the Temple with a great deal of fanfare, marching to the *Kodesh Hako-dashim* to participate in this phenomenal concentration of holiness. Yet that is not the case at all—because *kedushah* does not prosper in the presence of masses. It does not thrive under the gaze of the many, in openness, in revelation, in exposure. Rather, it is the opposite of exposure—hiddenness—which is the natural environment of *kedushah*. Holiness grows in the unobtrusive recesses of the soul, not on the stage of one's public persona.

Another example of the Halakha's preference for hiddenness as a prerequisite for holiness is the *Sefer Torah*. The Torah is read on Monday and Thursday, and twice on Shabbat. It is forbidden to touch the inside of the parchment of the Torah scroll, the side on which the writing appears, which is why we use a metal or wooden pointer. Indeed, if one does touch it, his hands are considered "defiled," *tamei yadayim*, and he therefore must wash his hands. The *Sefer Torah* confers impurity upon the hands because otherwise one might become over-familiar with *kedushah*; if that happens, one detracts from the *Sefer Torah's* sanctity. When there is too much exposure, holiness is diminished. Indeed, when the Talmud speaks about not touching the parchment of the *Sefer Torah*, the language it uses is: *ke'she'hu arum*, "when it is naked." At such time, it is, as it were, exposed, naked or: lacking in *tzeniut*.

The Greeks, the Rav says, saw the human body primarily in aesthetic terms. They were obsessed with beauty. But their notion is that beauty does not thrive in hiddenness. Beautiful objects require that they be displayed and admired. Hence, if you accept the body primarily in aesthetic terms, an object of beauty, it demands exposure. This indeed was one of the major elements that occasioned the great collision between Athens and Jerusalem: the Greeks introduced gymnasia into Israel, where sports were engaged in the nude because the body was an object of beauty. But Judaism does not look upon the body primarily in aesthetic terms. That is what, to a large extent, caused the Hasmonean revolution which we celebrate on Hanukkah.

That is not to say that there is no aesthetic in Judaism. When, for instance, the Talmud says that *benot Yisrael yafot hen*, that Jewish women are beautiful, the Talmud was not engaging simply in an off-hand comment. But clearly, in the priority of values, *kedushah* takes precedence over aesthetics. The main approach of Judaism toward the human body was not as an aesthetic object but as a religious value, something sacred. But that which is sacred requires covering, distance, the opposite of exposure. Hence, Judaism legislated the laws of *tzeniut*, and demanded covering up, because if indeed the body is sacred and sanctity is more important than beauty, then beauty has to take second place. The laws of *tzeniut* therefore position Judaism as opposite to the Hellenistic tradition.

A few examples may be offered to support the Rav's thesis. In the beginning of Exodus, God calls to Moses out of the burning bush and says, *Moshe, Moshe*. Moses replies, *Hineni*. God continues: "Remove your shoes because the ground you are standing on is hallowed ground." And here God reveals Himself for the first time to the world's greatest prophet: "I am the Lord, the God of your fathers, the God of Abraham, Isaac, and Jacob." How does Moses react? With *tzeniut! Va-yaster Mosheh panav ki yarei me'habit el haElohim*. Moses covers his face because he is afraid to look at God. This fear is not lest God punish or devour him, nor is it the fear of the unknown. It is, more accurately, awe: Moses is overawed. In the presence of *kedushah* the proper response is to close one's eyes and to cover one's face. If *tzeniut* reflects the correct orientation of the human personality to the presence of *kedushah*, then the body, which encloses the human personality, requires similarly that it be covered up.

Another example: The sixth chapter of Isaiah, often referred to as the vision of the "seraphic songs," records the first divine revelation to this great prophet. Isaiah envisions the seraphim, or fiery angels, as they surround the very throne of the Holy One. As they do so, they call out to each other: *kadosh kadosh kadosh*, "Holy, holy, holy is the Lord of Hosts." It is most interesting to note how the prophet describes these angels: each angel has six wings. With two wings the angel covers his face, with two others the angel covers his feet, and with the remaining two he flies. Note: only two of the six are functional—the wings for flying! Four of the six represent *tzeniut*, covering up. Why do they cover up? Because *kadosh kadosh kadosh*; in the presence of *kedushah* there must be covering up. Exposure is abhorrent—even of angels, beings which have no *yetzer hara*, to whom sexuality is utterly irrelevant. In the presence of *kedushah*, there must always be concealment.

Tzeniut is an indication that a human being possesses a *neshamah*, a soul, and the soul is an aspect of *kedushah*. *Tzeniut* is therefore an acknowledgement that the human personality, which includes the human body, partakes of *kedushah*. The body is not just a fortuitous biological mechanism devoid of any transcendent meaning or higher moral obligation. Man may be an animal, but man is also an angel because he has the *tzellem Elohim*, the divine spark; he possesses *kedushah*.

The second dimension of *tzeniut* is connected with the experience of *kavod*, usually translated as "glory," "majesty," "honor," or "respect." But "dignity" is a better translation. The word "dignity" itself derives from a Latin root which means value, worthiness. A human being must have a sense of self-respect, an awareness of his own self worth. The source of this human dignity is *Ha-Kadosh Barukh Hu*, with regard to Whom we say *kevod Elohim haster davar* (Proverbs 25:2), the dignity of God lies in hiddenness. Dignity, like *kedushah*, thrives in *haster davar*, in obscurity, in concealment rather than exposure. This holds true for man as well: his concealment is both cause and effect of *kavod*. One who possesses *kavod*, a sense of dignity, will deal with it in a manner compatible with *tzeniut*. Modesty will characterize his conduct and personality as a reflection of that inner sense of worth.

Confronted by a person who is always bragging, always talking about his own achievements, boasting of his attractiveness or intelligence or talent or wealth, we know intuitively that such a person despises himself. He compensates for his poor self-image by proclaiming how great and superior he is, thereby seeking the approbation of others. A person who has self-respect has no need to wear his virtues like a badge and show them off to the world. One who lacks this sense of *kavod*, of inner dignity and worth, will expose himself, as if to say, "Look at me. Am I not beautiful?

Am I not smart? Do you not admire me?" The lack of *kavod* leads to exhibitionism, the opposite of *tzeniut*, whereas a sense of *kavod* will normally result in the practice of modesty or *tzeniut*.

As mentioned earlier, propriety of dress is an aspect of *tzeniut*, but that does not imply that *tzeniut* requires a kind of concerted attempt to look unkempt or unstylish. *Tzeniut* is not the antonym of attractiveness and pleasantness of appearance; it is the opposite of overexposure which, in turn, is a sign of the lack of *kavod*, of self-dignity.

Tzeniut implies *kavod* both with regard to oneself and to others. In its broader sense, the concept of *tzeniut* as *haster davar*, as concealment or hiddenness, bears upon interpersonal relationships. A relevant and significant example is *tzedakah*. The highest expression of this mitzvah occurs when the donor and the recipient do not know each other or of each other. Here, *tzeniut* ensures that *kavod* is extended not only to one's self but, primarily, to the other, in concern for the dignity of another sentient and sensitive human being. To give someone a handout directly is a good thing, but it is not the ideal way, for the recipient is aware of his status as a mendicant. The far nobler way is that of genuine modesty, where in addition to supporting somebody financially in a time of his need, you also support his personality by respecting his *kavod*.

Finally, I propose a third concept, privacy, for which no word exists in classical Hebrew. (The absence of a name does not imply the non-existence of the concept. One can entertain an idea or a value or a precept without consciousness of it as a separate entity and, hence, without a name.) Privacy is a very important concept not only in secular law generally, but also in Halakha where it was very well developed much earlier than in the Western world. (See the chapter on "Privacy in Law and Theology," in my *Faith and Doubt*.) It is part of Judaism's ethics of communication.

In a sense, we might say that the ethics of communication which Judaism prescribes, directly or indirectly, is based upon *imitatio Dei*, the imitation of God or, in the Biblical vocabulary, "You shall walk in His ways."

In order to define the boundaries of the ethics of communication, we must consider how God communicates with humans, so that we might learn more of how humans ought to communicate with each other. God both reveals and conceals; He communicates, but not everything, not always.

At Mt. Sinai, there took place *giluy Shekhinah,* the revelation of His presence and of His teaching, i.e., Torah. God communicated with Moses and with the emerging nation of Israel gathered about the mountain. It was a communication of self-revelation.

In turn, man communicates with God by "revealing" himself to His Creator. Such is the understanding of prayer by the author of *Tanya* and by Rav Kook, among others.

Hence, in imitation of the Creator, man too must reveal himself to his fellow men as a means of communication. But there is a limitation that is very important: God reveals Himself, but He also conceals Himself. There is a divine sense of privacy which affirms the boundaries of His personality. There are limits beyond which no human may trespass and into which the human intellect may not freely probe. Thus, King Solomon in his Proverbs teaches us, as was mentioned earlier, *kevod Elohim haster davar,* the honor or dignity of God is in concealing matters. And the Talmud (*Hagigah* 13a) quotes Ben Sira who warns us, "in what is wondrous to you do not probe"; in what is hidden from you do not explore; understand deeply what is permitted to you, but you have no business attending to the hidden things. There is enough unknown in matters available for man's search and research; there are areas, however, that are "off limits" to him. The essence of the Creator is forever concealed from man, and no matter how we will try, we shall never penetrate the inner sanctum of God's essence. He wishes to protect His privacy, as it were.

Similarly, *tzeniut* means respect for the inviolability of the personal privacy of the individual, whether oneself or another, which is another way of saying that *tzeniut* is a respect for the integrity of one's ego, of one's essential self.

Man, in the understanding of Judaism, is fundamentally inscrutable; as much as you know about him, you never know everything about him. Were you really to know everything about him, that would mean that he lacks a core of self and is nothing but a collection of reactions and molecules and organs but not yet a human being. One's humanity, in some sense, is contingent upon his inscrutability, his mystery, his privacy. Man, according to Torah, possesses not only nature—his natural self that can be weighed and measured—but also *personae.* The word originally meant a mask, because it symbolizes that aspect of man that is concealed from public view. Beyond that mask is a living, very real human being. This mysterious, vital center of personality transcends the collection of our natural physiological and psychological properties. Not only *is* man a mystery, but he *should be* a mystery. One is obliged to develop a proper sense of self, whereby one is happy with that self even though no one else knows about it, confirms it, or validates it. This does not mean that one ought to be catatonic; a state where one does not communicate with another human being is pathological. In a healthy human being, revelation and communication are balanced in that vital core that remains free and undetermined—the center of personality that has clearly defined boundaries of selfhood. It is this privacy which we confirm when we speak of *tzeniut*. The other aspects of *tzeniut* are but derivative expressions of this core.

The concept of privacy in Halakha is evident in the beginning of the Talmud's tractate *Bava Batra*. The Gemara discusses the question of *hezek re'iyah*, a tort or damage that consists of invading someone's privacy by looking into his property. This visual intrusion into his private domain is regarded as a *hezek* or tort, and is actionable in a halakhic court of law. To take the Gemara's example, assume two partners bought a parcel of land and later decided to divide it. The halakha is that if one partner wants to build a fence to maintain his privacy, even if the other does not, the fence must be built and each pays 50% of the cost. Why? Because privacy is a right; *hezek re'iyah* is a genuine concern.

Now, the partner who does not want the fence must still pay 50% not because he also derives the benefit of privacy, but for quite the opposite reason. The Gemara explains by posing the following case: the partners purchase and then wish to divide a piece of property that is on a slope or diagonal, with one taking the bottom half of the property and the other the top half of the property. They now want to build a fence. But in this case, only one party has to pay the entire amount—and that is the owner of the upper level property. Why? Because the law of *hezek re'iyah* is such that one must pay not in order to gain protection from the visual intrusion by the other party, but rather to prevent oneself from invading another's privacy by spying on him! Therefore, if the two lots are level, each partner has to pay half the expense of the fence to prevent each from spying on the other. But if one is on the upper level and can look into the other's property, especially his roof where the partner who holds the land below assumes he is safe from inquisitive eyes, but the latter can not see the former, the latter does not have to pay at all. Hence, the Halakha requires of one to respect the privacy of his fellow man and—to pay for it. This is the law, and is so codified by the Rambam and in the *Shulchan Arukh*.

Tzeniut is much more than a mitzvah or commandment embodied in the very texture of the Halakha. Consider this: a great deal of Halakha is ethical in nature. *Tzedakah*, the prohibition of gossip, the commandment to bury a corpse if there is no one else to do it, visiting the sick, and so many other laws, both positive and negative, are therefore treated in both the halakhic and Musar (ethical) literature. Are these ethical halakhot only to be considered as mitzvot—or something more than that?

The ethical mitzvot are more than disembodied commands, because they issue from the principle of *imitatio Dei*, the imitation of God. The Mekhilta comments on the verse *zeh Eli ve'anvehu*, "this is my God and I shall glorify Him," that the word *ve'anvehu* is composed of the two words *Ani ve'Hu*, "He and I," that is, God and I. The Rabbis teach that as He is, so must I be: just as He acts morally, so must I. As God is merciful so must I be merciful. So it is with regard to all the "ethical mitzvot"—God not only commands these acts as a matter of law, but He Himself performs them. With the "regular" mitzvot, for instance when God commands us to eat the *korban Pesach*, He Himself does not, of course, eat the Passover lamb. But when God commands us to be kind, gentle, compassionate, considerate, loving, generous—it is because He acts in that manner, and we must not only obey Him but also imitate Him. His actions become the norms. This is what the Rabbis meant when they said that "the Torah begins with *chesed* and ends with *chesed*." In the beginning of the Torah we read that Adam and Eve were naked. As an act of loving kindness, God prepared clothing for them. Thus, we humans must imitate Him, and we too must provide clothing for the unclothed, the poor. The Torah concludes with the death of Moshe Rabbenu. God performed the act of burying Moses, and because God did it, we do it. The highest realm that humans can reach is the imitation of God's ethical personality.

If we say that *tzeniut* is an imitation of God's ways, that means that God too practices *tzeniut*. But how is it possible to say of God that He is modest? If we take *tzeniut* in the conventional context, that it implies clothing that covers certain parts of the body, etc., it is an absurd irrelevancy. However, we can speak of God as having a sense of privacy. I therefore return to a theme to which I alluded earlier.

In the philosophic and Kabbalistic traditions, one aspect of God is His knowability, His accessibility to our intellectual curiosity, His readiness to allow us to seek Him out, His relatedness to us. To know God is, after all, a great mitzvah. In Isaiah's famous vision of the Messianic era, the culmination of the redemption will be *u-male'ah haaretz deiah et Hashem*, that the earth will be filled with knowledge of God as the waters cover the sea.

But at the same time that God is knowable by man, both Jewish philosophy and Kabbalah teach that in His essence God is absolutely unknowable. He is infinitely remote from man's inquisitive mind, totally impervious to man's unquenchable desire to know. That is why, in the Kabbalah, the essence of God is called the *Ein Sof,* the Infinite. However, R. Hayyim of Volozhin says that the real, inner meaning of the term *Ein Sof,* or endless, refers to our search for understanding of Him: that there is no end to our efforts to know His essence; we must fail. It is His nature to remain mysterious, infinitely remote. This vast inscrutability of God is the inner boundary of His privacy. He resists man's desire to know Him, and limits his longing theological curiosity. This is the concept of the privacy of God.

Of course, Judaism wants us to understand. It wants us to understand nature, all knowledge of the world and of man. It wants us to know Torah and to know God. To know Him is one of the loftiest ambitions and most heroic achievements of *Homo religiosus,* religious man.

But both philosophers and mystics have taught that only certain aspects of God are accessible to man's intellect. Thus, what God *does* can be pondered; His "actional attributes" are such that we may attempt to describe and understand them, and we are bidden to imitate them. But when it comes to the divine Essence, to what He *is,* His inner self, we can only know what He is not— His "negative attributes." We are strictly limited in our ability to apprehend Divinity: encouraged to know what we may, discouraged from the futile task of going beyond our ken. Just as man, if he were totally knowable, would be less than human, so God, if

He were totally knowable, would be less than divine. God is, as it were a very private Individual. Just as He reveals Himself, He conceals Himself.

The prophet Micah spoke words which remain one of the great formulations of man's duty on earth: "It has been told to you, O man, what is good and what the Lord requires of you, but to do justly and to love mercy and to walk humbly with your God." The last of these three items, "to walk humbly" or modestly, is, in the Hebrew, *hatzneia lekhet. Hatzneia* is from the same root as *tzeniut*. To live a life of *tzeniut* is a matter of imitating God—"to walk humbly with your God." As He is merciful, I must be merciful; as He is gracious, I must be gracious; and therefore, as He practices *tzeniut*, privacy, so must I practice *tzeniut* and I must be modest and establish my own privacy and refrain from encroaching upon the privacy of my fellow humans. We must imitate the Almighty and learn from Him how to relate to others and to ourselves.

Man cannot flourish in a meaningful way without revelation. Just as God reveals Himself, so man cannot flourish without self-revelation or communication. And he must supplement that with its opposite: *tzeniut* or privacy, keeping the center of his personality mysterious and unknown, unexposed, unbreached.

———

TZENIUT IN ITS larger sense reflects the faith in the human potential for sanctity, *kedushah*. It reflects a respect for one's self and for others—for their *kavod*, their dignity. It is also a halakhic and ethical expression of the inalienable and inviolable privacy of man, based upon imitation of God. *Tzeniut* is also, therefore, a statement about God: that He is *kadosh kadosh kadosh*, He is holy, and that *melo kol haaretz kevodo*, the entire world is filled with His *kavod*, His majesty or dignity. Finally, *tzeniut* is a characteristic of God: He is private and, therefore, the acme of religious and moral development takes place when, in our own lives—in every prosaic aspect of dress, of speech, of mannerism—we reflect the highest and ultimate demand of the Holy One as it came to us through the prophet Micah *ve'hatzneia lekhet im Elohekha*, to walk with *tzeniut*—with and in imitation of the Lord our God.

Chapter 5

EDUCATION

The first item in this chapter is my investiture address as President of Yeshiva University, in which I outline my vision for Yeshiva both as an institution and as an educational ideal. The second item speaks of higher education in general, and the role that morality could and should play in colleges and universities in America. The third article is my address at commencement, 23 years after I delivered my investiture address in 1976.

Thereafter, I discuss Jewish education on the primary and secondary level, concluding with some critical comments on Jewish education in Modern Orthodoxy.

~ 19 ~

A VISION FOR
YESHIVA UNIVERSITY

I am deeply moved by all those who have assembled this day to join me in this ceremony of investiture as president of Yeshiva University. It is on this very platform that I received my doctorate ten years ago. Even more am I honored by the confidence placed in me by the Trustees in entrusting to me the destiny of this great citadel of learning, which nurtured me intellectually and spiritually from the time I was 18 years old.

However, this sentiment is tempered by two factors: first, I fully appreciate that it is not I but Yeshiva University which is being honored by you at this occasion. It is Yeshiva to which you, and I, express our gratitude for 91 years of unexcelled academic and communal leadership.

Second, I feel humble indeed to have been summoned to follow two of the most innovative and gifted spiritual and educational leaders in the history of the American Jewish community—Dr. Bernard Revel, of blessed memory, the first president of Yeshiva University, and his successor and my immediate predecessor and teacher, Dr. Samuel Belkin, may he rest in peace. I revered Dr. Belkin as an inspired teacher; I loved him as a man, as a friend, as my mentor. His giant mantle feels all too large upon these narrow shoulders.

Nevertheless, I am mindful of the saying of an ancient sage, "(What the great) Samuel (was) in *his* generation, (the lesser) Jephthah (was) in *his* generation." I know that I cannot equal my predecessors. I pray only that I may prove to be of as much service to my generation as they were to theirs.

———

I SUPPOSE THAT every epoch produces its own *Weltschmerz* and issues its own solemn jeremiads. Yet it is undeniable that depression and gloom and foreboding seem to be the hallmarks of our particular time. We are the generation of Vietnam and Wa-

---

My address at my investiture as President of Yeshiva University on November 7, 1976.

tergate. Economic distress casts a pall over our country, and indeed the world, at the beginning of our third century. The United Nations, which began with so much promise, continues to lend the sanction of international respectability to terrorism and duplicity, and has soured mankind's hope into cynicism. And the State of Israel, which is for Jews the only meager, institutionalized consolation to emerge out of the unspeakable horrors of the Holocaust, and for the Western World the only shred of atonement for its sorry and sordid record during the war years, remains the only country in the world whose claim to national self-determination is questioned by most of the nations.

At a time of such justifiable pessimism, there is much unhappiness too in the world of education.

The position to which I have been called is no easy one even in the most favorable of circumstances. Today it is more difficult than it ever was before. The lead article in a current journal of higher education is entitled, "The Reeling Presidency."

———

Yet, limited though we are by unpleasant realities, we must and shall confront the future courageously. As the first century R. Tarphon taught, "you are not required to finish the task, but you are not free to desist from it."

When the philosopher Immanuel Kant formulated his categorical imperative, he was asked if it is at all possible to abide by such a sublime code. He responded: "I don't know if it's practical and I don't know if it's possible, but this I do know, that *du kanst weil du must*"—you can because you must.

So, maybe this isn't the best time, but it is the only time we have. And though society seems to be spinning, and institutions seem to be tumbling, and the world seems to have become unstuck, and university presidents are reeling, nevertheless I shall do the only human and honorable thing: I shall try, I shall persevere—and, with the help of God, we shall prevail together. We can, because we must.

A great American, Admiral Halsey, once said, "There are no great men—only great challenges which average men must somehow try to meet."

I should like to address myself to some of the educational challenges which all of us confront. They are problems that are not necessarily unique to higher education or indigenous to Yeshiva University. They are also philosophical and societal, and are reflected in the fact that a profound and hazardous confusion has insinuated itself into the prevalent philosophy of education in America. For an abrupt shift has taken place in the values that Americans place on education—a shift almost sharp enough to be termed a revolution.

There was a time when the American emphasis on education seemed quite extravagant. In 1830, that perceptive French observer, Alexis de Tocqueville, wrote from America to a professor friend in Paris, "The universal and sincere faith that they profess here in the efficaciousness of education seems to me one of the most remarkable features of America . . ."

In retrospect, this faith seems so pure, so ingenuous. But it soon became quite disingenuous.

For too long, American educationists and many colleges and universities mindlessly allowed themselves to fall into the trap of commercialism, as they corrupted the educational enterprise with the clever hucksterism of Madison Avenue. In our pursuit of more education for more people—an ideal not only defensible but quite noble—we promised young men and women that a college degree will open for them the doors to higher pay and better jobs, that a sheepskin will produce more greenbacks, that a Ph.D. will give them money and status. As a result, higher education has now been caught in its own trap. We promised that college is "an investment in future earnings," and now, suddenly, we discover that the financial return after graduation on the investment of tuition, estimated as between eleven and twelve percent some five years ago, is now only slightly above seven percent! The inexorable logic of our deceptive appeals to materialistic motivations clearly leads to the conclusion that it is now wiser to invest in tax-free bonds than to go to school . . .

———

It is because of this unfortunate linkage, both explicit and subliminal, between education and material rewards, that in these last several years Americans have begun to speak of people as being "over-educated." My Grandmother would have asked, in her earthy Galician Yiddish, "Is it a shortcoming if the bride is too beautiful?"

I would not want this criticism to be overstated. I fully subscribe to the need for vocational preparation of young people so that they may be gainfully employed as adults. It is economically necessary, eminently reasonable, and—for Jews who abide by the Jewish Tradition—religiously mandatory. But, speaking both as a committed Jew and as an academician, it is offensive, self-defeating, and dangerous to link career training with the *purpose* of study, to confuse culture with professionalism, to identify the beneficial economic consequences of the educational enterprise as its proper motives. This represents the antithesis and the undermining of true scholarship, and is what the Talmud called *shelo lishmah*—study pursued for unworthy and dishonorable motives.

I humbly suggest that Yeshiva University's distinctive philosophy of education has something of enduring value to contribute in this particular dilemma not only to the Jewish community, but to American society in general.

It is perhaps worthwhile to summarize briefly what we regard as our distinctive mission.

The guiding vision of this university, as it was formulated by my two distinguished predecessors, was the philosophy of "synthesis," the faith that the best of the heritage of Western civilization—the liberal arts and the sciences—was or could be made ultimately compatible with the sacred traditions of Jewish law and life or, at the least, that this dual program, with all its tensions, was crucial to the development of young Jews in an open society. The very name "Yeshiva University" symbolizes this article of faith.

During the course of time, this formula has been deepened and enhanced. Yeshiva has succeeded in raising several generations of young people who have thereby managed to gain the best of both worlds, the Western and the Jewish; and, by great effort and exertion, it has become a center of advanced research, extending the frontiers of knowledge in the arts, the sciences, and Judaic Studies.

We are committed both to unfettered scholarship, and to the quest for transcendent values, norms, and the wisdom of tradition. We see no essential conflict between our common humanity, shared with all people of all perceptions and all races, and our distinctive Jewishness; between the universalism of our intellectual pursuits, and the commitment to the study of the heritage of Israel.

Yeshiva University's role as the transmitter of two cultures, and the creative development of both cultures, is thus the first major element in Yeshiva's purpose.

The second is, quite simply, the commitment to excellence. The word, of course, comes easy to the mouth of any educator. I do not know of any university that does not lay claim to the pursuit of excellence. Yet if I mention it here it is not so much to persuade you that we are excellent, as to remind myself that the search for excellence lays a moral obligation upon me and my administration, that we must never cease from pursuing it, though we will never attain it in its fullness.

The recent period of rapid growth and expansion has come to an end, for Yeshiva as well as for the rest of higher education in this country. Now, in this period of restraint and consolidation, our emphasis must be on quality more than on quantity, on depth more than on breadth. Yeshiva University knows that it has two great goals: survival and excellence. And one without the other is impossible.

Third, and finally, what Yeshiva reaffirms for itself, and what it must urge upon American society in general, is the love of learning for its own sake—what in the Jewish tradition is known as *torah lishmah*. It is this third principle that I believe must be invoked and implemented if higher education in this country is to be spared the humiliation of trivialization.

———

DESPITE THE ACKNOWLEDGMENT by the bearers of this tradition of the need for vocational training, the theme of learning for its own sake remains a sacred goal—indeed, the preeminent value in all of the tradition. Whereas in the sources, this theme of *torah lishmah* refers exclusively to the study of the sacred literature, it becomes our duty to expand this concept from *torah* to *chokhmah* (secular knowledge), in the spirit of Saadia Gaon and Maimonides, so that the concept of learning for its own sake embraces not only sacred but worldly wisdom as well. For ultimately, as that profound sage and gentle mystic-poet, Rav Kook, taught, "the Holy of Holies comprehends both the holy and the profane."

It is this pursuit of learning for its own sake, without ulterior motives, this unadulterated love of the intellectual enterprise, that American universities must now, more than ever before, seek to inculcate in their students. Universities must, even while providing for career training, return to the original purpose of education, which is the transmission of culture and the advancement of knowledge for its own sake.

We know this in our very bones in this time of crisis. I wish that the policy-makers of our government knew this as well. If the present disengagement of government from support of education and research continues, it will be a long time indeed before America can again win so many Nobel Prizes in one year. Even self-interest, paradoxically, requires disinterested learning. The citizenry and government of America must learn that the cost of education is high, but the cost of ignorance is higher; that man is wedded to his intellect, and if he does not adequately provide for its upkeep, he may find that the alimony is even more onerous . . .

I would be less than candid—indeed, intellectually dishonest—if I stopped here. For what I have said about learning for its own sake does not exhaust the full meaning of *torah lishmah*. Is learning itself, indeed, going to save us? Do we have the right to subscribe to a kind of salvific mythology of education? Can we afford the luxury of a disengaged intellection and singleminded pursuit of research for its own sake in a society that seems to be undergoing a nervous breakdown? Dare we build ivory towers on the shifting sands of social instability and moral confusion?

Contrary to what Socrates taught, the knowledge of the good does not by itself lead to its implementation. Education alone is not the answer to the world's ills. Uganda's Idi Amin may be an ignorant boor, but he was far outclassed by the scientists who performed human experiments in Nazi concentration camps, and by the learned ideological hatchetmen of Stalinist Russia and Maoist China.

Perhaps our crucial problem today is not the absence of education but, on the contrary, its growth without spiritual directions and ethical dimensions. The disparity between, on the one hand, man's technological progress, made possible by his accelerated accumulation of knowledge, and on the other hand, his moral stagnation, goes back to the biblical tale of the Tower of Babel, those primitive builders who knew everything about bricks and mortar but nothing about heart and sensitivity and people. That condition still obtains; time has only exacerbated it—and we are only eight years away from 1984, the target date set for us by that modern prophet of doom, George Orwell . . .

———

THIS DISJUNCTIVENESS BETWEEN technology and morality, between know-how and know-what, between education and ethical deterrence, is reflected in an agonizing existential paradox of contemporary man: a tremendous feeling of self-sufficiency and power, accompanied by a growing awareness of his own triviality, his marginality, his insignificance. The more powerful he becomes, the more impotent he feels and the more self-contempt he develops. The more he takes things in his own hands, the more he comes to believe that he possesses nothing but "things" and *is* nothing but hands. Man *becomes* his own tools—heartless, soulless, pitiless, and ultimately even mindless. The philosopher Santayana wrote that men have come to power who, "having no stomach for the ultimate, burrow themselves downward towards the primitive." Barbarism is in the air, all about us.

But Judaism has taught all of us, Jews and non-Jews alike, that even when learning is pursued for its own sake, intellectually, it must never become an absolute, unrelated to moral dimensions. One must learn in order to do; and even if he learns for the sake of learning itself, it must be the kind of learning which makes him a different and better human being. King Solomon referred to Torah, the repository of Jewish teaching, as "a tree of life to them who take hold of it" (Proverbs 3:18). Note that the famed king (whose wisdom was legendary despite his lack of an earned doctorate) chose as the symbol of learning only one of the two trees that grew in the middle of the Garden of Eden: the Tree of Life and the Tree of Knowledge. Surprisingly, he equated Torah—essentially an intellectual pursuit—with the Tree of Life rather than that of Knowledge. For true Torah is more than knowledge, it is life. True education is more than learning, it is human experience and neighborly love and elemental compassion as well. True intellect leads to more than concepts, it leads to reverence. The mind in its furthest reaches must transcend the cognitive and lead to a humble sense of wonder.

That learning must be more than knowledge, that it must enhance life, was expressed in a startlingly poignant way by the Zohar, source book of Jewish mysticism. The biblical Tree of Knowledge, it taught, possessed within it yet another tree—in Aramaic, *ilana de'mota,* the Tree of Death. When man combines knowledge and life, he is capable of suppressing the Tree of Death. But if he pursues knowledge alone, unconcerned with the Tree of Life—with human compassion and love and gentleness— he thereby releases the noxious Tree of Death in all its many and ugly manifestations.

Our generation has repeated the mistake of Adam and Eve. We have learned nothing from our primordial forebears. We have blithely ignored the Tree of Life, and passionately bitten into the fruit of the Tree of Knowledge. But the fruit is poisoned with the taste of death. Within the contours of the Tree of Knowledge— science and technology and even philosophy and art and literature—there has taken shape the dreaded Tree of Death, with its variety of deadly fruit: nuclear disaster, ecological cataclysm, genetic manipulation for sinister purposes, art and literature at the service of pornography and propaganda. The Zohar's insight is the anticipation of Huxley's *Brave New World*—a paradise turned into a hell.

———

EDUCATION, THEN, must always strive for more than an arrogantly unresponsive quest for information or facts or knowledge alone. It must be concerned with the quality and dignity of human life.

It is this enduring principle which is embodied in Yeshiva University and which I suggest is worthy of consideration by a wider audience: study for its own sake—not corrupted by base motivation and cheap commercialization, but also not study which ignores human dignity and morality and the quality of life; the life of the mind which avoids the extremes of intellectual sacrilege and academic idolatry.

I have no doubt that there are many universities which subscribe to this ideal and strive with might and main to achieve it. Yeshiva University comes to this conclusion by extrapolating from the sources of the millennial tradition which gave birth to it and nourished it.

It is a tribute to my beloved teacher, Dr. Belkin, that he deliberately built this institution according to this ideal pattern. How else explain the Albert Einstein College of Medicine, where pure research on the frontiers of medicine and the biological sciences is wedded to the prevention and conquest of disease and infirmity? How else explain the Rabbi Isaac Elchanan Theological Seminary, where the intricacies of Talmudic learning are integrated into the ideal of Service—to the young and the very old, the poor and the infirm, as well as to the community at large? How else explain the Wurzweiler School of Social Work, where social theory and humane practice go hand in hand? Or the Belfer Graduate School of Science, or the Ferkauf Graduate School of Humanities and Social Sciences, or our new Cardozo School of Law, or the Gruss Institute in Jerusalem, or each of our fifteen graduate and undergraduate divisions?

Yeshiva's obligations to its student body and to the Jewish community are self-evident. Its contributions to its third constituency, America and society at large, should be equally obvious—not only in humanistic education and scientific research and medical and social and psychological community service, but also in the perennially relevant educational and philosophical insights it has culled from a tradition of study and teaching over the past 3500 years.

PERMIT ME TO close with a pledge and a prayer. To my alma mater, Yeshiva University, its faculties, students, and trustees, I pledge all my strength and whatever modest talents and wisdom my Creator has granted me. I well know that no matter what I do for Yeshiva, it will be inadequate to repay the infinite debt of gratitude I owe it for my own education.

To the Jewish community, I pledge that I shall exert whatever influence this office confers upon me to advance the welfare of our folk and our faith, of Israel and Torah, in the special ways Yeshiva has perceived them, the ways of *Torah Umadda*. Let the

word go out from here that Yeshiva is entering a period of renewal; that here is and shall be the greatest home of Torah in the
Diaspora, even while we remain fully abreast of the wisdom of
the world; that we will relate positively, warmly, and support-
ively to the State of Israel with pride and without apology—for
our destinies are intertwined and interlocked.

To the world of scholarship, I pledge that this university will
endeavor, to the limit of its ability, to contribute to the advancement of knowledge and research in all areas of the sciences and
humanities.

To the community at large, I pledge to continue and augment
our policies of communal service in the areas of health and welfare—striving for excellence and compassion even in the face of
political cynicism.

———

To MY DEAR father and mother and my beloved wife and children, I pledge to try my best to bring honor to our family to com-
pensate, however inadequately, for the sacrifices that they must
make to support my role in public life. Without their unquestioning faith in me and unswerving support of me throughout
the years, I would never have been able to undertake these ardu-
ous burdens of communal and educational leadership. And with
this pledge to my utterly devoted parents for whom no sacrifice
was too great for me, and to my always gracious and ever understanding, always patient and ever loving Mindella, and to my
four dear and precious children, who have made our family one
of Torah and song and laughter, go my apologies for the difficulties my career has visited and may yet inflict upon them, and
my gratitude for all they have done for and meant to me
throughout the years.

And finally—a prayer.

The Talmud (*Ber.* 28b) tells us that one of the early sages, R. Ne-
hunya b. Hakanah, used to offer a special prayer when he came
into the *Bet Hamidrash* (academy). On such occasions, he would
recite a prayer for divine guidance. It is his prayer which I now
recite as I am summoned to the presidency of Yeshiva University
at the beginning of this last decade of its first century:

"May it be Thy will, O Lord my
God, that no mishap occur
because of me; that I not
pronounce as acceptable and pure
that which is unacceptable and
impure, and that I not condemn as
wrong that which is right; that I not
err in any matter of principle, and
that my colleagues—trustees,
philanthropists, educators, faculties,
students, administrators,
alumni, the community at large—
have reason to be happy with me.
And may they too never err in any
important matter, and may I be
privileged to be happy and
fulfilled working with them."

So may it be Thy will. Amen.

A MORAL MISSION
FOR COLLEGES

Until about 50 years ago, as has been observed by President James T. Laney of Emory University (*Harvard Magazine* September–October 1985), it was commonly accepted that the university was responsible for offering its students moral guidance. For sure, professors regarded themselves as not only the teachers of knowledge and skills, but also as educational stewards of a special kind of wisdom: the nature of the good life; truth and goodness and beauty; and the value of thought and reflection.

In time, that received wisdom came under progressive assault. Universities began to disseminate knowledge without reference to this ethos. Intellectual inquiry became an autonomous enterprise. The moral mission of higher education was denigrated as too parochial and amateurish and, in the sixties, as being hypocritical, a cover for imperialism. Not long ago, a noted British philosopher observed that philosophers have been trying all this century to get rid of the dreadful idea that philosophy ought to be edifying. If this is true of philosophy, what can one say of other branches of knowledge taught in our ivied halls?

This despair about the larger questions of life having a claim on our attention has filtered down to our lower schools. Only a few weeks ago, New York's Governor Cuomo created a stir when he suggested that values ought to be taught in New York State public schools. Secretary of Education William J. Bennett has repeatedly urged public school leaders to teach moral and ethical subjects that represent a consensus of the community.

It is fairly obvious that this erosion of the teaching of values in our schools is a reflection of a deliberate turn of events in higher education and in the intellectual climate of this country. No wonder that George Bernard Shaw once said of us:

"I doubt if there has been a country in the world's history where men were ashamed of being decent, of being sober, of being well-spoken, of being educated, of being gentle, of being con-

---

This Op-Ed piece appeared in the New York Times *on October 14, 1986. It was adapted from my address at the convocation celebrating the 100th anniversary of Yeshiva University.*

scientious, as in America." As usual, Shaw was exaggerating. But there is an undeniable kernel of truth in his criticism.

Such value-agnosticism in the academic enterprise is, first of all, self-destructive. To be value-neutral means to abandon the very premise on which the search for and transmission of knowledge is pursued. If the university does not teach the moral superiority of education as opposed to ignorance, of reason over impulse, of discipline over slovenliness, of integrity as against cheating—then its very foundations begin to crumble.

An educational system that is amoral in the name of "scientific objectivity," thus devours its own young. They fall prey to a variety of predators that rob them of their confidence in the life of the mind, the significance of culture, the intrinsic worth of knowledge.

Moreover, permitting a generation of students to grow up as ethical illiterates and moral idiots, unprepared to cope with ordinary life experiences, is a declaration of educational bankruptcy. It is no excuse to say that for moral instruction people ought to look to their churches and synagogues. Most of them never show up in churches and synagogues, and too many religious institutions, affected by the prevailing secularism, are afraid to use the words "right" and "wrong."

In addition to allowing academic values and general social-moral principles to come out of the closet and into the lecture hall, we must reassert the existence and value of the spirit. It is my hope that the counsels of sophisticated despair will soon be decanonized in the academy; that our society will learn that there is a larger wisdom that awaits our patient inquiry; that man is a spiritual as well as a biochemical, psychological, political, social, legal and economic animal.

An openness to spiritual dignity does not imply denominationalism. It does mean that the prevalent dogmas of scientific materialism and philosophical despair are not the only points of view worthy of scholarly attention; that belief in the reality of the mind and the existence of the soul does not condemn one as intellectually inferior and scientifically backward; that faith and hope have equal claim on the heart and minds of educated people and deserve to be presented without coercion on the one side or derision on the other; that not all authority is authoritarian, not all morality is moralizing, not all religion is Khomeinism, not all spirituality is illusory.

If the marketplace of ideas cannot find place within itself for the idea that maybe man is more than man, that just possibly there is more to the world than the world, then all the other huckstering that goes on in that pathetically depressed economy may lead to the conclusion that humans are less than human and that there is less to the world than meets the eye.

From the inevitable tensions that arise between fidelity to a sacred tradition and the search for universal knowledge, some general principles emerge which, even if disputed by some, are of value to all: that the pursuit of knowledge is deserving of sacrifice; that knowledge ought to ripen into wisdom; that whether or not one believes that human beings are the purpose of creation, they are certainly the purpose of education; that the effort by man to transcend himself is admirable, even if he often fails; that there are verities that are eternal, though they may be ignored for generations; that men and women possess spiritual dignity that makes them worthy of our respect, our reverence and our dedication to their welfare.

A modern university should not be "spooked" by the specter of sectarianism. It should encourage a moral climate that elicits respect for the human spirit, for honor, for law, for the pursuit of knowledge and love of learning, for the human capacity for self-transcendence.

~ 21 ~

COMMENCEMENT
ADDRESS, 1999

After 22 years of inviting speakers from elsewhere, I decided to deliver the commencement address myself this year, in honor of my classmates who today celebrate the 50th anniversary of their graduation from Yeshiva College in 1949—and, of course, in honor of this year's graduates.

I hope you do not think I am compromising your special celebration by taking note of the jubilee anniversary by me and my classmates. I am reminded of an incident that occurred to one of the most distinguished philosophers of our times, Ludwig Wittgenstein. He was preparing to take a train at the Oxford Depot in England, and was deep in philosophic conversation with two of his most eminent students—Prof. Hart, and a woman whose name I forget. At one point, they noticed to their dismay that the train was beginning to pull away from the station, whereupon they all began to run for the train. The two younger scholastics made it just in time, but the older Prof. Wittgenstein was left behind, huffing and puffing, a look of disappointment written all over him. A kindly lady who noticed the professor's discomfort assured him, "Don't worry, the next train departs in just one hour." "But you don't understand," he replied, "*they* came to see *me* off . . ."

So, we have gathered to see you off, and it may sound to you that we are sending the class of '49 off. But worry not. By the time these ceremonies are over, all of us will have been sent off successfully.

I offer you my apologies as well for being the hapless victims upon whom I am visiting my maudlin recollection and gratuitous advice. My only excuse is that years alone endow one with certain privileges, and that half a century from now you probably will inflict similar punishment upon your students and grandchildren. May you all live that long and longer—in health and happiness.

Delivered at the 68th annual commencement exercises of Yeshiva University on May 26, 1999.

Then vs. Now

What a difference between my graduation and this class! Consider the numbers alone: in 1949, the faculty, both full-time and part-time, consisted of 38 men—no women. And the graduating class counted 38 men—no women. Today, we celebrate the graduation of 2200 men and women, of whom 650 are undergraduates and 836 graduates. And the faculty of the undergraduate colleges consists of 267 men and women, and the total faculty—full-time and part-time—numbers 1015 scholars. Then we had no Kollelim, today—five. Then we had but one building, and today we have five campuses in New York, and one in Israel. So we usher out this foul but fascinating century, so blood-drenched yet so glorious, in far better condition than we were in mid-century.

The cultural differences are also fascinating. Then, as a well-known writer observed, chips were made of wood, hardware was hammers and wrenches, and software wasn't in the dictionary. Grass was something you mowed, Coke was something you drank, crack was something you repaired, and pot was something you cooked in. If you were lucky, life was "swell" or "neat"—not "cool." And we had to ship arms clandestinely to Israel—not fly openly and happily for a year or two of learning there.

Despite all these changes, many things have remained fundamentally the same, especially for Yeshiva students. We then were, and today you are, basically respectful of teachers and parents—with only an occasional aberrant personality to spoil the record. Yeshiva students mostly do have intellectual concerns, despite worry about career and future. They were, and you are, loyal to our great country and passionately committed to the State of Israel—which then was only one year old. Above all, they did, and you do, cherish the wholeness and holiness of the Jewish heritage. And for this we are most grateful.

Independent Thinking

I direct my remarks this morning to the newly minted bachelors concerning two of the things that have not essentially changed in 50 years—and that are in apparent conflict with each other. One is the need for every person to think for himself or herself, and the other is the need for us to speak and act as one, for the sake of unity in the community.

The pressure to conform, the means by which discipline is enforced in society, opposes the need to think critically for oneself. It acts in conjunction with the herd instinct which, as the term implies, reduces humans intellectually and morally to our basic biological level—that of animals. Now, as then, society demands conformity with its values, opinions, styles of dress or speech—in every sphere of human activity.

Nowadays we experience the same tyranny but with a slight twist: apparently we must conform to non-conformity itself. If every kind of dress, however fashionably skimpy or morally repugnant, is acceptable, whether at the office or at home, at the beach or in the house of worship, then everyone must dress different and down. If speech must be laced with "you know" and "like," then, like, everyone, you know, must speak in a kind of like linguistic static . . . If everyone indulges in the collective pursuit of mindless hedonism and permissiveness, then people of decent instincts sheepishly follow suit and disguise their thoughtlessness with phony euphemisms. The tendency to submit to the icons of fashion and accept the *diktat* of the barons of campus or industry by wearing only designer *clothes* may be forgivable. Not so the easy capitulation to designer *ideas*. The darker forces of our culture flourish in the murkiness of the critical intellect.

The Jewish tradition celebrates thinking for yourself. "This is the Torah, and I must study it," is the formal introduction by many of our medieval halakhic authorities to a declaration of critical ideas, as if to say: I must learn Torah as I understand it, with my own mind, even if I have to question the views of eminent predecessors. The giants of the Jewish tradition were notoriously independent thinkers—independent even of their own beloved teachers. R. Asher (1250–1327), of Germany and Spain, instructed us that the Torah demands that we speak the truth and that we not play favorites for any individual. And R. Hayyim Volozhiner (1749–1821) taught us that to differ with a revered teacher is a *milchemet mitzvah*, a holy war, in which we give no quarter to an intellectual opponent because of his station or prestige. These, and others, were eminent halakhic authorities who rejected authoritarianism.

I shall never forget an incident that occurred when I was a student of our late master, Rabbi Joseph B. Soloveitchik, of blessed memory. "The Rav" had been propounding a fascinating interpretation of a Tosafot for about two weeks of *sheiurim*. At the beginning of the third week he called upon me to present the Tosafot and, intimidated as I was, I gave back to him what I thought was a full exposition of his arguments. I was confident that I would receive at least a word of commendation—but got the exact reverse. "What are you telling me? Don't you think I know what I said? I want to hear what *you* think! I want my students to think for themselves and not just to parrot what I say."

A year ago, both India and Pakistan shocked the world and caught its leaders unawares when these two antagonistic countries exploded nuclear devices, throwing the international balance of terror into chaos. Why, it was asked, was the government unprepared for this? The answer: there exists in the CIA an obscure post in charge of "contrarian thinking" whose job it is to argue against conventional wisdom. (There is an established place for contrarian thinking even in the stock market.) This time the intelligence officer in charge failed to think in a contrary manner, resulting in the worst American intelligence debacle in recent years.

I am not advocating that you be perversely different on principle. But when it comes to the important decisions in life, in the quiet of your own mind, be wary of the tyranny of dogmatic opinions and untested ideas and the demand for uniformity of thought. You who have studied Talmud in depth know that of the 526 chapters of the Mishna, only one—*Eizehu mekoman*—contains laws with no controversies, no differing views!

The lesson for us is clear: each of us must have tucked away in some corner of his or her brain a contrarian—or *ipkha mistabra*—compartment whose function it is to seek out views other than those we readily consent to because they swarm around us. The devil's advocate can well turn out to be an angelic emissary. And swimming against the stream may be the best way to avoid drowning.

The Need for Unity

However, we must not ignore the countervailing need—that of unity as an alternative to chaos. Hence, I am not advising you to be non-conformist on principle on every issue. Just as we are rewarded for *derisha*—speaking out—so, the Talmud teaches us, are we rewarded for *perisha*, for keeping silent, for squelching the urge to proclaim and declare. To choose properly and wisely between them, *sekhel*—good judgment—will always remain indispensable. Offsetting the need for individual independence is a crying need to hold together a society whose fabric seems to be unraveling. Kosovo and Serbia, Syria and Lebanon, the Basques in Spain and the Kurds in Turkey—these and many others illustrate the centrifugal tendencies abroad in the world, fueled by hatred and the resurrection of ancient enmities. And here in America, diversity and cultural pluralism overemphasized may yet lead to social incoherence.

For Jews, the situation is even worse. The recent election campaign in Israel highlighted an ethnicism and tribalism that portend a movement from attractive diversity to dangerous fragmentation—a peril already evident, as well, in American-Jewish life. We hurl invectives at each other with the enthusiasm of a manic pitcher in a fateful game of denominational hardball. The Shinui party in Israel spews forth anti-Orthodox hatred bordering on the anti-Semitic. Politicos on *all* sides, both here and there, use inflammatory rhetoric to humiliate even minor dissenters in their own bailiwick. So deep is the fissure that families on opposite sides of the several divides choose not to marry with each other, so that we are faced with the terrifying possibility of breaking up into two peoples, as mere resentment curdles into cold and hard hatred.

How has it come to pass that such virulent factionalism and partisanship, the illegitimate scions of smug self-certainty, are allowed to run amok in the land? We are faced with more than a civil war amongst Jews. We are faced with an *un*-civil war. We seem to be going beyond a *Kulturkampf*, a war of cultures, to adopting a *Kampfkultur*, a culture of war, a battle psychology—against each other. For all our rhetoric about Jewish unity, we are on the precipice, staring into the abyss of communal self-destruction—and there is enough blame for all sides to share in the guilt.

Reconciliation and Tolerance

How then, you may ask, do we reconcile these two apparent opposites—the need to be unified and avoid chaos and anarchy, and the imperative to think for ourselves and allow for contrarian thought?

There are several answers. First, reserve your intellectual independence for the truly important things. Not every issue is worth arguing for, and not everything that comes into your mind should come out of your mouth. And second—speak humbly, without arrogance. No one is an expert on everything.

Third, and more important: Our tradition teaches us that the *tefillin shel rosh*, phylacteries worn on the head, must be exposed, while the *shel yad*—those on the arm—must be covered. So, in the realm of ideas and attitudes whose provenance is in the head, always feel free to air your questions and entertain contrary views. But when it comes to action and working for the common weal, symbolized by the arm, then after decisions are democratically arrived at, all dissident views must be held in abeyance—covered up with dignity—as the majority view prevails. Speak your mind, but act in concert with others.

Hence, group action—yes; group thinking—no. Mutual commitment to ideals—yes; the stifling of all dissenting notions—no. And physical or even verbal violence—no, never.

Finally, there is really no *necessary* conflict between independent thinking and unity of action. Certainly, there are times when fundamental principles must be defended at any cost. There are red lines that may not be crossed. But these lines must be short, few, and well defined. And remember: most often it is not diversity of thought that causes disunity, but the *way in which the views of the disputants are expressed*. If there is a lack of mutual respect, of civility, of *derekh eretz*, of acknowledging the right of others to maintain different opinions, then a crippling disunity is inevitable. If, however, the arguments are conducted in a spirit of tolerance and dignity and a readiness to compromise on tactics and less-than-fundamental matters, unity and amity are certainly attainable. This attitude most often characterized the Talmudic debates throughout its long history. The lack of such comity is what led to the destruction of the Second Temple and Jewish independence two millennia ago.

I am grateful to our Dean Purpura for drawing my attention to something the historian Shelby Foote has pointed out: Before the Civil War, the United States was referred to in the plural—"the United States *are*." After the terrible war that claimed 620,000 lives, the United States became singular—"the United States *is.*" We became one nation.

Tragically, it seems that the opposite grammatical transformation is afflicting us as Jews: we are going from the singular to the plural. And we have got to reverse that trend.

Making a Difference

I address myself specifically to those today graduating from our three undergraduate schools. Your generation dare not wait for blood to be spilled or reputations besmirched or schisms perpetuated in order finally to conclude that unity must be achieved— a unity invigorated by lively debate in mutual respect. As you grow into leadership positions, Yeshiva alumni should not allow it to be said that the Jewish people *are* this or that, only that the Jewish people *is* one thing or the other.

I repeat: there are boundaries beyond which, as men and women of principle, we dare not go without injuring our integrity. But draw those lines with exceeding care. Do not be tempted by easy solutions expressed in slogans and cliches and buzz-words. And do not be seduced by the extremists' meretricious claims to consistency. Life is too complex, too full of ambiguity and paradox, to be captured by facile consistency. Remember that extremism can rip off the thin veneer of civilization and reveal the ugly, venal visage of violence.

Instead, advocate the primacy of Torah with strength but with humility, with conviction but with compassion, with vigor but with reverence—and even with love for those outside your own circle. Sometimes that demands the most courage.

In only a few years, you will be in a position to make a difference. If you, as graduates of Yeshiva College and Stern and Syms, are truly *benei Torah,* you will strive mightily to achieve that modicum of unity. As the Talmud put it so quaintly (*Berakhot* 6a): The Almighty too dons *tefillin,* and in them is inscribed the verse (II Samuel 7:23) "Who is like unto Thy people Israel, one nation on the earth?" One who fails to promote the oneness of Israel, disqualifies the *tefillin* of the Almighty and in effect denies the unity of God.

So, as you leave Yeshiva bear in mind that as the people of Torah we are each of us summoned to our sacred mission to act on behalf of the peace and unity of the community, and all mankind: "Its [the Torah's] ways are the ways of pleasantness, and all its paths lead to peace" (Proverbs 3). Let us exercise our critical intelligence honed by the study of both our sacred texts and the richness of worldly culture. And let us insist that only in an atmosphere of civility and tolerance can vigorous disagreement enhance the welfare of all. This, after all, is of the essence of *Torah Umadda* which Yeshiva stands for and what we have been teaching you—and what I hope you have learned and learned well.

Be proud of your heritage, proud of your alma mater, and proud of our sublime mission. Know that we are proud of you, the fruit of our labors over the years. Remember at all times that in the eyes of the world each of you represents Yeshiva University and all that it stands for. I am confident that you will reflect well upon us.

In the words we proclaim when we finish reading every one of the Five Books of the Torah, as you close the covers on this chapter of your lives, *chazak chazak ve'nit'chazak*—Let us be strong, very strong, and let us strengthen each other.

~ 22 ~

TAKHLIT
Teaching for Lasting Outcomes

I

The Talmud (*Ber.* 17B) uses the term *takhlit*, purpose, in discussing what should be the lasting outcomes of Jewish education. Rava used to say: the *takhlit* of wisdom is *teshuvah* (the transformation of personality) and *ma'asim tovim* (good deeds).

A parallel that immediately comes to mind is the Platonic tripartite soul. Plato divides the soul into three: the cognitive, or intellectual; the affective, or emotional; and the volitional, that which commits a man to action. In medieval Hebrew thought these were known as *sekhel, regesh,* and *ratzon.* What Rava does, is to place the first at the service of the latter two.

In contemporary terms we would say: the purpose of learning, the *takhlit* we seek, is the commitment to Jewish action and to the sense of Jewish identity. Jewish education endeavors to produce, first, young men and women who will live their personal lives in a Jewish manner, and participate fully in the affairs and concerns of the Jewish community, both locally and throughout the world. Second, and even more fundamental, it seeks to secure in them an inner sense of identity as Jews, the transformation of the student's personality from something Jewishly *un*formed to something Jewishly *in*formed: its Judaization. We want the products of all our efforts to be Jewish both inwardly and outwardly, psychologically and practically. Of course, those who have different Jewish commitments will vary in their interpretations of these ideals. From the standpoint of Jewish tradition, it would be necessary for a young person, for instance, to be acquainted with Talmud, to study Torah every day, and to observe *kashrut, Shabbat, taharat hamishpachah.* For others, the standards may be different. But all Jewish edu-

Published by the Jewish Education Committee of New York, this was adapted from an address at the Pedagogic Conference of the Committee in February 1970.

cators can agree on the general rubric of "feeling Jewish" and of acting Jewishly.

II

Now, teachers today—and perhaps it was always that way—are caught in a terrible bind. Economically, socially, culturally, and often politically, they are beset by forces that are usually beyond their control. Because of these various pressures, they sometimes are prone to stultifying discouragement. True, such despair is an all-too-human tendency, but it can corrupt the best of skills and the finest of intentions, and frustrate the *takhlit* to which they aspire.

In seeking to counter this pervasive discouragement, it is well to treat it in the form of three components, three cardinal sins that bedevil and tempt the Jewish teacher, namely: *defeatism, pessimism,* and *cynicism.* These are the three manifestations of despair: in himself or herself and his ability to succeed in his tasks; in his students' ability to "catch on," to be ignited by the spark of Jewishness; and in the very subject matter he endeavors to transmit to them. Against this *yeiush* (despair) the teacher must set his *bitachon* (faith, hope): his confidence in himself and in his ability to perform; in his students and their capacity to respond; and in the rightness of whatever it is that he teaches.

III

Self-confidence and defeatism are, especially in education, self-fulfilling prophecies. If we believe that we are not going to succeed, then indeed we shall not succeed. If we believe that we will, then most probably we will. Of course, by the nature of things Jewish educators are confronted by certain stubborn and irreducible facts that cannot be overcome by mere willpower or wished out of existence by faith. But there are many aspects of the situation that are malleable.

Jewish teachers, *qua* Jewish teachers, have no choice but to commit their hearts and minds, their efforts and faith, to the proposition that they are going to succeed. They have a special moral *obligation* to succeed. We are commanded, as the Israelis say, by "General *Ein Bererah*" (No Alternative), because it is primarily *our* task to call a halt to the cultural-spiritual geno-suicide that threatens the existence of the Jewish community and tradition in the United States.

Prof. Dov Sadan of the Hebrew University, one of the world's most eminent authorities on Hebrew and Yiddish literature and folklore, who has in the course of his career written over 40 major books and hundreds of articles, tells the following about his early youth in a small town in Galicia in explanation of his literary productivity. Throughout his childhood, his father kept reminding him that when his mother was about to give birth, she took ill, and the doctor presented her with a very cruel choice: either the baby must die in order that she might live, or if she wanted the baby to live, she would have to die. She chose the second alternative, and died as she delivered the child—Dov Sadan. "So," his father would often remind him, "for the rest of your life you have got to work not only for yourself, but bear the responsibility as well for living for your mother and for all the children she might have had, had she chosen to live at the expense of your life." That awareness—of having to create and produce not only for himself but for many others—is what gave him that enormous, vital energy to produce what he did.

It is a similar awareness that weighs heavily on the conscience of the Jewish teacher. If he is an authentic Jewish teacher, he is hounded into success by the ghosts of martyred colleagues whose burdens he must now assume. He has got to teach as well for three million of today's Jewish community of Eastern Europe who, if not for their tragic fate, would have been the great fountainhead and resource for Jewish education in America. He has got to teach for those millions of American Jews who have opted for assimilation, fading out of the Jewish community. He must produce, must succeed; he has no choice, no moral alternative.

In addition to a sense of moral obligation, a realistic and penetrating view of our contemporary predicament reveals three factors that augur well for the success of Jewish educators. The first of these is the cultural revolution. For some reason that is quite understandable but not always excusable, we are accustomed to view all change as harmful. Hence many of us greet the present socio-cultural turbulence with assorted jeremiads. We fear it, we bemoan it, we are outraged by it. But we may be overreacting. It is good to remember that we were always in deep trouble with the established social order against which youth is rebelling. The "Establishment," with which we sometimes identify emotionally, was always inimical to the most sacred values and cherished interests of Jews and Jewish educators. The present chaotic situation represents a tremor of revulsion against the whole Western self, against the self-indulgent, philistinic existence of the parents of many of today's students. That self and that existence were never overly sympathetic to what Judaism and Torah have had to teach. They forced Jewish educators into an apologetic, defensive, and compromising pattern that was alien to them. We therefore ought to recognize in these new social convulsions that have gripped all of society not only a danger, but also the possibilities of opportunity. As Western civilization, in the form we have known it, approaches its moment of truth, what we have to say, if we say it articulately and honestly, may get us a better hearing.

We have unwittingly ignored a powerful ally for Jewish education in the rebelliousness of contemporary youth. Actually, we have taken advantage of it to some extent, but only semi-consciously, and without defining it. There are many students now at Stern College for Women and the James Striar School of Yeshiva University, and probably in corresponding Jewish schools elsewhere, who have come from almost totally non-Jewish Jewish backgrounds, and whose original motivation was a rebellion against their parents. They came because someone was able to harness these enormous energies that have been released in our times. There was a time when a young person rejected parents and, along with them, God and Jewish tradition and affiliation. Today too some of them reject their parents and the god of these parents: materialism and hedonism—all the values which have been the bane of our existence and against which we have always fought. Hence, even while we may be losing many of our children from Judaism, we have got to make a conscious effort to attract those who are beginning to question the premises of their parents' lives.

A second promising element in society's new situation is the Black Revolution: We have told ourselves, these past several decades, that America had come of age in accepting cultural pluralism, and that therefore Jews have the right and even the socio-cultural duty to enhance and develop their own religious and cultural patterns and thus preserve the integrity of their people and way of life. But that was just an illusion—pleasant, but dangerous. Cultural pluralism was really an empty slogan, because all along it was really the "melting pot" which effectively prevailed as the dominant social mechanism, while cultural pluralism was just talked about. But if there is anything that can transform cultural pluralism from a wish into a reality in this country, it is the Black Revolution. What the Black man is saying is, "I am Black. I can't pass as White and in fact, I don't want to. I want my identity to be recognized as legitimate in this country. I want to live my own culture. I don't want to be patronized, I don't want the White man's condescension. I want to be accepted for what I am, as I am." If the Black man can succeed, then Judaism will prosper that much more, because it will mean that practicing Jews will be accepted for themselves, as themselves, without having to apologize for their existence. It is this passionate assertion of Black identity that inspires many of the radical Jewish groups that are now beginning to express themselves as Jewish today, overseas as well as in America. Many of these young Jewish radicals, like their Black contemporaries, are discovering their own identity and asserting their unapologetic right to be Jewish, not necessarily because of any ideological or religious commitment, but on an even more fundamental psychological level.

The third favorable element is the State of Israel. Of course, the State has been with us for a whole generation. The troubling thing is that it has not been sufficiently exploited these past twenty years. It is amazing how matter-of-factly our own children accept the fact of Israel. The inescapable conclusion is that it is our very own fault. In our desire, instinctual rather than conscious, to shield our children from the Holocaust horrors to which we were exposed, we never really told them the story. And unless one has experienced the personal threat of the Holocaust, even vicariously by study and reading, one can never appreciate what the State of Israel really means. No matter what our own ideological orientation as to the relationship between the Holocaust and Israel, they must always be coupled pedagogically, in order for young people to understand in the depths of their being that Israel is something ineffably vital to them as well as to us, and that it must never be taken for granted.

IV

In addition to confidence in what teachers can do as teachers, they have got to have faith in their students' capacity to be moved.

The following paragraph has a contemporary ring to it:

> Our present generation is a wonderful one, a generation that is altogether amazing. It is difficult to find another like it in all our history. It consists of many opposites, light and darkness coexisting in it. It is lowly and despicable, yet elevated and lofty; altogether guilty—and altogether innocent! It is a strange generation: mischievous and wild, yet exalted and noble . . . You find, on the one hand, increasing *chutzpah,* the son unashamed before his father, youngsters insulting their elders; and on the other hand—charity, decency, justice, and compassion gaining strength, idealistic and intellectual power breaking out and ascending. A generation of this kind, ready to meet death bravely because of goals it considers worthy, often solely on account of inner feelings of righteousness and justice, cannot be considered lowly, even if its goals are all wrong.

Thus spake Rav Kook, in his *Chazon Ha-Geulah,* some five decades ago. So, today's "crazy, mixed-up kids" who are carried away by noble, idealistic intentions are a new phenomenon compared to their parents' generation, but not compared to that of Rav Kook's contemporaries. Certainly there are differences between today's youth and the one of some fifty years ago. Their generation had abandoned Judaism, but at least had a fierce ethnic-national identity. Rav Kook, of course, was speaking about the *chalutzim* in Palestine. But nevertheless, Rav Kook taught, wherever you find idealistic fervor, there will you find an opportunity for Torah. And much of today's youth *is* idealistic; indeed, if such a thing is possible, they are in some ways *too* idealistic. A prominent social philosopher has attributed the negative features of the youthful cultural revolution to its perfectionism which, powered by idealistic zeal and invariably leading to disillusionment, pushes them over the brink to moral nihilism. But the process can be halted midway and utilized constructively, if we are sympathetic and wise, if we listen to them, if we appreciate their criticism without being patronizingly masochistic, if we consider their protest without either dismissing it or swallowing it uncritically.

Another important element in this new spirit that inspires a sense of optimism with regard to this generation's students, is that it is not exclusively vocation-oriented, as was the last generation. Their parents are sufficiently well-to-do for them not to have to worry about how to make money. It no longer interests them that much. They can afford to be repelled by the whole present educational system which is geared to teach them how to make a living instead of how to live. On a certain level, this re-orientation holds the promise of a genuine epistemological revolution.

Why is this important for Jewish education? For a long time we were caught on the horns of what might be called the pragmatic dilemma. Jewish learning seemed totally "irrelevant" to the career goals which society considered the purpose of all education. Of what earthly use could the history of the Maccabees or the debates of *Bava Metzia* be to a budding lawyer or doctor? Hence that tired retort offered by parents to appeals to give their children a Jewish education: "I don't want my son to be a Rabbi." In truth, while it hit Jewish educators hardest, they were not the only victims of this educational vocationalism. It was a problem for the teacher of Shakespeare and Chaucer and world history as well. "So what?" was the prematurely hard-headed challenge little boys and girls flung at teachers who were condemned to trivialization and obsolescence because their courses could not, at the lowest level, get them a better job or, at the highest, get them into a graduate school or discover the cure for cancer. But that vulgar pragmatism is now increasingly being brought into question. And Jewish education, which was afflicted much more than general education, may now be able to emerge in a new light, unhampered by this handicap. Judaism, with its insistence upon *Torah lishmah*, is now presented with new opportunities.

Of course, this does not mean that children in Hebrew schools at any level are ready to study *Torah lishmah* in its most ideal form. Scholarship-for-its-own-sake is not by any means triumphant. Indeed, one of the major complaints of the campus rebels is that so much scholarship is "irrelevant" to their lives.

Now, that word "relevance" has been abused of late. It has been undone by popularity. "Relevance" has become a sacred

232 | SEVENTY FACES

cow that has been milked of all its real meaning and importance. What has been overlooked is that a certain amount of "irrelevance" is always relevant in teaching culture, let alone religion.

Nevertheless, despite these strictures, we must accommodate our teaching to these rightful demands for relevance to the student's spiritual, psychological, and cultural problems and concerns. Certainly, this is far more legitimate and exciting than the vocational challenge. The relevance that we ought to strive for is contained in the Talmudic dictum mentioned at the outset:

Education ("wisdom") must be related to the two elements of *maasim tovim* and *teshuvah*.

Study must be made relevant, first, to *maasim tovim*, or ethical and social idealism. This particular relevance of Jewish teaching ought to be explicated quite early, before our students reach their teens and are inspired by social idealism from the outside world and the youth culture, and then discover that their teachers lamely confirm it. Judaism should not be put in the position of "me too" in the realm of social justice. Students at Jewish schools must know that, as the Sages put it, "the Torah bespeaks generosity and kindness from beginning to end," and that the outside world is merely confirming now what is already knowable from Jewish sources. Passover and Hanukkah as expressions of the ideals of freedom and self-determination are cliches by now, and have probably been overdone or at least overstated. But there are other examples of Jewish concepts and institutions that are equally exciting and germane. *Shabbat,* as the sense of freedom from the tyranny of technology, is but one illustration. Young people are becoming progressively more conscious and resentful of the hold that technology has on the spirit of man and its encroachment on our freedom. *Shabbat,* specifically in its halakhic formulation, gives man the opportunity one day of the week to liberate himself from depersonalization by technology, to live as a human being amongst human beings, without this constant and slavish reliance on the various mechanical and electronic implements that have given us convenience at the expense of anomie, alienation, and a collective schizoid apathy. Young people, who are so much more sensitive than their elders to the mixed blessings of technology, can appreciate *Shabbat* as a summons to responsibility for the welfare of Nature, which we have not only tamed but very nearly wrecked; and as a day when man speaks to man, when there is genuine dialogue, because we appear as ourselves without the mechanical props which disguise and stifle us all the rest of the week.

Kashrut too may be taught in a "relevant" manner. (An ideal conjecture: what can be more in tune with the times than "selling" *kashrut* as "Jewish soul food"? Today no less than in antiquity, a case can be made for it as a cultural means of ethnic identity.) The newest concern of the young liberal world is the mindless way in which we are poisoning life on this planet by interfering with the basic ecology of the planet. By our single-minded pursuit of our technological, commercial, and pecuniary interests, we have risked an end to all human life. Only a few years ago, we referred to such ideals as "the reverence for life," borrowing Schweitzer's phrase. But what is *kashrut* if not an expression of the Jewish reverence for life? It can be viewed not as a completely new, Sinaitic prohibitive legislation, but as a partial reversion to the original vegetarianism of the Torah. Adam was forbidden to eat animal meat. It was permitted only as a concession to Noah. At Sinai, as part of our commission as "a holy people," sensitive to the sanctity of life, we were commanded to reaccept a partial vegetarianism. Even as difficult a commandment as *shaatnez* can be treated in this manner. It expresses symbolically a reverence for the integrity of the original species of creation, thus declaring as immoral the overexposure to radioactivity or pesticides, etc., which can cause mutations, and thus raise the specter of the disappearance of whole species. *Shaatnez* is an affirmation of man's respect for the universe, for the integrity of creation, by keeping the separate species apart.

A note of caution must be sounded, however, in this effort to relate the teaching of Judaism to social idealism or *ma'asim tovim*. First, the *mitzvah* must be the starting point, only afterwards proceeding to the contemporary ideal. Otherwise, we run the risk of trivializing Torah, for as soon as a contemporary concern has passed out of fashion, the "relevant" *mitzvah* may suffer the same fate. Second, related to this, we must teach it as a religious norm and beware of the danger of oversecularization.

The second element in the effort to make Jewish learning relevant to Jewish students may be termed, for the sake of the rubric, *teshuvah*: Judaism as an experience, principally a religious experience. The current cultural mood is favorably inclined to a reaffirmation of the validity of feelings, of subjectivity, of *regesh*—long banished in today's technopolitan "Secular City." Today, however, we are confronted by a romantic movement which has rediscovered the affective side of human personality. This obligates teachers too to loosen up and moderate their rationalistic fixations without necessarily abandoning reason altogether. Intellection and ratiocination, for all their transcendent value, must not degenerate into a "hangup." The emerging society of the young and the youthful is experiencing a new search for roots and for experience—even for the ecstatic experience—and it must be both respected and encouraged.

The current adult generation had already begun to feel this spiritual restlessness, this dissatisfaction with the cold scientific *Weltanschauung* and faith in technological "progress" which failed to heal the fractured quality of life, the dim awareness of the incoherency of all our existence. We have seen signs of its expression in what may be called a spiritually neurotic manner. Thus, the search for antiques, really certified junk, is a way of recovering roots, some linkage with the past, with tradition. Just below the level of consciousness, we have become aware of the depressing fact that the shiny new exteriors in which we live cover up a great inner vacuum, a gaping emptiness, a frightening nothingness that is discontinuous with the past, that promises no future, and that threatens to expose the sham of the present. So we express our search for past, for roots, for inherited meaning neurotically—old furniture and trinkets. Even more indicative of our inner sickness is that fashionable new—really ancient—madness: astrology. Some very "in" people no longer consult their stockbrokers, ministers, or psychoanalysts. They consult their astrologers. More seriously and respectably, a distinguished (Christian) sociologist, Peter L. Berger (*A Rumor of Angels*) speaks of the search for the signals of transcendence, the supernatural, in daily life. What was once dismissed as religious fiction is coming into a new prominence even in sophisticated circles.

With our children, the need and desire to fill the inner void which the previous generation has bequeathed to them, often latches on to fruitless and dangerous goals: the psychedelic experience, pot, heroin, LSD. In a remarkable reversal of the old Marxist formula, opiate is fast becoming the religion of the masses. But there is a genuine spiritual underside to this drug culture: the striving for experience, for *regesh*. It now becomes the task of Jewish educators to satisfy that need and provide them with what they seek from within Judaism, which possesses untapped reservoirs of genuinely elevating and "exciting" experience—as well as doctrine and thought. Even if we agree that the current popularity of "mysticism" and "Hasidism" in the circles of the Jewish young is really a fad, still such fads do tell us something important. They are symptomatic of a deep malaise and an even deeper spiritual hunger. To meet this new situation, we in Jewish education must rid ourselves of our own rationalistic prejudices and liberate ourselves of our own self-images as intellectuals, misunderstood philosophers, frustrated professors. We must see ourselves again as whole human beings, as sentient beings who must speak and communicate with students not only by skills and techniques and not only through ideas, but through real, genuine experience and emotion. We must kindle the spark of Jewish feeling in ourselves if we are to communicate successfully with this segment of the rising generation. We have got to add more *drama*, not dramatics, to the material that we teach—and even to our own selves. There has got to be more *devekut*, more heart, and less inhibition and bashfulness in demonstrating to our students our own capacity for religious experience. There has got to be more emphasis on the ecstatic and less on the aesthetic, even a willingness to risk and sacrifice the aesthetic in favor of effective, inspired living. Judaism, as my distinguished teacher, Rabbi Joseph B. Soloveitchik, has said, has not only a *masorah* of ideas, but one of *regesh* as well, a tradition of experience and affective orientation. In our desiccated, uninspired, and disingenuous age, we have almost abandoned that *masorah* and we must now begin to rediscover it.

Using *Shabbat* again as an example of a new direction or emphasis, this would mean that in addition to teaching laws and customs and literature and folklore and social ideals of *Shabbat*, our primary emphasis has got to be communicating, non-verbally as well as verbally, *Shabbat* itself as an *experience* here and now. This means teaching not *about Shabbat*, but living *Shabbat* itself. There must be a cooperative venture of teacher and students in searching in *Shabbat* for Berger's "signals of transcendence"—what we in our *Zemirot* call *me'ein olam ha-ba*—a foretaste of Eternity. That means that teachers have got to learn how to sing

Zemirot again. I intend by this not better choral groups or fine, cultured, liturgical music conducted by a competent cantor, but singing from the soul, with a feeling of abandon, including Hasidic dancing—all without shyness. At Yeshiva University, notable successes have been scored with such ten-day seminars, geared primarily to young people who come from almost totally non-traditional backgrounds. What inspires them is not the intellectual but the experiential: they manage to throw themselves into *Shabbat* with song and dance. We "turn them on" and that gives us at least a fighting chance.

Of course, it is a difficult assignment for those of us in or approaching or past middle age, who have grown up in a more sedate and solemn atmosphere than that of the New Romanticism. But the time has come to rethink the problem of Jewish schools with an eye to creating the optimum conditions for this environmental-affective approach, instead of the present direct-informational orientation. The most radical of several alternatives is, perhaps, the idea of the boarding school, where it is possible to create an almost totally controlled environment, as some out-of-town Yeshivot now do. However, this will always remain a solution for the chosen few, never for the masses. Less radically, we might think of including *Shabbat* as a major part of the school program and curriculum. Saturday would become a day without writing and with no formal instruction or use of textbooks, but a day of *actually* experiencing and living what we otherwise teach them *about*. Such an experiment is foredoomed unless the group is first "seeded" with a few inspired people—pupils or faculty—who can create and sustain the mood. Similarly, the program of the school should be broadened to include summer camp and special youth seminars during winter vacation and towards the end of the summer. These should be regarded not as incidental supplements, but as basic parts of the Hebrew school and day school curriculum. Experience thus far with such techniques—as supplementary to rather than part of the program—is unusually promising. We have discovered that youngsters are willing to have their deepest emotions engaged—and it is exhilarating. When they later enroll in our formal schools—at the secondary and university level—they experience an understandable emotional let-down. But soon the affective appetite is transmuted into an intellectual hunger and these same young people then complain that our curriculum is not strong enough, that they are not getting enough Jewish information, that they want to learn more.

V

Finally, what must be overcome is an externally induced cynicism that sometimes infects the Jewish teacher, against his or her better judgment. For effective teaching and the attainment of the *takhlit*, genuine personal belief in the subject taught is a *conditio sina qua non*. It is good to remember that with all our justifiable efforts at professionalizing Jewish education, Jewish teaching is not really a profession. It is a mission. In a profession, it is sufficient to show skill and produce results even while remaining essentially impersonal to the subject. A mission, however, implies passionate commitment and reverence for what and for whom you are teaching. If Jewish teaching is only a profession, then I may mold and shape and select from my subject at will. But if it is a mission, I may highlight, I may emphasize, but I may never truncate and betray what I am teaching.

This is, in other words, a plea for more honesty and less apologetics for Judaism. It is time to let Judaism, our material, speak for itself. For a long time now Judaism, through the medium of Jewish educators, both rabbis and school teachers, has been presented in this country as a confirmation of all the major presuppositions and prejudices of Western civilization. Consciously or unconsciously, we have acted as if we wanted to be more Western than the West. Judaism, according to the version preached and taught these last several generations, has been made to appear more liberal, more patriotic, more pro-integration, more full of "happiness" (whatever that means), and more of whatever the "Liberal Establishment" espoused at the time, than anything else that Western civilization had to offer. Teachers became brokers for this form of acculturation.

The effort to identify Judaism with "happiness" is a case in point. To a generation that blinded itself to the misery abounding all through life, and that aspired "to be happy" and secure, Judaism was distorted into just such an image. Thus, the attempt by some people to project Judaism as such a happy thing that it even looks with favor on sexual permissiveness. Hucksters of pseudo-liberalism in Jewish dress tried to sell us what Rollo May

(*Love and Will*) has called "the new puritanism": inhibitions = ill health = sin. Hence, permissiveness = fun = happiness = a *mitzvah*. Less drastically, but quite revealing, several years ago one of our "defense agencies" published a book designed to introduce Judaism to the Gentile world. Turning from page to page, one was amazed to discover that "Judaism" was one big party, a funthing. Everything was happy. Always. Pesah was joy, Shabbat was fun, Shavuot was exciting. Then one came to Tisha Be'Av— and that too was a "happy day" for some reason that still eludes my most persistent theological inquisitiveness. The image of the Jew emerged as someone who is a prematurely senile semi-idiot. We are always happy—in this post-Auschwitz era . . . Our apologetic impulses, benevolent as they are, thus caused us to miss the heart of Judaism. We failed to transmit the sense of the tragic, as well as joy, the pathos, a sense of the presence of the demonic which we should certainly have learned from the Holocaust.

The same obsolescence has returned to haunt us like a counterfeit coin with regard to other apologetic dogma as well. "Patriotism" has become questionable; it is "square" and, for some, "dishonest." Integration has been preached not as a pragmatic and fair solution to a social problem, but as the essence of all Judaism—as if it would have been sufficient had Torah been given for this alone. What will happen if most blacks and white liberals eventually agree with the Black Power movement and ask not for integration, but for separate but dignified and equal treatment? What does "Judaism" say then about the problem?

Quite frankly, if Judaism will continue to be taught as that which invariably confirms all the prejudices and value judgments of our enlightened and liberal segment of society, then who needs us? And who needs Judaism? The only responsible alternative is to be humble and present Judaism, if necessary, as an alternative to the dogmas of society. We must allow Judaism to speak for itself—and show that we believe in it even when it is unpopular. We must have the confidence to stick by it and know that ultimately it will prevail, even if it must go into eclipse for a while. Even while showing Judaism's relevance to the new generation's social idealism and quest for experience, we have got to have the elemental honesty to resist cultural pressure and oppose what we consider wrong from a Jewish point of view. For instance, we must tell our students clearly what the sexual morality of Judaism is—even if we know that their parents violate it and that they too are probably going to violate it. Honesty requires of us to acquaint our students with the fundamental supernaturalism of Judaism, even for those who are not willing to accept it. Even those whose attachment to Jewishness is primarily cultural rather than religious, must possess the integrity to acknowledge and teach that classical Judaism is, as the late Rabbi Maimon once said, not *kultura* but *kol Torah*. "Culture" alone cannot neutralize the countervailing pressures in our society. Perhaps such bald honesty will alienate many from Judaism and even from the synagogue and community. But it is worth the risk. I would rather hold the few honestly than the many under false pretenses. Jewish education has to aim, largely, to *maladjust* children to those premises and principles of the world at large that are at odds with Judaism's great ideals of righteousness and judgment and man's and Israel's responsibility before God.

VI

To summarize: teaching for *takhlit*, for lasting results, requires of teachers to renew their confidence in themselves; to reestablish their faith in their students; and to strengthen their belief in what they teach, without fear of becoming dissenters by presenting Judaism as an alternative.

The difference between teaching for lasting results and teaching without permanent effect is revealed in a key verse in II Kings 12:3. "And Jehoash did that which was right in the eyes of the Lord all his days wherein Jehoiada the High Priest instructed him." The term "all *his* days," according to one commentary, refers to Jehoiada, for later in life, after Jehoiada departed, Jehoash turned away from the right way. Why so? Malbim briefly points to the word *horahu*, translated as "instructed him," and comments on its contrast to *limdehu*, "taught him."

The difference lies in this: *horahu* means to point in a certain direction. *Limdehu* derives from *malmad*, the harness one places on cattle and which keeps them going in the right direction. Pointing out the right way is a benevolent act—but it is fairly impersonal, and does not last; when the "pointer" has left, the instructed may very well lose his way again. That is what happened to Jehoash after Jehoiada died. But harnessing—that is teaching in its profoundest sense, that is communication with intimacy of personal contact and, moreover, the "harnessed" goes straight even after the teacher has left. He who practices *horahu* may well experience eventual frustration. The one who engages in *limdehu* will be teaching for lasting results.

It is time for us, as Jewish teachers, to stop being *morim* and return to the honorable profession of being *melamdim*.

It is time for us to strive for lasting results as an act of *imitatio Dei*, for He too is a *melamed*—a teacher: *ha-melamed Torah le'ammo Yisrael*. "He teaches Torah to His people Israel."

~ 23 ~

FOUR
MYTHS

I concede, at the outset, that I have many more questions than answers, and that contemplation of the subject assigned to me leaves me more puzzled than enlightened. At the beginning of this century, Ambrose Bierce defined "education" as "that which discloses to the wise and disguises from the foolish their lack of understanding." The truth in that statement does not diminish with age. In an effort to avoid playing the fool, I shall make no pretense to greater understanding than I possess. I shall bear in mind what Alfred North Whitehead said after hearing Lord Bertrand Russell lecture on quantum theory at Harvard: "I congratulate Lord Russell for leaving the vast darkness of the subject unobscured."

Permit me to do just that: to respect the "vast darkness" of the subject, to make no effort to unravel the fundamental mystery that lies at the heart of the educative process and the teacher-student relationship. I shall merely endeavor to remove some of the obscurity covering the darkness and the mystery by discussing four myths or half-truths that have afflicted us this past half-century. Perceptive teachers recognize these sanctified untruths for what they are; however, as long as they remain unidentified they impair the work of the Jewish educator—and have done so these past 50 years and more.

MYTH NO. 1: "Children Don't Want to Learn." This unspoken assumption imposes an obvious handicap upon the teacher. But it does not stand up under criticism.

On a general, theoretical level, it is true that there is a natural resistance to school and learning. The Sages, commenting upon the reluctance of Israel to stay on at Sinai after the Revelation, compared the Israelites to "a child fleeing from school." The aversion of children to learning is no new phenomenon. Yet, that

This appeared in Jewish Education *Spring 1977 under the title,* "The Jewish Educator and Jewish Education: Four Myths", *and was based on a lecture at the National Commission for Jewish Education Conference.*

can hardly be the whole story. It may be as much a reflection on the school system in the days of the Sages as an expression of some universal, innate anti-intellectualism. At any rate, this tendency is counterbalanced by a healthy and powerful curiosity, allied to a quest for meaningfulness and self-transcendence. I suggest an analogy from Hasidic literature. R. Shneur Zalman of Liadi teaches, in his *Tanya*, that the Jewish soul possesses an *ahavah tiv'it u-mesuteret*, an inborn and concealed love of God. Man is a *Homo religiosus*, a natural lover of God, but that love is an undeveloped talent which we are called upon to express or "reveal." What is true for *ahavat ha-Shem* is true for *ahavat ha-Torah*: there is an innate but undeveloped love of learning, and it is the task of the educator to "reveal" this hidden love.

This myth was more true than untrue at the beginning of this jubilee, when secularism reigned unchallenged and Judaism was treated with something worse than hostility—namely, apathy and indifference. But today it is more fiction than fact. I believe that the Counter-Culture has had a lasting effect on the perception of Americans. It has altered our epistemological presuppositions. It has caused us to question our questions and doubt our doubts, and has left in its wake a residue of thirst for that which is suprarational, for that which transcends our senses, our logic, and our contrived technologies. It is a thirst which can be slaked either with fetid waters from the putrid sewers of contemporary culture—or by the pellucid "living waters" of Torah and its transcendent message. We are now in possession of a great opportunity, such as we have not had in close to fifty years.

MYTH NO. 2: "He Who Can, Does. He Who Cannot, Teaches."

This Shavian put-down is a piece of devastating cynicism that has had an incalculable effect in eroding the self-image of a noble profession. It has confirmed the worst fears of self-abnegating educators about their vocation—that it is the last resort for incompetents, ne'er-do-wells, and malcontents.

This self-deprecation is largely a self-fulfilling prophecy, abetted by the hitherto inexorable expansion of economic opportunity, the changing perceptions of status, and the stubborn facts of materialism in a technological and urban culture. With Jews, this is aggravated by an assimilationism which considers the whole Jewish enterprise as irrelevant, and teachers therefore superfluous.

Certainly in classical Jewish life, teaching had status—but no money. The lack of financial advantage always posed a problem that evoked many attempted solutions—but the status of the *talmid chakham* and the teacher remained unaffected. It is only in the modern age, with its hedonism and materialism, that status became linked to money, and the absence of the latter caused a diminution of the former.

As a result, we are left with a situation today which I do not believe is significantly different from that of fifty years ago: education attracts the best and the worst. The best—the most idealistic, the most committed, the most principled. And the worst too— those who couldn't make it in pre-med or pre-law, those who didn't have fathers or fathers-in-law with a family business. (For whatever the consolation is worth, the situation is worse in the Rabbinate, and I believe it is improving in teaching.)

The task of undoing this myth is the responsibility of educators—the best of them. There must, of course, be constant pressure to improve material means. But there must be a deliberate effort to avoid submitting to society's insidious confusion of salary and status. Propaganda for the recruitment of the potential teachers of tomorrow must originate with teachers themselves, not only schools, philanthropists, and Federations. And it must be proved by a collective pride in our sacred profession.

MYTH NO. 3: "Our Problem Is the Lack of New Techniques."

Supposedly, Jewish education is lagging behind general education because we are behind in research, in technology, and in applying new methods. The *bête noire* is usually some part of the "Establishment"—the Boards of Jewish Education, the Federations, the wealthy philanthropists, the universities.

However, while I certainly do not gainsay the value of technique and technology and methods, this is more a counsel of despair than the consequence of sober analysis. It is a cop-out. Undoubtedly, certain techniques are helpful: some methods are more effective than others. But these cannot substitute for the personal, human encounter in the substantive, non-skill teaching whereby Judaism is transmitted from generation to generation. Perhaps here is the most important difference between general education and religious, especially Jewish, education: Jewish education is more than cognitive.

In a remarkable metaphor, the Zohar teaches that within the Tree of Knowledge of Good and Evil there existed an *ilana de'mota* a Tree of Death. Hence, when Adam ate the forbidden fruit of the Tree of Knowledge, he and his descendants after him were sentenced to mortality. But if so, how can man avoid having the fruit of his hard-earned knowledge lead to death? Only when knowledge is tasted in conjunction with the Tree of Life. And Tree of Life is the symbol of Torah—"It is a tree of life to them that grasp it, and of them that uphold it everyone is rendered happy" (Prov. 3:17).

Science and technology in contemporary life have taught us with cataclysmic finality that knowledge is power—but that it is not necessarily virtue; that, contrary to Socrates, *knowing* the good does not perforce lead to *doing* the good. The Tree of Knowledge encloses a Tree of Death.

The Torah tradition has always avoided, therefore, an interpretation of Torah study that would justify a theory of "knowledge for knowledge's sake." Even the Lithuanian Mitnagdic teachers, who emphasized the cognitive moment in the precept of *talmud torah*, saw Torah as an organum which was fundamentally spiritual, only that the key, the way, was primarily cognitive and intellectual.

Hence, the Jewish educator must be more than a Jewish scholar, though certainly that is indispensable. And he must be more than a Jewish scholar who possesses effective educational techniques. Above all, he must be a complete Jew, a complete human being—a *mensch*.

Here is where the most intense efforts must be made in the attempt to improve the efficacy of the educator and the state of the art—here, in the personality and development of the educator himself, and not primarily in the gadgets, devices, and methodology that mediate between teacher and student.

MYTH NO. 4: "We're Fighting a Losing Battle."

I refer here not to the occasional, fitful bout of pessimism that seizes the most sanguine of us every now and then, but rather to the seasoned conclusion that Judaism has no future in this country, that we are at best postponing the inevitable quietus for another few years. This is the most pernicious and baneful myth of all, one that insinuates itself slowly into the minds and hearts of the careless and the faithless. It was, I feel, the myth most responsible for the debacle of Jewish education early in the history of the American Jewish community.

No one can put his heart into a failing business, and what is Jewish education without heart? One who has no doubt that "we're fighting a losing battle," and considers himself/herself a person of integrity, had best look for a more promising occupation.

But how can the Jewish educator, surveying the often bleak scene both in this country and elsewhere, even in Israel, avoid generalizing about the future of the enterprise to which he is devoting his life—and coming to a sad conclusion?

First, by a quick glance back at the past, when it was often feared that there would be no future. Now, I am not a sociologist, and I am neither a futurist (the sophisticated contemporary term for a prophet) nor the son of a futurist, but an amateur historian who has learned something about jeremiads and gloomy predictions by the best of us—even in pre-Enlightenment days. Consider this: in the days of the Prophets, the worshippers of Baal predominated and the devotees of One God were a persecuted minority in Israel—and so Elijah was at the brink of despair. To offer some other examples haphazardly, and with disdain for chronology: Maimonides, in a letter to the "Sages of Lunel," expressed the nagging fear that they were the last Jewish scholars left in the world—this, before Nahmanides and R. Asher in Spain and the Tosafists in Germany and France. Closer to our own day, the famous head of the Yeshiva of Volozhin, R. Naftali Zevi Yehudah Berlin (known as "the Netziv," in his responsa, *Meshiv Davar*, No. 44), had to assure East European scholars that theirs is not the worst generation in history. So, let there be no easy slide into despair. We are summoned to the historical perspective which gives us far more reason for hopefulness. (One thinks of the Israeli who announced that he was an optimist, and upon being challenged as to why, if that were the case, he looked so worried, answered, "Do you think it is so easy to be an optimist?")

Second, such defeatism in what sociologists have called the "cognitive minority" is one of the ways that the majority culture seeks to overwhelm and undermine non-conformists and enforce a cultural homogeneity upon society. If I were to express this same thought aggadically, I would find it ready-made for me in the Talmud (*Shab.* 89a). What caused the sin of the Golden

246 | SEVENTY FACES

Calf? The tradition answers that Moses was late by some six hours in descending from the mountain. Still, the Israelites were not upset until Satan confused the world by projecting onto the clouds a picture of Moses lying in his coffin. It was then that they cried out, "Moses is dead!," and proceeded to that abomination which became the archetypical sin in Jewish consciousness.

Third, no matter what our orientation within Judaism or towards Jewish education, one noble dogma unites all of us: that our future has been secured for us in the past; that the covenant between God and Israel guarantees the eternal existence of the Jewish people and its return to Eretz Israel. We are covenanted to survive, to succeed in the end.

So, it all boils down to faith—faith in the surpassing endurance of the sacred legacy we are commissioned to pass on; faith in the ultimate success of the enterprise of Jewish education—which engages our labors, our thought, and our destiny; faith in the resonance which the Torah we teach will find in the young people we educate. Or, to state the articles of faith of the Jewish educator in the last quarter of this century as antitheses to the four myths:

1. Faith that there is in the heart of the Jewish child something that responds to Torah.
2. Faith that he who can, does; and he who can do best—teaches.
3. Faith that the greatest contribution to Jewish education comes not from techniques but from teachers; not from methods, but from men and women and hearts and souls.
4. Faith that despite all difficulties, we are determined that we shall not be defeated; that we shall counter pessimism with persistence; that the covenant continues; that *am Yisrael chai* because *ode Avinu chai* and that therefore the Torah is a *Torat chayyim*.

It is this faith which will keep us "in business" and will guarantee that fifty years hence Jewish educators will assemble for another hand-wringing, yet heart-warming celebration—unless, of course, the Messiah comes first.

~ 24 ~

TORAH EDUCATION IN THE MODERN ORTHODOX COMMUNITY

In addressing this topic, I make certain assumptions which it is best to declare at the outset.

I speak of "Torah Education" as it is known and practiced in Centrist or Modern Orthodoxy. This means, Jewish education in that community which subscribes to *Torah Umadda* as a desideratum and not a concession, to tolerance and moderation, to the State of Israel; and to the unity of the Jewish people. But these admirable qualities and values are ancillary to the primary principle of Torah as the very source of our lives, both individual and communal, and the study of Torah as the pre-eminent *mitzvah* of Judaism. My remarks might be viewed as self-critical, maybe negatively constructive. Although I shall dwell upon our faults and failures and flaws, and forgo self-gratulation, do not conclude therefrom that we are hopelessly inadequate and doomed. Quite to the contrary: If I am critical of our educational efforts, perhaps harshly so, I ask you to consider the public airing of my displeasures as a sign of collective self-confidence and strength. Were I less confident of our past achievements and future triumphs, I would not risk exposing our weaknesses.

I shall cluster my remarks about two poles or centers of concern: *Torah* and *Mitzvot*.

Torah

The Torah component in the theme of "Torah Education at the Crossroads" may be divided into a discussion of motivation, continuity, and axiology (or: the role of Torah in the hierarchy of values).

This appeared in Ten Da'at *(Fall 1989) as* "Torah Education at the Crossroads" *and adapted from a lecture at Cong. Kehilath Jeshurun in New York City.*

Motivation

One of the most fundamental, difficult, and persistent questions which Jewish educators have to confront is that of the motivation to learn. This is universally the case, but it is especially nettlesome for children or adolescents of our community who are exposed to the whole gamut of contemporary experience in which Torah learning is not a prestige item.

The perennial problem is getting more difficult of late. Why, after all, should a young person study Torah when it is so easy to be accepted, successful, and recognized without a whisper of Jewish literacy? It is even possible to attain eminence in national and international Jewish leadership while remaining profoundly ignorant of Jewish classics, practice, or values; or worse, one can be married out and aggressively assert that the dogma of "pluralism" qualifies the ignorant, the Jewishly illiterate, and the intermarried to be "Jewish" leaders equal with all others. Why study Torah when it hardly articulates with anything familiar in secular life, when it has barely any resonance in the general studies which a child undertakes for all of his/her youth in our society?

For most of the 70's there seemed to be certain segments of Jewish society for whom this question seemed less acute. This was the era of the Counter-Culture, when many young Jews rebelled against the Jewish "establishment" and its insensitivity to cultural and spiritual values, by seeking out Jewish study in one form or another. This was the period of ethnic self-assertion, of the proliferation of Jewish studies courses in universities throughout North America, and a conscious rejection of many of the symbols and institutions of our technopolitan society.

That period, however, quickly passed away—and I rue its untimely demise. The 80's generation on our campuses has been as humorless, as intensive, and as grimly serious as the 70's generation—but about altogether different things. They are overconcerned with their vocations, their professions, their security, their social acceptance. With the shift from marijuana to booze has come the change from Marcuse to money, from society to self and status, from the New Leftist to the All-Rightnik . . .

Our tasks, therefore, promise to be more difficult, not less so. With the obsession with vocation and money-making seeping down to high schools and even lower, culture as such is in eclipse, and Jewish learning especially threatens to become the private preserve of a priestly class—once rabbis, now mostly *roshei yeshiva* and, in other circles, university professors of Judaic studies: the new monastic order, the Essenes of the Academy. But that, of course, jeopardizes the existence of Torah which must be *moreshet kehilat Yaakov,* a possession of *all* our people.

Continuity

The criterion of success in Torah education is not how much or how well our pupils learn in their schools, but how much and how often they learn *after* they leave school, when they are at work and building families and running businesses and raising children.

Of Torah we say daily *Ki hem chayenu ve'orekh yamenu,* "They [the Torah and its commandments] are our life and the length of our days." The test of whether we are truly committed, of whether Torah is really "our life," is whether or not it is indeed "the length of our days." If you want to know if Torah is central to your life—*ki hem chayenu*—check to what extent you turn to it in *ve'orekh yamenu,* after your formal schooling is over. How often do you open a *Gemara* or *Chumash* or attend a regular *sheiur?* The test results for most of us—most of us Orthodox Jews, let alone the others—are probably quite dismal. And that means that we must take an honest look at the educational system which produced us, as well as our society in general.

I submit that to improve this situation, to make sure that, to the maximum extent possible for us, Torah becomes a part of our adult lives, we must make a serious attempt to induce and inspire the best and brightest of our high school students to continue their full dual-curriculum of Torah and general studies into their college years.

In elementary Jewish schools, we teach skills and love. In high schools we teach ideas and ideals. But it is primarily Torah study on the level of higher education that can succeed in encouraging the study of Torah as a life-long occupation, as an act of the love of God expressed in the idiom of the intellect.

Regular Torah study on the college level is critical to developing the habit of Torah study for the rest of one's life. Only if Torah education is continued on a higher level for an ever larger number of Centrist Orthodox Jews, can we hope to achieve credibility—in our *own* eyes—as an authentically Orthodox voice, and thus validate our approach to secular studies and the Gentile world and the non-Orthodox communities and the State of Israel.

Axiology

The question of axiology is that of the scale of values, and what role we assign to the study of Torah, what emphasis we place on it vis-à-vis other activities.

The Mishnaic teaching *ve'talmud Torah keneged kulam* means that Torah study outweighs not only all the other *mitzvot* but, remarkably, even non-*mitzvot*, such as vacations, entertainment, proficiency in every conceivable sport, and so on. . . .

To the largest extent, this emphasis on Torah as the chief value of life and of Judaism is transmitted, or not transmitted, to our charges in indirect as well as direct ways: not only by construction of curriculum, but also by our own conduct as parents and teachers, our tone of voice, our body language, and the clues and hints they pick up from us and from their fellow students.

We must beware of reducing Torah to a "course" or subject or discipline or field of knowledge alone. Torah is and must always be presented as a deeply religious and spiritual enterprise. The Sages taught that Torah study by man is an act of *imitatio Dei:* we imitate the Creator, who spends most of His time studying Torah. And God learns Torah; He doesn't just "take a course" in Torah in His heavenly Yeshiva Day School. . . .

I am not advocating that we teach only Torah. I am philosophically committed to *Torah Umadda.* I do not expect or want all boys to become rabbis or *roshei yeshiva* and all girls teachers (although we could use many more recruits to both callings). I want our children to be proficient in all their secular studies too. But I want all of them, no matter what careers they will pursue, to keep Torah as their prime spiritual commitment, and *talmud Torah* as a regular and ongoing part of their lives.

That, I maintain, must be the end-product of our form of Torah education: greatness as human beings, but always as great Jews. And that cannot happen without the proper emphasis on the primacy of Torah as a life-long enterprise of the first importance. No form of Orthodoxy can flourish without that emphasis.

Mitzvot

The Facts on the Ground

We turn now from the question of the study of Torah to that of *shemirat ha-mitzvot,* the problem of the observance of the commandments, and thus the whole "lifestyle," as it is now called, of our school population both during and after their years of formal education.

When I do so, I refer not only to the matter of "observance" in a way that can be quantified and projected in a sociological survey: how often do you lay *tefillin;* how often do you light candles?

I am concerned by the *quality* of the observance, the emotional dimension of our *shemirat hamitzvot,* the investment of our deepest feelings, the enthusiasm we bring to our religious acts, the faith in the transcendent One that must always underlie our expressions of Jewish living.

There was a time that our elementary yeshiva schools and even high schools were models of disorganization, pedagogical disasters. Today almost all of our educational institutions are efficient, systematic, and professional. Our teachers are pedagogically competent, psychologically sensitive, well trained. Lesson plans are submitted, conferences are held, and the classes hum.

Everything that is needed for the success of the educational venture is there.

Everything except *neshama,* soul.

Our children are taught to recite *berakhot* before eating, and their knowledge of which blessings to recite and when is often quite sophisticated. But I do not find these children actually reciting them, as a normal and accepted part of their lives, at home. Moreover, even when a *berakha* is recited, I rarely detect a note of genuine feeling. The schools seem to be fighting a losing battle against the homes, purveyors of emotional thinness.

I sometimes attend services at one yeshiva high school or another and, with a considerable number of very happy exceptions, find them depressingly similar to the "davening" of their parents. The *tefillah* is by rote, without *kavanah*, without heart. The prayers roll off their lips fluently—and fall to the floor, shattered and splattered. If our children are no better than we are, what hope is there for the future? (It was Elijah who said, "Enough! Now, O Lord, take my life, for I am no better than my fathers"—I Kings 19:4.) And if our schools cannot correct the situation, who will?

The Problem in Perspective

We must remember that our educational concerns embrace not only the transmission of knowledge—of the cognitive and abstract elements of culture per se—but the whole gamut of Torah, which is as broad as life itself. For the Jewish educator, character and religious conduct and morality are not merely ancillary consequences of learning, but the very substance and stuff of education. Moral behavior and the spiritual life are the *telos* or goal of education: *"Takhlit chokhmah teshuvah u-maasim tovim"* (*Ber.* 17b): The purpose of wisdom is repentance (the spiritual transformation of personality) and good deeds (practical moral conduct).

It is this disjunctiveness between, on the one hand, the moral life and the spiritual aspirations that are the purpose of Torah education and, on the other, the deprecation of such values in contemporary Western culture, that makes the enterprise of Jewish education so problematical today.

The kind of conduct expected of a young Orthodox Jew and Jewess—regular *tefillah*, set times for study of Torah, modesty in dress and speech, respect for elders and Torah scholars—is often alien to what is expected of them as "typical Americans" in their socioeconomic class, where the norms are more often set by television rather than the *sheiur* and by the agenda of the political liberals rather than by the *Shulchan Arukh*.

The question of "lifestyle" or *shemirat ha-mitzvot* ultimately relates to what Victor Frankl has called the "noogenic vacuum" in the life of contemporary man; it boils down to a metaphysical pain: the lack of transcendent anchorage or roots for all values and all of life. Our students and the homes they come from are afflicted by a creeping emptiness that our society insinuates into our very selves, by an axiological void which demands to be filled. It is a very depressing question that modern man usually attempts to suppress: without God, without something beyond me and beyond my physical existence, what is life all about? What meaning is there to all this? Why struggle? Why live? Why not suicide?

Such questions have disturbed Western society at least for the past forty years. We probably can pinpoint the most recent outbreak of such concern as 1949, when Karl Mannheim published his essays on "Diagnosis of Our Time" and "The Crisis in Valuation." He recognized that the twin sources of the deep crisis and malaise in Western civilization were the erosion of legitimation and the loss of meaning. As legitimation became attenuated, the usual sources of authority began to lose their significance—from Presidents and Prime Ministers to Popes and Professors. The sense of purpose is gone. Our lives and our acts are hollowed rather than hallowed. We look about in vain for something worthy of our commitment and our love. We have relativized good and evil and trivialized reward and punishment. God has been dethroned by man, and as our other idols have been found to have clay feet, apotheosized man has been discovered to be flat-footed.

Hedonism is the unspoken and unchallenged assumption of the times. Indeed, it is the metaphysical cataclysm which we have sustained from the loss of legitimation and authority which gives rise to hedonism. As Amitai Etzioni wrote a few years ago, "Hedonism further develops when norms which define meanings disintegrate without being replaced by new norms. Hedonism thrives amidst a spread of normlessness." ("The Search for Political Meaning," in *The Center Magazine*, March/April 1972.) In other words, for the Jew the loss of *halakhah*, of a life of *mitzvot*, leads to a life of gross and empty pleasure-seeking.

Often, this hedonism—sometimes in quite vulgar form—coexists ironically with the trappings of Orthodox observance. Examples: shameless public expression of sexual affection—while wearing a *kippah*; Orthodox men and women filling their minds with the most dreadful pornographic trash, far more polluting to the imagination than the smokestack exhaust that fouls our air and against which some of these same people rail with all the passion of trendy indignation; parents taking their Day School children to Club Med for their "winter vacation."

Allied with hedonism is an individualism run rampant: self-centeredness, egocentricity. Hence, all those "self" movements: self-realization, self-expression, self-fulfillment, and the variety of weird "therapies" which grow wild in the fertile soil of California. It is an orientation that stems from Swinburne's "Man is the measure of all things." This ultimately becomes, "I am the measure of all things." In *Teahouse of the August Moon*—a Broadway play popular many years ago—a little Okinawan recites an insightful soliloquy in which he says "There is East, there is West, there is North, there is South; I am in the middle, so I am the center of the world."

But such narcissistic self-indulgence is misleading. It is a living lie. And it leads right to the contempt for Torah.

Judaism, while focused on man, holds that man is important only because he stands before God, and it is this which gives him his significance despite the fact that he is finite, fallible, imperfect.

Jewish education thus has a massive task of resisting this regnant, unspoken philosophy of the world about us, and—without overstating the case and without detracting in the least from the need for self-esteem for the child—teaching, in ways they understand, that self-fulfillment comes from self-transcendence, that finding the self is achieved by losing the self in a great cause: the study of Torah; the life of *mitzvot;* Israel; concern with oppressed Jewries and the homeless and the sick and the underprivileged.

The central mission of Jewish education is to fill the metaphysical void creatively and truthfully. I am certain that it will not be possible to do so with nationalism, e.g., Zionism or Israel alone; not by language alone, whether Hebrew or Yiddish, not by a warmed-over liberalism and meliorism presented as the totality of Judaism; not by the academic study of Judaism, for if man does not live by bread alone, neither does he thrive by disembodied text alone.

Our response will have to be a spiritual one, a religious one, a metaphysical one. We must provide the raw material of Torah from which students can construct their personal Jewish answers for themselves to such ultimate questions. And that means taking *mitzvot* seriously as the practical expressions of truth, of trust, of a deepening sensitivity to the One, the commanding Presence. If we are to answer that need and in that manner, then we must impart not just knowledge but life; teach not just *how* to do *mitzvot* but *to* do them; present Torah not as just a way of being Jewish, but as its very essence.

The mission of Orthodox Jewish educators, therefore, is to influence the home rather than be influenced by it, and to present Torah expressed in a life of *mitzvot* as the source of legitimacy, authority, value, and validity. Unless we strive to do so, all our other educational efforts will be in vain. We must never submit to the benevolent trivialization of Jewish life and learning as something secondary and merely ethnic—a kind of intellectual equivalent of gefilte fish.

The Need for Renewal

What I am calling for in our educational institutions is a sense of renewal, a turn from technique to *takhlis*, a reinvigoration of both our external and internal lives from the sources of *emunah*, of Jewish faith of all the ages.

It is simply not enough to be identified proudly as Jews. There has got to be study, study of Torah. And there has got to be *shemirat ha-mitzvot*, observance—on a level higher and more intensive than is present in our homes.

And observance in and by itself is not enough. We have got to raise a generation of religious Jews. And Jews, as a sympathetic and wise Gentile observer once said, do not merely *have* a religion; they *are religious.* Or should be.

We have got to aim to educate a generation of Jews who care—who really and truly care about their Judaism, who worry about it, who identify their destiny with its destiny, their fate with its fate.

Another way of saying the same thing is that we must so raise our children—and ourselves—that we are capable of being indignant when Torah is ridiculed, mocked, scorned.

The Capacity for Outrage

Permit me to go to the enemy camp to find a striking example of what I mean when I plead for a sense of indignation as the criterion for faith and commitment and seriousness of purpose.

An Indian novelist, a disaffected Moslem living in London, wrote a book that shook the world. Salman Rushdie incurred the wrath of the Islamic world because of what it considered blasphemy of all it holds sacred. Ayatollah Khomeini promptly condemned him to death and ordered his execution.

Now, there is no doubt that Khomeini was a religious butcher who lacked the most elementary qualities of humaneness, compassion, or sensitivity. The Ayatollah was a disgrace to all religious folk of all faiths. Indeed, he even gave fanaticism a bad name.

But that is not my concern now. What I am intrigued by and what I admire is the capacity of Moslems world-wide to be indignant. Moslems really *care*; they were angry, irate, furious. Their capacity for outrage is a clue to how deeply they feel about their religion.

Not too long ago, fundamentalist Christians were also deeply disturbed and upset by a movie which they thought showed terrible disrespect to their central religious figure. Some of the protesters went overboard in demanding censorship of the movie, and others went even further in transforming their protest into ugly manifestations of anti-Semitism. But their protest showed that they care about their beliefs, that they take them seriously.

I admire those Moslems and Christians who possess this capacity for outrage, and I am jealous—even as I am fearful of the excesses of some of them.

I also admire, *le'havdil*, the *Haredim* in Jerusalem who refused to suffer the insensitive commercialism of those who put up advertising posters, which they considered immodest and salacious, in their neighborhood bus stations. The lunatic fringe that decided to torch these stations was and is fanatical and overreactive and deserves condemnation. But the peaceful protesters were right on target. They showed that they cared, and that is why they were angry and indignant enough to demonstrate their fury by marching and shouting. Can you imagine our prim, proper, well-behaved youngsters of our day schools, elementary and high and college, doing the same because their moral sensibilities as *benei Torah* were outraged?

Now, most Jews care deeply about things too. We organize against signs of anti-Semitism, we demonstrate against Soviet treatment of its Jews, we march in defense of Israel. And so do our day school youngsters—with even more verve and zeal than their parents. But all this concerns *Jews*—not *Judaism*. It refers to the physical and political security of Jews, but has nothing to do with faith, with religion, with morality, with Torah, with soul.

We get terribly nervous about the threat of censorship of any group, but that is either because we fear the consequences for ourselves or, even if for objective reasons, it is a cherished political belief, not a holy Jewish tenet. American Jews can summon the emotions of anger at a threat to free speech, which is as it should be, but not about scorn heaped upon Torah. We are ready to man the ramparts for the First Amendment but not for the First Commandment; most Jews do not even know what it is.

We have so much fiction by American Jewish writers that scoffs at Judaism and Jewish tradition in the most devastating and heart-breaking ways, that we have become inured to it. Israeli writers are even more blasphemous than their American Jewish counterparts. Some of the diatribes we read here or that Israelis write there make Rushdie's anti-Islamic stuff seem so tame that we might call them "Angelic Verses." Yet, who is outraged by all this? Who is ready to mount a protest against Woody Allen's anti-Judaic writings equal to our angry reactions to his Op-Ed piece in the *New York Times* against Israel, or to the Nazi march in Skokie a number of years ago? Whose blood boils when an Israeli playwright holds all that is sacred to us as believing Jews up to contempt and ridicule, belittling all that is dear and precious and holy in our tradition? I am not speaking of philosophical or theological arguments—which must be met civilly and respectfully—but of cheap ridicule, of literary "shmutz."

Hardly anyone, really. We greet it with a shrug. We are so used to it that it no longer bothers us. And maybe that loss of the sense of outrage really bespeaks a loss of faith, a condition of being uncaring, cold, callous. Or at least of not being sufficiently committed.

In a word, our loss of the capacity for outrage is an indictment of our whole community, which has absorbed uncritically the hedonistic and narcissistic ethos of the larger society, and of the educational system, which has failed, despite heroic efforts, to change it. With all the marvelous, wonderful, even incredible accomplishments of which we can be truly proud, there is a dangerous worm gnawing away unseen in our vitals, and this problem must be addressed and solved soberly and deliberately, and not overlooked and ignored.

The most critical problem facing Orthodoxy, which preaches *Torah Umadda*, moderation, tolerance, and openness, is: Can we be all these things without sacrificing that *"bren,"* that enthusiasm, that zeal and commitment and powerful love without which we are condemned to spiritual superficiality and religious medioc-rity? Can our youngsters, some of whom aspire so mightily to be "cool," learn the ambition to be warm and even ablaze with the dream of achieving spiritual authenticity?

What is needed for all this to occur is a new assertiveness of Orthodoxy, grounded in both commitment and openness, tough-mindedness and tolerance; a new injection of single-minded dedication; a refusal to be passive about our future; a willingness to face criticism and react to it constructively; and a resolve that we will make Torah education grow in both quality and quantity.